*W*ildlife
Travelling Companion
GREAT BRITAIN
AND IRELAND

*W*ildlife
Travelling Companion
GREAT BRITAIN
AND IRELAND

Martin Walters

The Crowood Press

First published in 1992 by
The Crowood Press Ltd.
Ramsbury, Marlborough
Wiltshire SN8 2HR

Field Guide plates 1–12 by **Chris D Orr** and plates
13–20 by **Amanda Yektaparast.**
Maps by **Kathy Merrick.**

Title page photograph: the dramatic valley of Glencoe
in the Scottish Highlands.
Photograph this page: Greenshank (*Tringa nebularia*).

British Library Cataloguing in Publication Data

A catalogue record for this book is available from the
British Library.

ISBN 1 85223 586 1

Edited and designed by
D & N Publishing
DTP & Editorial Services
5 The Green
Baydon
Wiltshire SN8 2JW

Phototypeset by FIDO Imagesetting, Witney, Oxon

Printed and bound by Times Publishing Group,
Singapore

CONTENTS

SECTION I: COUNTRY GUIDE   7

   Introduction   7

   The Landscape   7

   The People   10

   Flora and Fauna   12

   Habitats   12

   Climate

   Conservation   17

   Travel Tips   19

SECTION II: SITE GUIDE   21

   1. Northern Scotland   31

   2. Western Scotland and Islands   40

   3. Eastern Scotland and Highlands   51

   4. Southern Scotland and Borders   59

   5. North-West England   67

   6. North-East England   77

   7. Eastern England   90

   8. South-East England   106

   9. Southern England   118

   10. Midlands and Welsh Borders   129

   11. South-West England   142

   12. Wales   161

   13. The Island of Ireland   178

**SECTION III: FIELD GUIDE TO
COMMONER ANIMALS
AND PLANTS**   195

Useful Addresses   236

Bibliography   236

Index   237

SECTION I
COUNTRY GUIDE

INTRODUCTION

This book is not a travel guide, but rather it is a companion to the natural history of Britain and Ireland. As such, it aims to locate and describe a selection of the best natural history sites to be found in this region and to point out some of the typical animals and plants which might be seen there.

The area is of course well served with field guides and monographs dealing with the identification of many plant and animal groups, presented at all levels of readership, from the academic to the general. This book, which is one of a series of regional handbooks, aims to complement such guides by providing concise information about the natural history of the area and where to see prime examples of the major habitats and interesting species.

The continuum of plant and animal communities making up our countryside can broadly be divided into major, more or less distinct habitat types, most of which are immediately recognizable by the amateur naturalist. The essence of each of these habitats is described, to give something of their flavour and distinctive character and to introduce the characteristic species they contain.

Most of the book is devoted to the site guide, which is organized on a regional basis. Here we have selected from the cream of natural history sites to provide the reader with a guide to some of the very best, be they of

Opposite: *view across the River Spey, near Grantown-on-Spey.*

interest because of their plant life, for their birds, or for other aspects of their natural history. In many cases, the sites selected are nature reserves, or have some form of protected status, but all are proven sites well worthy of a visit.

The natural history of the British Isles is very diverse, encompassing as it does the bleak rocky sea-cliffs of St Kilda, the majestic massifs of the Scottish Highlands, the flat East Anglian fenland, the gentle wooded coombes of the south-west, and the windswept blanket bogs of western Ireland. In addition, the long intricate coastline includes fine estuaries with their associated mudflats and coastal marshes, many of which are internationally famous for the wildlife they support.

Although not primarily an identification guide, we have nevertheless included a field guide section which should help with the identification of some of the more familiar vertebrates, butterflies and plants likely to be seen in the sites described in the book.

THE LANDSCAPE

Britain and Ireland have very varied landscapes which contain many contrasting features. Within a comparatively short distance the traveller can experience windswept hills with Alpine flowers and mountain birds, gentle damp low-lying woodland and open saltmarsh and estuary alive with the calls of waders and wildfowl.

Most places in Britain and Ireland are reasonably close to the sea, which is one of the dominating features affecting the wildlife of these islands. No other European area has such a varied coastline, nor so much marine wetland habitat to offer.

By the standards of much of continental Europe, Britain and Ireland are countries of rolling hills, rather than of high mountains. Nevertheless, even our modest 'mountains' dominate the landscape in many places,

Flowers in a coastal pasture with Bunowen Bay and the Twelve Bens, Eire, in the background.

Mountain on the Dingle Peninsula and Slieve League in Donegal. The Irish coastline is rather rounded in the east, but heavily indented in the west, with bays, coves, cliffs and a multitude of inlets and headlands, providing a good variety of habitats, from grassland and dunes to rocky promontories. The Burren, centred on County Clare, has an unusual karst landscape with domed limestone pavement and a special flora. Ireland has very little woodland remaining, and large areas are covered by blanket and raised bogs, particularly in the central plains.

In Britain, only parts of Scotland and Wales are truly mountainous, with high hills and plateaux dominating the overall landscape. The Cairngorms massif is the highest range and has its own very characteristic fauna and flora. The highest peak, however, at 1344m is Ben Nevis, a relatively isolated hill not far from Fort William.

notably in Central and West Scotland. This is partly because, although the altitudes reached are not great, many of the ranges rear up close to the sea, starting from a low base level.

In Ireland, especially in the south and centre, low-lying grassland and peatland dominates, with blanket and raised bogs covering large areas. From the lowlands, occasional ranges of hills and mountains thrust upwards, such as the Mountains of Mourne (in Northern Ireland) and, in the Republic of Ireland, the Bens of Connemara, the Wicklow Mountains, Magillicuddy's Reeks and the imposing coastal peaks of Brandon

Wales has fine mountain ranges too, most notably Snowdonia and the Brecon Beacons. The Lake District in the north-west of England has scenery recalling parts of Scotland, although its particular combination of lake and hill is unique.

In England, the high ground is mainly to be found along the backbone range of the Pennine Hills, which extend from Derbyshire, north to the Scottish borders. Other isolated pockets of high ground include the moors of Bodmin, Exmoor and Dartmoor in the south-west.

Elsewhere, Britain is a landscape of undulating, mostly farmed country, with pasture and grazing land concentrated in the damper west, and arable cereal and other crops in the more intensely farmed midlands and south-east. Woodland generally increases towards the west, and East Anglia is the region with the fewest trees and least woodland cover.

The geology is complicated in detail, with a wide range of rock types making up the hills and underlying the soils of lowland areas. However, a few useful generalizations are possible. The upland mountainous areas with high rainfall tend to be on neutral rocks, with a neutral or acid soil developed over them. Acid-loving vegetation tends therefore to be prominent in upland sites, and in boggy habitats in the high rainfall regions of the north and west. Interesting exceptions provide some of the best flower-hunting areas on outcrops of calcareous rock in uplands, such as at Ben Lawers or the limestone pavements of the Burren and the north-west Pennines.

Other areas with acid soils include those developed over sandstone or pockets of heathland, where leaching has impoverished the surface soil by removing minerals. Lowland heathland occurs mainly in Dorset, Hampshire, Surrey and in parts of East Anglia. Here the plants tend to include heather and related species, and there is a very characteristic assemblage of both animals and plants, with several rarities.

In eastern, central and south-eastern England, the soils are often lime-rich, especially along the chalk and limestone ridges of the North and South Downs, the Chilterns and the Cotswolds. The flora again reflects the geology, with flower-rich chalk grassland a much cherished habitat in southern England. Chalk grassland is also an excellent habitat for butterflies and other invertebrates, as well as for flowers.

THE PEOPLE

Britain and Ireland have been inhabited by people and their associated animals for many thousands of years, and this long history of settlement has left indelible marks on the natural history of the region.

Neolithic settlers first began clearing the native mixed deciduous forests about 6,000 years ago and the loss of original woodland has steadily proceeded ever since. During Roman times, the forests had already been reduced to less than half of their original extent as farmland and grassland encroached further.

Woodlands were very often used to provide a renewable source of wood for fuel and timber, and were managed by traditional methods such as coppicing. Many woodland plants and animals became adapted to such management regimes and today many woodland reserves (such as Hayley Wood) are retained in these semi-natural states, specifically for the benefit of the wildlife.

The Industrial Revolution brought with it not only accelerated destruction of natural habitats, but also initiated a phase of pollution which is still a major problem today. Waste gases from industry and cars are causing acidification of some habitats, particularly upland lakes, lowering the range of species which can survive. At the same time, nitrates and minerals from fertilizers find their way into rivers, streams and lakes and cause destructive algal blooms. Technology and the industrial society also introduced chemicals such as pesticides, several of which had unforeseen and dramatic effects on wildlife, reducing, for example, populations of birds of prey such as the Peregrine. Thankfully, curbs on the use of these poisons has led to a revival of the Peregrine and several other predatory birds.

Naturally wet habitats, such as the once extensive fens of East Anglia, were carefully drained to provide yet more fertile soil for planting crops. Today this habitat has almost entirely gone, with very few remnants, such as Wicken Fen, to remind us what it must have been like.

It is doubtful whether any of the habitats we see today are natural in the sense that they are unaltered by human influence, with the possible exception of the high mountain tops, inaccessible rocks and cliffs, both inland and at the coast, and some mudflats and saltmarshes.

Elsewhere, what we see as today's wildlife refuges, and what we seek to preserve, are at best only semi-natural, in that they are a

This limestone cutting between Buxton and Ashbourne has a rich flora, and associated insect life.

product of centuries of close interaction with people and their ways of life. Examples of obvious semi-natural habitats are legion, and range from established ancient woodland (most of which is or has been managed in one form or another) through lowland heath (certainly man-induced) to chalk grassland (a product of regular grazing). Indeed, many of our richest and most interesting habitats rely upon regular management to keep them in what we now regard as their most interesting state. Such habitats include heath, water meadow, machair, upland heather moor, chalk grassland and coppiced ancient woodland.

This at once proves that land-use and conservation are by no means incompatible, and that it is possible for each to go hand in hand and be of benefit to the other. Although it is clearly still important to retain and protect certain types of site and habitat from the more directly damaging influences of people, conservation today must be to some extent an element of land-use, especially in an area as densely populated as the British Isles. However, conservationists cannot afford to be complacent, and some of the statistics about habitat loss are chilling: about 40 per cent of ancient woodland and lowland heath, 50 per cent of lowland fens and mires, and a staggering 95 per cent of lowland neutral grassland lost since 1945; at least forty internationally important estuaries threatened by development.

A growing threat is now also posed by the damaging effects of tourism, especially at certain very popular sites. As leisure time has increased, and the population has become more mobile, so has access to wild country improved. The result is that certain areas are now definitely 'honeypots' for holidaymakers, especially during the peak summer holiday months. This is resulting in damage, some of it likely to be long-lasting, to sites such as parts of the Lake District and Peak District National Parks. In some places, the sheer pressure of feet (and also more recently of mountain bikes), has actually worn away the very footpaths which were made to make access easier. Despite this problem, it is still surprising how easy it is to escape the crowds and to experience the wildlife even of a region as crowded as this.

Whilst this book gives priority to sites which are relatively easy of access, it also includes many places which are not so well known, as well as those which for various reasons are more famous. The hope is that it will encourage visitors to seek out and see for themselves the rich wildlife of the splendid range of reserves and sites so readily available to the interested and enthusiastic naturalist.

FLORA AND FAUNA

The flora and vegetation of Britain and Ireland are closely related to those of the European continent. This is because the separation of these islands from mainland Europe has happened very recently in geological history, and has had little effect. This is in sharp contrast to ancient oceanic islands where a large proportion of the species are endemics, that is, they are unique to that area.

As a result of this very recent separation, the flora of the dry, sandy heaths of the East Anglian breckland, for example, closely resembles that of the North German and Polish heaths, and contrasts very strongly with the Atlantic bogs and moorland of Ireland and Wales. In fact, a diagonal line drawn across England from the Severn to the Wash roughly separates two very different kinds of countryside. South and east of the line there

Yellow Iris (Iris pseudacorus) is often seen brightening up a river or canal bank, as here at Carlton Bridge.

are no mountains, the soils are generally very fertile, being mostly derived from young rocks or base-rich glacial clays, and the climate is more continental, with relatively low rainfall and relatively hot summers.

However, if we compare the variety of British native flora with that of a Mediterranean country of comparable size, such as Italy, we see that ours is much smaller; for higher plants about 1,750 compared with about 5,000 species. This large difference is explained by the Ice Ages, which wiped out the earlier vegetation which covered what we now call Northern Europe. Of course the ice also covered, and denuded, areas of high ground elsewhere, such as the Alps, but these areas were quickly recolonized from a large pool of species in adjacent lowlands, or other protected sites. The native flora we now have is also largely a re-immigrant one, but whole groups of plants that we know from fossil remains once grew in Northern Europe never succeeded in returning until some were introduced by people into gardens. Good examples are Magnolias and Plane Trees (*Platanus*).

Gannets (Sula bassana) nesting on Bass Rock, a steep-sided island in the Firth of Forth which supports 20,000 pairs of these magnificent birds.

Most recently, human activities, either directly or indirectly (as through grazing animals) have very radically altered the face of Britain and indeed of the whole of Europe. The destruction of the native re-immigrant forests which once covered the lowlands began in Neolithic times in Britain and has continued, with interruptions, to the present day, so that our familiar landscape, with its discrete patches of woodland, its hedgerows and green fields, is very largely an artificial product of an agricultural society. Gross pollution and destruction, following on from the industrial revolution and the rise of dense urban communities is part of our modern history, and the major cause of the

movement for the conservation of nature. Moved and alarmed by the increasing pace of destruction, we have in recent years set up a network of nature reserves and protected areas so that we must now visit such areas to see many of the less common lowland species which were much more widespread in earlier days. We might therefore expect that recent total extinctions from the flora would be very numerous indeed: that this is not the case is itself a tribute to the conservation movement and to the general success of education about our own responsibilities towards rare animals and plants in the wild. But we are warned that although total extinctions (since the 17th century) are only about 1 per cent, many more species have moved into the 'endangered' category, and need positive action to preserve them.

A survey of more than 300 threatened species published in the *British Red Data Book* reveals that the largest single group threatened are arable weeds, or plants of disturbed habitats. It is easy to see why this should be the case. Since the Second World War agriculture has undergone a revolutionary change which has involved the increased use of machinery and chemicals. There is no place in modern farming for many familiar wild flowers that were weeds of arable land, such as poppies, Cornflower or Corn Cockle. Nor is it easy to create nature reserves for this type of flower, whose presence in the countryside is directly dependent upon the farmers' activities.

The second largest group of threatened species are wetland plants. Here the factors are more complex, but the general picture is clear enough. Marsh, fen and bog habitats have all declined or disappeared in living memory, not just in Britain and Ireland, but in Europe as a whole. Such wetland habitats as are preserved suffer constant threats of pollution and the lowering of the water-table. Extinctions or serious decline due solely to over-collecting seem to be mercifully few, but orchids in particular continue to suffer from the unscrupulous collector who cannot be content with a photograph.

The fauna of the region is also relatively poor compared with the continent, especially in groups which are unable to fly, such as most mammals, reptiles and amphibians. For example, there are forty-five species of amphibians and eighty-five non-marine reptiles in Europe, but only six of each are native to Britain, with three amphibians and a single reptile (Viviparous Lizard) in Ireland.

There are over 170 species of mammal in Europe (including marine mammals), but only about seventy-five of these (or about 44 per cent) occur in Britain and Ireland. Of the approximately 430 European species of bird, however, about 255 either breed here or are seen regularly, representing about 60 per cent. Birds are very mobile, and most species can overcome the physical barrier of the Channel and other stretches of sea with ease. In addition, the very varied habitats, augmented by the long coastline with its rocky islands, provide arguably the greatest potential for birds of any European country.

Britain and Ireland hold populations of a number of internationally rare or endangered bird species. These include Red Kite, in its Welsh stronghold, Golden Eagle, centred on the Scottish mountains, Peregrine, now increasing around our coasts and on rocky inland crags, and Corncrake, breeding in the remoter areas of the Hebrides and west of Ireland. Other species which have their main or major populations here are Red-throated Diver, Manx Shearwater, British and Leach's Storm-petrels, Gannet, Red Grouse, Curlew, Great Skua, Sandwich, Arctic, Roseate and Little Terns, Guillemot, Razorbill, Twite and Scottish Crossbill.

HABITATS

MOUNTAIN AND HIGH MOORLAND

Although the mountains of Britain and Ireland are little more than hills when compared with the major ranges of Europe, such as the Alps and Pyrenees, they do nevertheless have a significant affect upon the ecology of the country, and they carry very distinctive habitats. Scotland has the lion's share of mountains, with over 90 per cent of high ground over about 915m.

Extensive areas of the uplands are clothed by bog, or heather moor. Moorland is usually an artificial community in that much of it is carefully managed, largely for rearing grouse or deer. If left to its own devices, upland heather moor would often revert, perhaps only quite slowly, to Birch or Oak woodland, and most of the region is potentially capable of supporting woodland as a climax community.

Upland moors are best developed on hills and mountains, in areas of high rainfall or humidity, such as in the major mountain ranges of Scotland, Wales, and Ireland, and in the three major upland areas of South-west England (Bodmin Moor, Exmoor and Dartmoor). These moors, which are mostly managed for Red Grouse, are usually above about 300m, and upland heath, upland grassland

13

and the coastal northern heaths of North Scotland, Orkney and Shetland form the largest semi-natural habitat in Britain.

Typical plants of the high moors are Heather, Bell Heather, Bilberry, and Cross-leaved Heath. These bushy species are often accompanied by Purple Moorgrass, Mat-grass, and the vigorous, invasive fern Brack-en. In wetter areas, shrubs like Bog Bilberry appear, along with cottongrasses and rushes. In very wet sites bog mosses proliferate, and these peaty communities also include the insectivorous sundews and butterworts.

Moorland and mountain birds include Golden Eagle (about 425 pairs, or about 20 per cent of the western European popula-tion), Golden Plover (about 96 per cent of EC's population), Curlew, Dotterel, Dunlin, Purple Sandpiper, Red Grouse (about 60 per cent of EC's population), Ptarmigan, Twite, Peregrine, Merlin (about 600 pairs, virtually all of the EC's population), Hen Harrier (about 400 pairs, or 10 per cent of western Europe's population), Ring Ousel, Red-throated Diver, Wheatear, Snow Bunting, Shore Lark, Lapland Bunting and Raven.

Mammals commonly associated with mountain and high moorland habitats include: Field Vole, Mountain Hare, Red Deer and Wild Cat.

HEATH AND SCRUB

Heath is the name given to bushy communi-ties, dominated by Heather and related species, that develop on rather poor, well-drained sandy soils, usually in the lowland parts of North-west Europe.

Lowland heath is one of Britain's most threatened habitats, and therefore one of our most precious. Nearly 80 per cent has been lost in the fifty years from 1930. This habi-tat, which is rare on a European scale, has long been under pressure from agriculture, and has steadily decreased in area over the last few decades, threatened increasingly now by building developments. Lowland heath is found mostly away from the more extreme oceanic climates of the west and north, and is particularly well developed in the sandy soils of southern and south-eastern England, for instance in Dorset, Hampshire and Sur-rey and in the Breckland of East Anglia.

Heathland shrubs in-clude Heather, Gorse and Broom. Some com-mon heath flowers are Tormentil, Thyme, and Heath Bedstraw.

Like heather moor, lowland, heath is main-tained by a regime of grazing or occasional burn-ing, and will normally revert slowly to a climax woodland, usually of oak and birch, if fenced off and isolated.

Upland grassland and stream in Argyll, Scotland. Intensive grazing by sheep restrict tree growth to protected sites, such as stream-side rocks.

Birds of heathland include the Tree Pipit,

Heather and Bracken dominate in this view of Roydon Common Reserve near King's Lynn, Norfolk. Roydon has a fascinating mixture of heath and bog habitats.

Yellowhammer, Stonechat and Whinchat. Several rare or unusual birds are also found in this habitat, such as Hobby, Nightjar, Woodlark, Stone Curlew and Dartford Warbler.

Southern lowland heaths are Britain's last refuge for the rare Smooth Snake and Sand Lizard, where they occur along with commoner reptiles such as Adder and Viviparous Lizard. Some heaths still have colonies of the threatened Natterjack Toad.

Small Heath, Grayling and Small Copper are characteristic butterflies of heath habitats, as is the rare Silver-studded Blue.

Scrub is a loose term which refers to rather unstructured areas where bushes dominate. It is most commonly found where grassland or pasture begins to revert slowly to woodland, a process which may take decades, or even hundreds of years. Common shrubs of scrubland are Blackthorn, Hawthorn, roses, Bramble and Elder, with climbers such as Traveller's Joy. Scrub is important as a nesting habitat for many of the commoner and familiar birds, and its flowers also attract adult butterflies to feed.

Cliff-top heath is a special community mainly found on sea cliffs in southern England and Wales. Here, amongst the wind-pruned Heather, Bell Heather and Western Gorse, can be found species such as Tormentil, Wild Thyme, Spring Squill, Thrift, Sea Campion, Scurvygrass, Sea Plantain and stonecrops.

DECIDUOUS WOODLAND

Before the dramatic effects of people and their livestock began to change the landscape of the British Isles, much of the lowland was covered by an interconnecting mosaic of mainly deciduous wild woodland. Little of this original woodland now remains and today we see just pockets, restricted to valley sides or discrete patches of managed woodland on level ground.

The major tree dominants are oaks, Ash, Lime and elms, and these probably formed a mixed tree-layer in much of the original lowland 'wildwood'. Beechwoods occur in some areas, particularly on shallower soils in the south, such as on the crests of chalk and limestone outcrops like the Downs and Chilterns.

Nodding Bluebells (Hyacinthoides non-scripta) carpet many lowland deciduous woods in spring. This wood is at Ashton Wold near Peterborough in early May.

In the north, Ash plays a much more dominant role in damp woods on calcareous soils.

Birch is another very common tree. It tends to prefer sandy, acid soils and is usually found mixed with other species, such as oaks, or Scots Pine. In Scotland in particular, birch may form fairly pure woods, especially at fairly high altitudes, but there are relatively few such remnants left. Further south, birchwoods also occur as a mosaic in lowland heathland.

Wet soils, especially along river valleys, may develop Alder woods. Examples of these can be seen in and around the Norfolk Broads where the soils are very swampy and where other trees find it hard to survive. One rather special type of wet scrub woodland is known as carr. Carr develops in fenland and represents a stage in the succession from sedge and grass-dominated fen to wet and damp woodland. Fen carr tends to be dominated by shrubs such as Sallow, Buckthorn and Alder Buckthorn, and fine examples can be seen in areas such as the Norfolk Broads, and at reserves like Wicken Fen.

Typical woodland birds include tits, warblers, woodpeckers, flycatchers, thrushes, owls and Sparrowhawk. Deciduous woodlands also provide safe homes for Badgers, Foxes, squirrels, mice, voles and shrews. Rarer birds nesting in deciduous woodland are Red Kite, Honey Buzzard, Goshawk, Black Grouse, Fieldfare, Redwing, Brambling and Firecrest.

Some woods are managed in a traditional manner, in what is known as a 'coppice-with standards' regime. This used to be much more widespread when people relied more on a crop of natural wood for poles and branches. Coppicing consists of cutting back certain species, such as Ash, Field Maple and Hazel, to stumps. These then regenerate and produce a regular crop of fairly straight poles, which can be harvested. Occasional tall 'standard' trees are left to develop fully, and these too are felled from time to time to give timber. Coppicing was a form of exploiting the woods, without destroying them. It also allows a wide range of woodland animals and plants to flourish, because there is more variety of habitat in a coppiced wood. Some woodland reserves, such as Hayley Woods, continue to be managed in this way, and the wildlife certainly benefits.

CONIFEROUS WOODLAND

The only truly native coniferous (evergreen) woodland in Britain and Ireland are the remaining patches of Caledonian Scots Pine forest in Scotland. Several remnants of these fine communities are now carefully protected but are threatened in many places through overgrazing by deer. Scots Pine also forms woods elsewhere, as for example on sandy well-drained soils in the heathlands of southern and eastern England, but these are mostly at best semi-natural.

Planted conifers are not without their wildlife interest. The edges of this Breckland plantation provide habitats for rare birds, such as Nightjar, Woodlark and Hobby.

Large tracts of countryside, especially in the hill country of the north and west, have been steadily planted with coniferous trees, usually with species of spruce, and particularly with the North American Sitka Spruce. These trees grow well on 'poor' soils and rapidly give a crop of timber. Plantations such as these, which are felled by rotation, although not without their own wildlife interest, certainly have a less rich fauna and flora than the native mostly broadleaf woods they have replaced. Furthermore, recent research is implicating them in channelling and concentrating the effects of acid rain. Fortunately, the move now amongst foresters is back towards a mixed planting strategy, using broadleaved species as well.

The most interesting coniferous woods for the visiting naturalist are those mature forests in which the trees are naturally regenerating, and which also include open areas and clearings. Here light penetrates, a rich ground flora can develop, and scrubby stands of pioneer birch often intermingle. This contrasts with the dark, serried ranks of exotic spruce, all destined to be felled together, with little or no natural regeneration allowed.

Birds of the coniferous woodlands include Long-eared Owl, Capercaillie, Black Grouse, Goshawk, Coal Tit, Chaffinch, Firecrest, Goldcrest, Crested Tit, Redpoll, Scottish Crossbill, Crossbill and Siskin. Mammals include Pine Marten and Red Squirrel. In felled or newly planted sites birds such as Nightjar, Woodlark and Hen Harrier may breed.

GRASSLAND (INCLUDING PASTURE AND DOWNLAND)

Grassland is a habitat under multiple threat from farming, building development and, in recent years, from major road-building programmes as well. Some of the most interesting types of grassland for the naturalist are

This headland just south of Torbay, South Devon, has breeding Guillemots and Razorbills (unusual on the south coast), and rare flowers such as White Rock-rose.

undoubtedly the unimproved chalk downland and sheep pastures, where traditional grazing regimes maintain a close-cropped sward with a rich and fascinating flora, including many beautiful flowers such as Horseshoe Vetch, Common Rock-rose, a whole range of orchids, and the rare Pasqueflower. These habitats are also the haunt of butterflies such as blues, and in places Marbled White.

Birds associated with open fields, pasture and farmland in general are Skylark, Kestrel, Grey Partridge, Lapwing, Jackdaw, Rook and Little Owl, as well as rarer species such as Stone Curlew, Cirl Bunting, Barn Owl and Montagu's Harrier.

Hay-meadows are another wildlife-rich habitat, but one sadly much diminished. Unsprayed hay-meadows, with a regular, but not too frequent regime of cutting, have many beautiful flowers and also provide nesting opportunities for birds, including the rare Corncrake. Dunlin, Lapwing and Ringed Plover also nest here. Some of the best are now only found in the machair habitats of western Scotland and in Ireland.

Wet lowland grasslands are rapidly disappearing as a wildlife habitat, mainly because of drainage schemes and changes to the water table. Many interesting birds depend on these grasslands for breeding or as a feeding ground, including Garganey, Pintail, Pochard, Spotted Crake, Ruff, Black-tailed Godwit, Curlew, Barn Owl, Montagu's and Marsh Harriers. In winter, flooded grassland attracts large numbers of wildfowl and waders such as Bewick's and Whooper Swans, Brent, Bean and White-fronted

A fine area of saltmarsh at Burnham Overy Staithe, on the north Norfolk Coast, with purple flowers of Sea Lavender (Limonium vulgare) and Shrubby Sea-Blite (Suaeda vera) in the background.

Geese, Pintail, Shoveler, Wigeon, Gadwall, Teal, Pochard, Shelduck, Redshank, Golden Plover and Black-tailed Godwit. Important areas of lowland grassland pasture can be found for example in the Broads of East Anglia, on the Ouse Washes, at Pennington and Keyhaven Marshes and on the Somerset Levels.

Flowers of wet meadows include Marsh Marigold, Meadowsweet, Yellow Flag, Ragged Robin, marsh orchids, and the rare Fritillary.

ROCKY COASTS AND ISLANDS

Britain and Ireland are superbly well-endowed with rocky coasts and islands, from the isolated and daunting fastness of remote St Kilda, to the proud Cliffs of Moher in western Ireland, to the crumbly chalk cliffs of southern and eastern Britain. These habitats contain some of our most important wildlife, particularly the often huge colonies of seabirds. Sheltered rocky coves also provide a haven for seals and otters.

Over 60 per cent of the world's Gannets (more than 160,000 pairs) breed on rocky islands and cliffs around the coasts of Ireland and Britain, as well as about a third of all British Storm-petrels (about 20,000 pairs) and about a fifth of the world's Razorbills (about 145,000 pairs). Other notable species associated with these habitats are Manx Shearwater, Leach's Storm-petrel, Fulmar, Shag, Cormorant, Kittiwake, Guillemot, Puffin, Black Guillemot, Great Skua, Arctic, Sandwich and Roseate Terns, Rock Dove, Golden Eagle, Peregrine and Chough.

On sea-bird cliffs, heavily manured by droppings, certain characteristic plants can be found, often growing luxuriantly. Examples are Tree Mallow, Sea Beet, Sea Campion, Scentless Mayweed, Common Chickweed, Red Campion, Cow Parsley and Angelica. Salt-tolerant species found on cliffs in general include Thrift, Rock Samphire, Sea-spurrey, Sea Aster, and Sea Spleenwort. In the north, this is the habitat of Scots Lovage and Rose-root.

ESTUARIES, MUDFLATS AND SALTMARSH

Estuaries and mudflats act as magnets to the large flocks of migrating waders and wildfowl which stop over every year from northern Europe, Iceland and even Siberia. There are about 170 estuaries around the coasts of Britain and Ireland, and many birds depend upon them for winter survival. Because the estuaries have a wide tidal range, large areas of food-rich mud are regularly exposed, offering easy pickings to the birds. In addition, the mild oceanic climate of the region and the relatively salty water means that they rarely freeze over.

Dunes often have interesting flowers, such as this stand of Everlasting Pea.

Many estuaries support good growths of eelgrasses (*Zostera*) and also a green seaweed, *Enteromorpha*. These are the staple diet of several wildfowl, in particular Brent Geese and Wigeon, which flock in their thousands to favoured sites.

Slightly firmer soils on saltmarshes are the habitat of the succulent glassworts, with Annual Sea-blite and Sea Aster appearing to the landward. The vigorous Common Cordgrass also spreads rapidly over muddy saltmarshes in many areas. In somewhat drier sites, at the edges of creeks, the Sea-purslane thrives, often covering wide areas. Higher up still you may find Sea Lavender, Sea Wormwood, Thrift and Sea Milkwort.

Birds of shore and estuary include wildfowl such as White-fronted, Barnacle, Pink-footed and Brent Geese, Whooper and Bewick's Swans, Wigeon, Mallard and Pintail, terns, gulls, and waders like Dunlin, Knot, Redshank, Oystercatcher, Ringed Plover, Grey Plover, Bar-tailed and Black-tailed Godwits, Turnstone and Curlew.

Some examples of estuary sites are: Eden, Ythan, Caerlaverock, Aberlady Bay, Ribble, Pagham Harbour, Langstone Harbour, Bridgewater Bay, Exe Estuary, Dovey Estuary and Strangford Lough.

DUNE SYSTEMS

Sand dunes are fairly common around our coasts, and they form wherever light sand accumulates in exposed sites under the influence of regular strong winds. On such coasts, the wind is constantly building up new dunes, which develop roughly at right angles to the prevailing wind direction.

Amongst the first colonists of new dunes are Marram Grass, Sand Couch, Lyme-grass and Sand Sedge, with plants such as Sea Rocket and Sea Sandwort growing on the nearby strand.

Purple Loosestrife (Lythrum salicaria) is often common in marshy habitats and is here seen emerging from reeds in a mixed fen community.

As the dunes stabilize, other plants such as Sea Holly, Sea Bindweed, Ragwort and Rose-bay Willowherb join the community. In the west, such habitats may have the delicate Dune Pansy.

In still older dunes, mosses are common in the ground-layer and the number of other species rises to include flowers such as White Clover, Restharrow, Bird's Foot Trefoil, Wild Thyme and Viper's Bugloss. The natural succession from this stage, seen in many places, is towards scrub with woody plants such as Sea Buckthorn, Privet, Elder and Blackthorn.

Many dune habitats have wet hollows between and to the landward side of the dunes themselves. These can be very rich for both plants and animals and often have fine displays of orchids. Pools in dune slacks are also a favoured breeding site for the Natterjack. In addition, dune grassland tends to support good butterfly populations.

LOWLAND BOG AND FEN

Peatlands, which include the upland bogs as well as these lowland bogs and fens, are a speciality of the British Isles, a direct result of our wet Atlantic climate. As with heaths, Britain has a major responsibility on a European scale for the conservation, protection and management of these most precious and delicate of environments.

In the west, and particularly in Ireland, lowland peatlands cover large stretches of the

Highland streams are characterized by fast-flowing, clear water, and rocky beds. This is the haunt of Dipper and Grey Wagtail.

landscape, clothing the lower slopes of hills with blanket bog. In hollows and on flatter land, valley bogs and fenland replace the blanket bogs. All peatlands have a very special assemblage of characteristic species, including the fascinating insectivorous plants, the sundews and butterworts. They are also home to birds such as Hen Harrier and to unusual butterflies such as the rare Marsh Fritillary.

In England, especially in the south-east, lowland fen still clings on in pockets, representing a habitat that was previously much more widespread. Fen differs from bog mainly in being developed in alkaline rather than in acid conditions, and its flora differs accordingly in interesting ways.

The lowland fens often have associated reedbeds. These have their own characteristic mix of birds, amongst them some rather rare species, including Marsh Harrier, Bittern, Water Rail, Spotted Crake, Garganey, Bearded Tit, and Reed, Sedge, Savi's and Cetti's Warblers.

LAKES, RIVERS AND STREAMS

The high rainfall and varied landscape and geology combine to create a great range of water courses throughout the region.

In highland areas, mountain streams and rivers surge over their rocky beds. These are the haunts of birds such as the Dipper and Grey Wagtail, and their damp rocks create a fern enthusiast's paradise.

At the other extreme are the slow rivers meandering through their fertile flood-plains in the lowlands. These fine habitats with their pools and reed-beds have a very rich flora and also attract good numbers of breeding birds, particularly wildfowl and other waterbirds such as Great Crested and Little Grebes, Mallard, Tufted Duck, Moorhen, Coot and Grey Heron.

The clear, chalk streams of southern England with their Water-cress beds are the haunt of Kingfisher, and, where the natural vegetation is allowed to flourish, they also attract many invertebrates such as damselflies and mayflies, many of which provide food for healthy populations of trout.

The nutrient poor (oligotrophic) lakes of upland and northern Britain represent a rather special habitat with a small number of specialized plants and other wildlife. This is the habitat of the pretty Water Lobelia and the odd Quillwort. There are also characteristic breeding birds, including Common Sandpiper, Red-breasted Merganser, Red-throated Diver and Goosander, and some rather rarer species such as Black-throated Diver, Osprey, Goldeneye and Common Scoter.

By contrast, nutrient rich (eutrophic) lakes are very fertile, having a good supply of minerals and organic matter. These are commonest in lowland sites, mainly in southern and eastern Britain, especially where the rocks are calcareous. The Cheshire and Shropshire Meres are examples of natural nutrient-rich lakes, but many artificial lakes, gravel pits and reservoirs also fall into this category. Such lakes tend to have well grown, often reed-fringed, margins with abundant wetland and water plants. They also support good populations of insects and birds, and in winter they are magnets for visiting migrant waterfowl.

CLIMATE

Britain and Ireland are strongly influenced by the North Atlantic Drift, which swings warm water up towards this coast from the southern Atlantic. This means that the climate here is milder than one might expect

The Natterjack (Bufo calamita) is smaller than the Common Toad and has a clear pale line along its back. Natterjacks live in colonies in shallow pools, especially in dune-slacks, near the coast.

from latitude alone. The seas around our shores also vary little in temperature between winter and summer, so that the effect of the prevailing westerly and south-westerly wind is to warm the land in winter and cool it in summer. On average, the summers are cooler and wetter than those further east, and the winters, which are also wetter, are also considerably warmer. The average temperature difference between winter and summer in the west of Ireland is only 8°C, but this rises to about 11°C in eastern England.

The growing season is long, and this is essentially a tree and woodland climate, trees being able to grow almost everywhere in this region, at least potentially. The only dry-land sites which are probably naturally tree-less are the extreme mountain tops and very exposed offshore islands and coasts.

The western and northern areas have the highest rainfall, being exposed to the waves of westerly depressions which characterise the climate. Since much of the high ground is also in the north and west, the rainclouds tends to form and drop their precipitation first in these areas, whilst the land further east gains some protection by being in a rain shadow. This same combination of geology and climate also results generally in poorer, thinner soils in the north and west, contrasting with more fertile, deeper soils in the south and east.

The high rainfall results in many upland streams and a fine network of rivers, ponds and lakes, adding to the variety of habitats.

Even though the climate is mild compared with more continental areas, the winters can occasionally be fierce, and in some highland regions snow lies almost throughout the year. Many species, particularly some birds, cannot survive such rigours and have evolved strategies for escaping when times are tough. Many insect-eating birds, such as Swallow, martins, Swift and most warblers migrate south in the autumn, to richer feeding grounds in southern Europe or Africa. By contrast, there is also a big autumn and winter influx, particularly of waders and wildfowl, which flee their largely frozen northern breeding grounds and select the coastal and inland wetlands of Britain and Ireland for feeding. This region has some of the finest wetland habitats in the whole of Europe and the estuaries in particular are vital for many thousands of wintering ducks, geese, swans and shorebirds..

CONSERVATION

Although Britain and Ireland are relatively heavily populated, and their natural habitats have been largely destroyed or altered, nevertheless the conservation movement here is perhaps stronger and longer-established than anywhere else.

In Britain, the main agency responsible for conservation is the Nature Conservancy Council (NCC), currently undergoing a reorganization and re-emerging as separate bodies for Scotland, Wales and England. It establishes and manages reserves and identifies and notifies Sites of Special Scientific Interest (SSSIs).

In addition, voluntary bodies such as The Royal Society for the Protection of Birds (RSPB), The Royal Society for Nature Conservation (RSNC), The National Trust (NT), The National Trust for Scotland, The Botanical Society of the British Isles (BSBI), The British Trust for Ornithology (BTO), and The Wildfowl and Wetlands Trust bear witness to the popularity of wildlife conservation. The RSPB alone has over 870,000 members and over 115 reserves throughout the country. The RSNC has over 250,000 members and owns or manages more than 2,000 nature reserves.

The National Trust, founded in 1895, owns 1,235,500ha of land throughout England, Wales and Northern Ireland, with over fifty nature reserves and 400 Sites of Special Scientific Interest. The National Trust for Scotland owns over 247,000ha, with some of Scotland's finest mountain and coastal scenery.

The United Kingdom has 279 National Nature Reserves (of which forty-five are in Northern Ireland), mostly managed by the NCC. In addition, there are over 5,000 SSSIs, which are not as well protected, being often on private land. However, owners of SSSIs are legally obliged not to damage them, although in practice many have been harmed or lost. There are also about 150 Local Nature Reserves (LNRs) established by local planning authorities.

There are ten National Parks in England and Wales, generally covering large areas of mixed upland landscapes in the north and west. In the National Parks, there are rather strict controls over land-use which might damage the environment. The Norfolk Broads and New Forest areas also have a National Park-like status. Planning restrictions also apply in the forty-eight Areas of Outstanding Natural Beauty (AONBs). Scotland also has forty National Scenic Areas.

In Ireland, the Wildlife Service is the main government agency involved in conservation. An Taisce (The National Trust for Ireland) is the leading independent environmental body, and The Irish Wildbird Conservancy is also a major voluntary conservation organization.

Most of the organizations mentioned own or manage nature reserves, many of which are featured in this book.

TRAVEL TIPS

Always plan your trip carefully, taking full advantage of detailed maps and published information. Many of the reserves make available useful leaflets which help explain features of the wildlife and provide maps of routes, footpaths and tracks. In coastal sites always pay full attention to signs and notices giving information about safe paths, and especially to the times of low and high tides. Always respect other restrictions, such as fenced-off areas of shingle, which may protect rare nesting birds, such as terns or easily damaged vegetation.

Adequate protective clothing is essential, particularly in the winter months and when visiting exposed sites, such as hills, or coasts and estuaries. Cold, wet weather, especially when combined with a strong wind, can quickly chill, even if the thermometer reading is not unduly low! By contrast, it is also surprisingly easy to get sun-, and wind-burnt when out walking in the open. For extended hill walks take an anorak and gloves, with a spare jumper and socks, and dry trousers if possible. Shorts may be comfortable in good weather, but it is wise to have dry and warm clothes handy. Take sufficient food and drink and eat little and often; this keeps up energy levels most efficiently.

A good, supportive pair of walking boots is desirable when walking over rough or wet ground. Some people prefer lighter footwear however, which is fine as long as the soles give an adequate grip – test them on wet, sloping grass first. For very wet areas, waterproof rubber boots are really the only sensible choice.

Always take a good map when out walking for a long period in relatively wild country, travel in pairs or small groups whenever possible, and always tell someone else where you are going, giving them an estimated time of arrival. You should also take a compass, a first-aid kit, a loud whistle and a portable torch plus spare battery. If caught in a thunderstorm, avoid exposed positions such as hilltops or ridges.

Good, portable field guides are also useful to take out into the field, as is a handy notebook and pencil. The bibliography at the end of this book lists some recommended guides.

For the birdwatcher, a pair of binoculars is well-nigh essential and I would recommend either **x** 10 (if you have a reasonably steady hand) or **x** 8 magnification, as being about right for most situations. Some keen birders use a telescope as well, mostly for looking at waders on estuaries, or for sea-watching.

Always take care to follow the guidelines for visiting a particular site. Sometimes, a permit is required from the controlling body or owner. In other cases there is easy and open access. Always follow public footpaths when these are marked (they are clearly shown on the Ordnance Survey Landranger maps). Watch out for, and respect, restrictions imposed by local landowners. This is especially important in upland moorland, particularly in Scotland during the Grouse shooting season (August 12th to 10th December) and during the deer stalking season (August to October). In the Republic of Ireland there is no network of public rights of way, so it is best to seek advice when planning a walk in open country.

Above all, perhaps the best advice for the naturalist is keep quiet, to move slowly and watch carefully. It is often surprising how much can be seen by selecting a good vantage point and observing. A good naturalist needs patience as well as knowledge.

The **Country Code** should always be adhered to as far as is possible:

1. Guard against fire;
2. Keep all gates closed;
3. Keep dogs under proper control;
4. Keep to paths across farmland;
5. Do not damage walls, fences or hedges;
6. Take all litter home;
7. Safeguard all water supplies;
8. Protect all wildlife;
9. Walk with care on country roads;
10. Respect the life of the countryside;
11. Do not make unnecessary noise;
12. Leave livestock, crops and machinery alone.

SECTION II:
SITE GUIDE

Although Britain and Ireland cover a relatively small area, and all parts of these islands enjoy a broadly similar temperate, oceanic climate, there are sufficient regional differences, both of climate and of associated vegetation, to make it convenient to divide the area into several regions.

In this book I have recognized thirteen such regions, following landscape features to some extent though of necessity the borders are determined partly by county or country boundaries. These regions are, very roughly, similar in size, and I have selected from within each a comparable number of sites.

For each region there is an introduction to the landscape and the main habitats to be found there, with a mention of any plants or animals which are particularly characteristic of that region or restricted to it. The box at the end of each introduction highlights fifty species which are associated with that region. These include some which are only to be found there, and also others which are especially common there or otherwise characteristic.

For each site described the information box provides a quick summary of the main features of interest to the visitor, including how to find the site, when best to visit it, with notes on any restrictions and an indication of the most impressive wildlife to be found there. Some sites are primarily of interest to the birdwatcher, while others have important collections of unusual wild flowers or insects. Occasionally, a single site combines excellent birdwatching with a rich flora and insect fauna.

The aim of this book is to provide a selection of sites, chosen in the main to represent a good cross-section of the varied habitats of these islands and their associated wildlife. All the National Parks are included, and the selection strives to include sites, usually reserves, which are scenically appealing as well as of interest to those who visit for the wildlife. Sites known for one particular rare species or group of species, and very small sites, have not been included.

After some of the numbered site entries there is a shortlist of other interesting sites which can be found nearby. For these, only brief notes have been provided on location and specialities, and the intention is that the reader will find these comments helpful when planning a holiday or visit to the region concerned.

For England, Wales and Scotland the information box gives an Ordnance Survey grid reference and the Landranger map number (L) to help pinpoint each site accurately. For all sites, mention is made of the nearest town or village, with an indication of the direction and distance from this place to the site in question.

Opposite: *burnt Gorse (Ulex europaeus) on the cliffs of Whitsands Bay in Cornwall.*
Overleaf: *maps of Great Britain and Ireland showing the positions of the main numbered sites described in Section II, and the boundaries of each of the thirteen regions.*

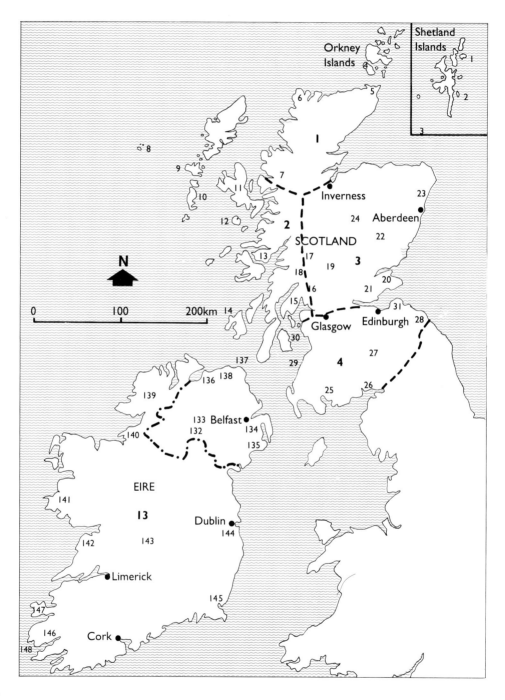

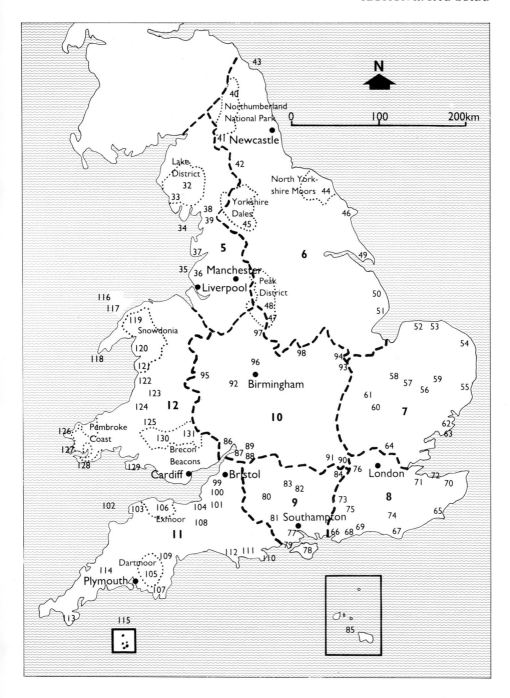

1. NORTHERN SCOTLAND

In the Highlands, Shetland and Orkney, the scenery can be really spectacular, especially on the outlying islands and stacks, but it is largely a very exposed area with regular high winds and storms. Despite this, the summers often have warm periods, and the days are long. In winter, by contrast, day-length is short and the hills and mountains are bleak, windswept and cold. The Flow Country in the north-east is one of the largest remaining expanses of peatland and moor.

There are many fascinating birds in this region, particularly those associated with sea, cliffs and moorland. Gannets abound in the coastal waters and breed in several large colonies, as do Fulmar, and auks such as Guillemot and Puffin. The rocky coasts and sheltered inlets attract Eider, and both Red- and Black-Throated Divers can be seen, either offshore or at breeding lochs inland.

Shetland attracts many birdwatchers and offers a wide range of seabirds and northern specialities, including British Storm-petrel, Great Skua, Red-necked Phalarope, Whimbrel and the occasional Snowy Owl.

Siskins breed in many places, and Twite

Eider (Somateria mollissima) is a large sea-duck which breeds around the coasts of Scotland and Northern Ireland. The male has a striking black-and-white breeding plumage.

can be found on the open moorland, especially near the coast. Old Scots Pine woods are the choice of the only truly endemic bird of the British Isles, the Scottish Crossbill.

Peregrines patrol the sea-cliffs on the lookout for likely prey, such as Rock Doves, and the higher hills and mountains are the haunt of Golden Eagles. Ravens and Hooded Crows are both commonly seen.

The northern coast, from Cape Wrath to John o' Groats, offers much to the botanist too. The most famous botanical treasure of this coastal strip is the pretty little endemic Scottish Primrose, happily still quite locally frequent in the short turf near the sea-cliffs. Where the limestone outcrops, especially near Bettyhill, the flora is very special, with Mountain Avens at sea-level, together with Pyramidal Bugle and Purple Oxytropis. Another characteristic plant of the north coast is the Curved Sedge.

Further south, and inland, the Inchnadamph area provides many botanical delights. The low limestone cliffs have large colonies of Dark-red Helleborine, abundant Mountain Avens and the very local Arctic Sandwort. Also in this area is the Whortle-leaved Willow.

On the moors and mountains two northern shrubs can be found. The Dwarf Birch is frequent around Ben Loyal, and Alpine

Opposite: *the Jay (Garrulus glandarius) is a common woodland bird throughout much of Britain and Ireland.*

Bearberry is found in many parts of Sutherland and Caithness.

Orkney and Shetland offer comparatively little special botanical attraction, although Shetland does boast a very special subspecies of Arctic Mouse-ear.

The Red-necked Phalarope (Phalaropus lobatus) is a rare breeding bird of the extreme north and west of Scotland (mainly Hebrides and Shetland) and the far west of Ireland. It is occasionally seen as a migrant, particularly after autumn storms.

I FETLAR (SHETLAND)	
Location:	Off E coast of Shetland island of Yell. Reserve is in N of island of Fetlar, around Vord Hill and Stackaberg, and covers about 690ha
Grid Reference:	HU 6292; L2
Access:	By regular ferry via Yell and Unst. Best in summer. Access to reserve mid-May to end July only
Terrain:	Rocky and grassy island, with patches of heather moor, peat bog and scattered lochs
Specialities:	Snowy Owl, Arctic Tern, Red-Necked Phalarope, British Storm-petrel, Otter, Common Seal

Fetlar lies about 6.5km east of the Isle of Yell and a similar distance south of the Isle of Unst, in the Shetland group, and is one of the most northerly spots in the British Isles.

FIFTY INTERESTING SPECIES TO LOOK FOR

Arctic Skua	Leach's Storm-petrel	Snowy Owl	Pyramidal Bugle
Arctic Tern	Merlin	Twite	Roseroot
Black-throated Diver	Puffin	Whimbrel	Scots Lovage
British Storm-petrel	Raven	Wood Sandpiper	Scottish Primrose
Eider	Razorbill	Alpine Bearberry	Whortle-leaved
Fulmar	Red Grouse	Arctic Mouse-ear	Willow
Gannet	Red-throated Diver	Arctic Sandwort	Common Seal
Golden Eagle	Red-necked Phalarope	Curved Sedge	Grey Seal
Golden Plover	Redwing	Dark-red Helleborine	Otter
Great Skua	Rock Dove	Downy Birch	Red Deer
Guillemot	Rock Pipit	Dwarf Birch	Wild Cat
Hooded Crow	Scottish Crossbill	Mountain Avens	Large Heath
Kittiwake	Siskin	Purple Oxytropis	

The terrain is bleak and treeless, consisting of rolling grassland, heather moor and bog. These habitats are interpersed with pockets of cultivation, rocky outcrops and the occasional loch or small pool. The coast is rocky, with small beaches and a few cliffs, particularly in the north.

The island became instantly famous in 1967, when Snowy Owls bred there. They bred regularly there between 1967 and 1975, and occasional birds have been present on and off there ever since. Breeding is probable again in the future. Besides the owls, Fetlar has a good population of Red-necked Phalarope, which are best seen at Loch of Funzie and Papil Water. Another bird of the lochs is the Red-throated Diver. Whimbrel are another speciality – look out for these on moorland sites, where they are fairly common.

This is one of the best places to see Manx Shearwater and British Storm-petrel, both of which breed in the south, particularly on the western slopes of Lamb Hoga. The shearwaters gather in the evenings in the Wick of Tresta before coming to land to find their breeding burrows.

In the north, the cliffs have breeding colonies of Fulmars, Kittiwakes, Shags, Puffins (about 2,500 pairs) and Black Guillemot also breed around the island. Fetlar has one of the largest concentrations of Arctic Skua, and Great Skua also nest here.

Both Grey and Common Seals are frequent, and Otters hunt regularly over the island and in the surrounding shallows.

The plants include interesting species such as Creeping Willow, Field Gentian, Northern Rock-cress, Northern Marsh Orchid, Frog Orchid and Moonwort.

Other important sites nearby: Hermaness (HP 6016), at the north tip of Unst, has over 10,000 pairs of Gannets.

2 ISLE OF NOSS (SHETLAND)	
Location:	E of Lerwick in Shetlands, immediately E of Bressay
Grid Reference:	HU 5540; L4
Visiting:	By ferry from Lerwick via Bressay and from Bressay to Noss (weather permitting). Open mid-May to end August (10.00–17.00, except Monday and Thursday)
Terrain:	Uninhabited island, with cliffs, grassland and heather moor
Specialities:	Huge seabird colonies, including a Gannetry

Noss is a National Reserve and covers about 300ha, rising to towering sandstone cliffs, reaching over 180m at the Noup of Noss. There are pockets of native heath and bog, but much of the land has been grazed for centuries and is much modified from its natural state. The coastline however is wild and unaltered, with rugged and fragile cliffs and scree, offering ideal nest-sites for a host of birds The cliff-tops have a rich array of flowers.

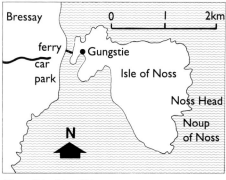

Map of the Isle of Noss.

On the cliffs the seabirds gather to breed in huge numbers, with over 100,000 pairs altogether, including about 38,000 pairs of Guillemot, 10,000 pairs of Kittiwake, 7,000 pairs of Gannet, about 6,000 pairs of Fulmar, and about 1,500 pairs of Razorbill. In amongst the boulders and clefts there are also Black Guillemot and Shag, and other specialities are Puffin, and both Great and Arctic Skuas. The Great Skuas breed very densely on Noss, and number about 400 pairs – a large population indeed for such a small island.

The nearby seas are ideal for both Grey and Common Seals, and watch out for Common Porpoises, particulary in Bressay Sound. As in many parts of the more remote areas of Scotland, Otters are still to be found along the rocky shore.

In the heaths, which are dominated by Heather, the flowers include Tormentil and Heath Bedstraw, and the pretty Heath Spotted Orchid. Roseroot and Scots Lovage are two northern species growing on the cliffs.

3 FAIR ISLE (SHETLAND)	
Location:	Midway between Shetlands and Orkneys
Grid Reference:	HZ 2172; L4
Visiting:	By air or ferry from Shetland
Terrain:	Small island with rough grassland, boggy heath, rocky shore, with sandstone cliffs
Specialities:	Migrant birds, including vagrants from North America and Siberia. Excellent bird cliffs and Grey Seal coves

Fair Isle is remote, lying about 40km due south of Shetland, and roughly mid-way between Shetland and the Orkneys.

Fair Isle's position puts it right on the main migration route for many birds and, since it is the only land for miles around, many small migrants use it as a stopping off point, mainly in the spring, early summer and autumn. The list of migrants, many of them rare, is impressive and includes regular Bluethroat, Icterine Warbler, Red-backed Shrike and Scarlet Rosefinch.

In the south, Fair Isle is crofted, whereas in the north it is more hilly, with heather moor, rising to about 215m. The cliffs, which reach about 150m, support good colonies of Kittiwake, Fulmar, and auks, and Common and Arctic

Otters (Lutra lutra) are sleek, mainly aquatic predators, found in waterways throughout the region. However, they have become rare over much of the lowlands and are very sensitive to disturbance and pollution.

Terns both breed on the island. At night, British Storm-petrels come ashore and several pairs also breed here. Leach's Storm-petrel is also seen regularly, and may breed as well.

The rocky coves and inlets are home to Grey Seals which can often be spotted hauled out, or bobbing in the water close to shore.

The rough grassy areas are dominated by skuas, with about 120 pairs of Arctic Skuas and about forty pairs of Great Skuas nesting. Watch out for the occasional Long-tailed Skua, and beware dive-bombing attacks, especially from the powerful Great Skuas!

The plant life is interesting too, especially in the cultivated crofted areas. Flowers include Roseroot, Thrift, Frog Orchid, Moonwort, Adder's Tongue, Spring Squill, Field Gentian, with many sedges and rushes.

4 NORTH HOY (ORKNEY)	
Location:	S and W of Orgill on island of Hoy
Grid Reference:	HY 2303; L7
Visiting:	From mainland Orkney by ferry from Stromness to Moaness Pier, or by car ferry from Houton to Lyness. Best in summer
Terrain:	Heather moor, bog and grassland, culminating in steep sea-cliffs and stacks
Specialities:	Seabird colonies, particularly auks, Kittiwake. Also Peregrine, Hen Harrier and Merlin. Mountain Hare

This RSPB reserve includes the summit of Ward Hill (479m), to the south-west of Orgill, at the north end of the island of Hoy. There are frequent ferries from Mainland Orkney.

This is a windswept, rather remote landscape, mainly tree-less, except in sheltered sites, the dominant habitats are bog, moorland and grassland, with inland crags and sheer sea-cliffs, especially on the west coast. A path leads from the west of the reserve, through Rackwick to the Old Man of Hoy, an impressive sandstone stack rising up to over 130m, and with nesting Fulmars. This area has some of the best seabird cliffs. A minor road skirts the southern edge of the reserve as far as Rackwick and ends in a simple car park.

Sandy Loch, a small loch close to the main track, has Red-throated Diver, and Great Skuas also breed in this area. The moors around support breeding Dunlin, Snipe and Golden Plover.

The cliffs west of Rackwick have large numbers of Guillemot, Razorbill, Puffin and Kittiwake, and you may also spot a Peregrine patrolling the skies overhead.

Other birds to watch out for are Stonechats perched on the top of bushes, especially on patches of Gorse, Wheatear amongst the rocks and rough pasture, and the Linnet-like Twite in small flocks over the moorland. Hen Harrier and Merlin may also be spotted in or near the reserve, and with luck, a Golden Eagle may soar over the hills on huge outstretched wings.

Interesting plants include Purple Saxifrage, Alpine Saw-wort, Alpine Bearberry and Dwarf Willow.

Other important sites nearby: Copinsay (HY 6001) is an island off the east coast of Mainland, and Marwick Head (HY 2224) on Mainland both have large seabird colonies.

5 DUNNET HEAD

Location:	NE mainland Scotland (Highland), about 10km NW of Thurso
Grid Reference:	ND 2075; L12
Visiting:	B855 N from A836 at Dunnet; ends at car park just short of lighthouse
Terrain:	Rocky headland with sandstone cliffs. Grassland and heather moor
Specialities:	Seabirds and local flowers, including Scottish Primrose (best May or June)

Dunnet Head juts out into the Pentland Firth as the most northerly point on the British mainland, and is easily reached by the Thurso to John o' Groats road. It may be visited throughout the year, but the best season is probably spring or early summer, when the flowers are at their finest.

In addition to colonies of Kittiwake, Fulmar, Guillemot, Razorbill, Black Guillemot and Puffin, the cliffs are a home to wild Rock Dove, and Raven.

In the Dunnet Bay area a few Arctic Terns breed and all three divers can be seen at certain times of year. Watch for small flocks of Twite, particularly around the crofts.

In winter the birds are equally interesting, and it is possible to see all three divers offshore and in the bay, together with sea-ducks such as Goldeneye, Eider, Long-tailed Duck, Common Scoter and Red-breasted Merganser. There are two small areas of freshwater nearby, namely St John's Loch and Loch of Mey. These attract small numbers of Whooper Swan and White-fronted and Greylag Geese, as well as Glaucous and Iceland Gulls, and waders including Purple Sandpiper and Turnstone.

The cliffs and nearby grassland have several unusual flowers, including the rare Scottish Primrose (also at Strathy Point), Spring Squill, Roseroot, Scots Lovage and Alpine Saw-wort.

Other important sites nearby: Dunnet Links is a reserve on Dunnet Bay. Strathy Point lies about 30km west along A836. Nearby Thurso harbour often has visiting Glaucous or Iceland Gulls in winter.

Scottish Primrose *Primula scotica*
This charming little plant is one of the few endemic members of the British flora. It is locally common in short turf on headlands near the sea on the north Scottish coast and on Orkney, where it flowers in June and July. The small, neat rosettes of leaves are a mealy white underneath, and the flower stalks, less than 10cm tall, have up to six small flowers, dark purple in colour with a yellow throat. Its larger relative, the Bird's-Eye Primrose, *P. farinosa*, grows in north England and south Scotland.

A rich coastal pasture at Bettyhill, in mid-July. Amongst the plants to be seen in this area are Scottish Primrose and Mountain Avens.

6 CLO MOR	
Location:	c. 10km NW of Durness (Highland), 5km SE of Cape Wrath.
Grid Reference:	NC 3073; L9
Visiting:	By ferry across Kyle of Durness from Keoldale, then by minibus towards Cape Wrath (alight at Kearvaig track)
Terrain:	Britain's highest mainland sea cliffs. Rocky shore, grass and heath inland
Specialities:	Seabird colonies, with one of largest British Puffin colonies. Golden Eagle

This spectacular site is best reached by walking from Kearvaig up towards the cliffs. The going is fairly rough and quite hilly inland from the cliffs.

The massive cliff rises to 280m and is alive with a mixture of seabirds, especially Puffin, Guillemot, Razorbill and Black Guillemot. The cliffs are another good site for wild Rock Doves which, together with other birds, provide rich pickings for the

Mountain Avens (Dryas octopetala). This pretty species prefers limestone rocks, especially in the mountains. It also grows at or near sea-level in the far north, and also in the Irish Burren.

local Peregrines. Golden Eagles also nest nearby and may be spotted soaring in the area. The hills just inland from the cliffs support Ptarmigan, at the surprisingly low altitude of around 200m, together with Red Grouse. Another speciality are Greenshank, which breed in damp areas alongside some of the streams.

Watch out for Great Northern Diver and Long-tailed Duck in the spring, particularly at Balnakiel Bay to the east.

Other important sites nearby: Faraid Head, just north of Durness, also has a large Puffin colony, and limestone heath vegetation with Mountain Avens.

7 BEINN EIGHE	
Location:	c. 2km W of Kinlochewe
Grid Reference:	NH 0065; L19/25
Visiting:	Visitor centre at Aultroy (open June–September)
Terrain:	Mountain country with heather moor and remnant Scots Pine woods
Specialities:	Golden Eagle, Merlin, Red Deer, Wild Cat, Pine Marten, Alpine flowers

This magnificent west highland reserve was the first British National Nature Reserve to be established, largely to protect the natural Scots Pine woodland fringing Loch Maree at Coille na Glas Leitire. It is also very large, covering about 4,800ha. Two trails lead into the reserve from a car park about 3km from the Aultroy Visitor Centre, one traversing woodland, the other mainly mountain country (the latter takes four hours to walk).

The lakeside woodland is being encouraged to recolonize higher ground by careful

A speciality bird is the Scottish Crossbill which is a scarce breeder in the old Scots Pine woods, where Siskins may also be spotted. Also breeding here are Sparrowhawk, Woodcock, Redstart, Wood Warbler and Redpoll. Watch for Greenshank in the wetter valley bottoms, and for Ring Ousel on the rocky slopes.

Red Deer and Roe Deer are quite easy to spot but there are other interesting but more elusive mammals here too, including Mountain Hare, Wild Cat, Pine Marten, Otter and Fox.

In the pine woods there are orchids such as Creeping Ladies' Tresses and Lesser Twayblade, together with some local and rare mosses and liverworts. On the moorland areas, the best flowers are found associated with calcareous outcroppings, with such species as Purple Saxifrage, Common and Intermediate Wintergreens and Roseroot. On ledges and other areas protected from grazing there are species such as Globeflower, Melancholy Thistle and Pyramidal Bugle. Occasional patches of acid upland heath with Dwarf Juniper, bearberries and Trailing Azalea add to the interest. Finally, at around 1,000m there are some Arctic-Alpine heath communities with Dwarf Willow, Mossy Saxifrage and Moss Campion.

The reserve also has a rich insect fauna, with thirteen species of dragonfly, including the local Azure Hawker and rare White-faced Darter.

The best time to visit is early summer, but the area is also impressive in the autumn, when the deer rut.

Other important sites nearby: Torridon (NG 9059) lies to the south-west and the whole area between Lochs Torridan and Maree form part of the Gairloch Conservation Unit, containing some of Scotland's wildest and finest scenery.

*Globeflower (*Trollius europaeus*). This giant buttercup is a flower of damp sites, especially in the north.*

management and the control of deer grazing. For this and other reasons, the Red Deer have to be carefully controlled and culled, and access is therefore restricted between 1st September and 21st November. On the slopes, upland grassland and bog take over, blending into scree slopes and Arctic-Alpine heaths at even higher elevations.

Mountain birds include Golden Eagle, Merlin, Peregrine, Buzzard, Ptarmigan and Snow Bunting. On the lochs there are both Red-throated and Black-throated Divers, and Redwing nest in the nearby birchwoods.

2. WESTERN SCOTLAND AND ISLANDS

The west of Scotland (north Strathclyde and the western Highlands) and the western isles have a magic all their own and contain some of the most beautiful scenery in the British Isles. They combine brooding mountains with gentle sheltered valleys and bays, as well as highly dramatic wild, rocky shores and cliffs. The relatively flat outer isles still have much unimproved traditional agriculture, particularly the species-rich hay meadows of the machair. By contrast, many of the inner isles, such as Skye and Mull, are hilly and mountainous, with imposing high ground, and bleak, exposed rocky coasts, as well as more sheltered coves and bays. This variety all adds to the natural history interest, making this region one of the most rewarding to visit.

Open well-grown Scots Pine woods are the prime habitat of the huge Capercaillie (Tetrao urogallus), which was re-introduced to the highlands in the last century. It is currently in decline, with perhaps as few as 1,500 birds left.

Buzzards are commonly seen over the more wooded valleys and hills, and Peregrines are fairly frequent on the crags and cliffs. A special raptor of this region is the White-tailed Eagle, now successfully re-introduced to Rhum, and ranging widely along this coast. Golden Eagle is represented here too, on the higher mountains and also on some rocky sea-cliffs. The Hebrides are one of the last strongholds in Europe of the Corncrake, and the Red-necked Phalarope also breeds on the outer isles. On wet moorland and along undisturbed upland valleys watch for the rather scarce Greenshank.

This is also Red Deer country, and controlled herds roam over many of the glens and hills. Wild Cat is commoner here than many imagine, but is very difficult to spot, being largely nocturnal and very wary, and the coasts and sheltered sea-lochs hold good populations of Otter.

Exciting botanical discoveries have been made in the western highlands and islands. Here there are unique localities for Alpine Rock-cress on the mountains of Skye, and on the mainland for the very rare Arctic cushion plant *Diapensia lapponica*, discovered as late as 1951. The extraordinary Pipewort can be found on Skye and Coll, and is otherwise restricted in Europe to the west of Ireland. A special pondweed, *Potamogeton epihydrus*, grows in lakes in South Uist: like the Pipewort, it has a mainly North American distribution. Finally, among these very special northern rarities, the remarkable little Arctic annual, Iceland Purslane, deserves special mention. On Skye and Mull this plant is probably at its southern limit in Europe. The curious Mossy Cyphel is by contrast not found in the Arctic, but also occurs in the Alps, Pyrenees and Carpathians.

Other characteristic flowers and ferns of this region are Northern Rock-cress, Narrow-leaved Helleborine, Irish Lady's Tresses, Hay-scented Buckler Fern and Holly Fern.

8 ST KILDA	
Location:	Isolated group of rocky islands, c. 70km W of the Outer Hebrides
Grid Reference:	NA 1000
Visiting:	By tour only. Permission required from NTS to stay
Terrain:	Sheer cliffs rising from ocean; sheep-grazed grassland and maritime heath
Specialities:	Vast seabird colonies, including world's largest gannetry

The St Kilda group of rocky islands stands as a bastion against the fierce Atlantic storms and forms a secure refuge for millions of seabirds. There are four islands: Hirta (or St Kilda), Soay, Boreray and Dun. Boats make regular trips in summer to the main island, Hirta. The north face of Conachair on Hirta rises some 430m from the sea, forming Britain's highest sea-cliff.

The main gannetry (with 50,000 pairs) is on Boreray and the nearby stacks of Stac Lee (172m) and Stac an Armin (192m). The islands also have over 230,000 pairs of Puffin (the colony on Dun is the largest in Britain), some 7,800 pairs of Kittiwake, 63,000 pairs of Fulmar (including Britain's largest colony), and about 10,000 pairs each of both Leach's and British Storm-petrels.

St Kilda has its own unique subspecies of Wren, which is larger than the mainland form and has a different song. Look for the Wren amongst the abandoned houses in the old village on Hirta.

Grey Seals breed around the islands, especially on Hirta and Dun, and feral Soay Sheep, an ancient brown breed, roam at will on Hirta as well as on Soay itself.

Interesting plants include Purple Saxifrage, Moss Campion, and the maritime fern Sea Spleenwort.

FIFTY INTERESTING SPECIES TO LOOK FOR

Black Grouse	Manx Shearwater	Otter	Northern Marsh
Black Guillemot	Peregrine	Red Deer	Orchid
Black-throated Diver	Puffin	Wild Cat	Northern Rock-cress
British Storm-petrel	Raven	Alpine Rock-cress	Pipewort
Buzzard	Red-breasted	Diapensia lapponica	Potamogeton epihydrus
Corncrake	Merganser	Hay-scented Buckler	Purple Saxifrage
Eider	Red Grouse	Fern	Sea Spleenwort
Fulmar	Red-necked Phalarope	Holly Fern	Chequered Skipper
Golden Eagle	Red-throated Diver	Iceland Purslane	Dark-green Fritillary
Greenshank	Short-eared Owl	Irish Lady's Tresses	Large Heath
Hen Harrier	Sooty Shearwater	Mossy Cyphel	Marsh Fritillary
Hooded Crow	White-tailed Eagle	Narrow-leaved	Scotch Argus
Kittiwake	Whooper Swan	Helleborine	Small Pearl-bordered
Leach's Storm-petrel	Grey Seal		Fritillary

9 BALRANALD (NORTH UIST)	
Location:	In NW of Hebridean island of North Uist
Grid Reference:	NF 7070; L18
Visiting:	Close to A865. Call at reception cottage on arrival. April–September
Terrain:	Marshes, rocky and sandy shores, machair and lochs
Specialities:	Breeding waders and wildfowl; seabirds (especially on passage); wild flowers; Corncrake

The Corncrake, a rare and threatened species, breeds regularly here in the machair and crops. You may be lucky and spot one, but the monotonous rasping call will usually give them away, most often in the early hours. There are probably about fifteen pairs in the reserve. May to July is the best season to visit for Corncrake and breeding waders, and for the myriad machair flowers. Sea-watching, from lookout spots such as Aird an Runair, can be very productive, with species such as Manx and Sooty Shearwaters, British and Leach's Storm-petrels, and Long-tailed and Pomarine Skuas a regular feature.

The machair has breeding Dunlin, Redshank, Lapwing, Oystercatcher and Ringed Plover, with Snipe in the wetter parts. Breeding ducks include Gadwall, Teal, Wigeon, Shoveler and Tufted Duck. Watch out for Twite and Corn Bunting. All three divers may occasionally be seen at some time of the year, along with Arctic Tern, which breed in the area. In general, Red-throated Diver breed on small lochs, the rarer Black-throated on larger lochs, and Great Northern are usually only seen at sea – the latter are non-breeding birds.

Grey Seals breed nearby and are worth looking out for in all the rocky inlets. There is also a thriving Otter population, and with patience they can be spotted fishing in the lochs.

Botanically the machair is fascinating. The soil is a mixture of shell-sand and peat and is very fertile, supporting a rich grassland which is partly cultivated, often as hay

Irish Lady's Tresses *Spiranthes romanzoffiana* The lady's tresses orchids, with their spirally arranged flowers, grow throughout the northern hemisphere. Only one is widespread in the British Isles, the Autumn Lady's Tresses. The best-known habitats of the Irish Lady's Tresses are in the west of Ireland, where it is rare but is found in several places. In west Scotland and the Hebrides it occurs in scattered populations, usually in damp, peaty meadows. There is an isolated site on Dartmoor, in England. It belongs to that very special group of species, like Pipewort, whose main distribution is in North America and which are not found anywhere on the European mainland. The spikes bear many large, white, sweet-scented flowers arranged in three spirally-curved rows. It flowers in July and August.

meadow. These traditional, semi-natural habitats harbour many pretty flowers, such as Ragged Robin, Early and Northern Marsh Orchids, Tufted Vetch, and in damper patches the beautiful Yellow Flag.

Other important sites nearby: Balivanich (Benbecula) has regular Glaucous and Iceland Gulls, and the causeway from North Uist to Benbecula offers excellent views of waders. Lochs Skealtar and Scadavay are good for divers, and are worth checking for Black-throated Divers.

View of North Uist from Eaval. This is a landscape of hillocks, blanket bog and lakes, the haunt of divers and waders.

10 LOCH DRUIDIBEG	
Location:	Towards N of Hebridean island of South Uist
Grid Reference:	NF7937; L22
Visiting:	On main A865 road. Permit required to enter reserve in summer (apply NCC or local warden in Stilligarry)
Terrain:	Mixture of open water, lochs, machair, moorland
Specialities:	Greylag Goose, Whooper Swan, divers.

This splendid loch has about seventy pairs of wild Greylag Geese, and a wealth of other wildfowl, including Eider, Teal, Shoveler, Shelduck, Wigeon and Red-breasted Merganser. Occasionally, Whooper Swans, regular in winter, stay on for the summer. There is also a colony of Grey Heron. The breeding waders are similar to those at Balranald, and watch out for Common Sandpiper and Dunlin. Common Gulls also breed here.

The whole region is good country for birds of prey, and for Short-eared Owls. Hen Harriers are frequent, but all the following breed in the area: Kestrel, Sparrowhawk, Merlin, Peregrine, Buzzard and Golden Eagle. On the east coast, it is worth remembering that White-tailed Eagles sometimes wander over from their Rhum stronghold, where they have been re-introduced.

Near the B890 towards Lochskipport Long-eared Owls breed in a mixed grove of trees and rhododendrons. From here it is well worth gazing up at the flanks of Hecla for Golden Eagle.

In spring and early summer the machair is bright with flowers, such as Lesser Meadowrue, Self-heal, Thyme, eyebrights, Kidney Vetch, Yarrow, Heath Spotted Orchid and Northern Marsh Orchid (and their hybrids). In the hay meadows there are poppies and Corn Marigold.

The acid waters of the loch itself and nearby peaty pools have species such as Bog Asphodel, cottongrasses, and the pretty Water Lobelia. Many of the lake's islands have stands of Scots Pine, Rowan, Juniper and willows, sometimes with Royal Fern in the undergrowth.

Other important sites nearby: South Uist Machairs (at Rudha Ardvule point, NF7330) has excellent machair vegetation. Loch Bee (to the north of Loch Druidibeg) is good for wildfowl.

The Peregrine (Falco peregrinus) is Britain's most powerful breeding falcon, here seen hunched over a kill in a moorland habitat.

Corncrake *Crex crex* L26

The Corncrake is a rarely seen, secretive bird which usually remains hidden in vegetation. It is a summer visitor, most often detected by its characteristic repeated rasping calls, often lasting hours, and frequently given at night as well as by day. It is a slimly built bird, light grey-brown above, with dark brown streaks. Its flight is ungainly and fluttering, showing trailing legs and chestnut wings. Moist grassland and traditionally managed tall hay meadows are where it breeds, and it is characteristic of the machair communities of the Hebrides and western Ireland. Unfortunately, populations of this attractive bird are in decline following habitat destruction.

11 OLD MAN OF STORR (SKYE)	
Location:	c. 10km N of Portree on Isle of Skye
Grid Reference:	NG 4954; L23
Visiting:	By path from car park close to A855. Best early summer
Terrain:	Heather moor, bog, grassland, cliffs, conifer plantations
Specialities:	Northern plants. Ring Ousel

Skye is easily visited by ferry from Kyle of Lochalsh. To reach the Old Man of Storr, take the A850 west and north from Kyleakin,

The Old Man of Storr. These strange pinnacles support a rich Arctic-Alpine flora at unusually low altitude.

via Broadford, through the magnificent coastal scenery to Portree (about 50km). Watch over the sea for Gannet fishing, especially in Scalpay Sound, and for Eider. The Old Man is to the west of the road soon after it passes Loch Leathan, some 10km north of Portree.

Follow a steep path through the conifer plantations, crossing a boggy area. This path leads on to The Old Man of Storr itself, an isolated rock pinnacle, 50m tall.

Like The Storr, a peak which rises up beyond, the rock is base-rich and many interesting wild flowers grow here, including Arctic-Alpine species at low altitude. Amongst these are Northern Rock-cress, Alpine Lady's Mantle, Moss Campion, Mossy and Starry Saxifrages, Iceland Purslane and Three-

flowered Rush. In boggy areas there are Bog-bean and Round-leaved Sundew.

Other important sites nearby: Tokavaig Wood (NG 6112) is a striking relict mixed Ash wood in the south of the island. It has a rich fern and bryophyte flora. Strathsuardal (NG 6322) has fine limestone pavement with Mountain Avens at low altitude. The Clan Donald Centre (NG 6105) has an arboretum and natural mixed deciduous woods.

12 RHUM	
Location:	SW of Isle of Skye
Grid Reference:	NM 3798; L39
Visiting:	By ferry from Mallaig or Arisaig. Permit needed from Scottish Natural Heritage to visit most of island. Limited accommodation in Kinloch Castle; some camping permitted. Best May–June. Beware midges!
Terrain:	Mountainous island with all major highland and coastal habitats
Specialities:	Golden Eagle, White-tailed Eagle, Red Deer

The whole of this magnificent island is a National Nature Reserve. There is a wide range of habitats, from rocky coast, to cliffs, bog, heather moor, grassland, and lochs, with some pockets of native woodland, and conifer plantations. The thriving Red Deer population is probably the best studied in the world. There are also feral goats on the island, and Otters and Common Seals in the bays.

Rhum is famed as the site for the re-introduction of the White-tailed Eagle to Britain. However, the eagles wander widely and a sighting is not therefore guaranteed on Rhum. There are up to five pairs of Golden Eagles nesting, as well as Peregrine, Merlin and Sparrowhawk. Over 100,000 pairs of Manx Shearwater breed on the mountain tops in the centre of the island (Askival and Hallival).

Red Grouse, Ravens and Golden Plover frequent the hills, whilst Woodcock, and the occasional Long-eared Owl breeds in the wooded areas. Along the streams, watch for Grey Wagtail, Dipper and Common Sandpiper.

Rhum has a rich insect fauna too, with Dark-green and Small Pearl-bordered Fritillaries, Large Heath, Emperor Moth, Fox Moth, Drinker and Northern Eggar.

Mountain flowers include Mountain Avens, Moss Campion, Stone Bramble and Northern Rock-cress, and in the lowlands there are orchids including Fragrant, Frog, and marsh Orchids, particularly near the sandy northern bays.

Other important sites nearby: The adjacent islands of Canna and Eigg are also well worth visiting.

13 RAHOY HILLS	
Location:	On Morvern Peninsula (Highland), opposite Isle of Mull
Grid Reference:	NM 6954; L47/49
Visiting:	Permit needed from SWT. Best from May–July
Terrain:	Mountain country; streams, lochs, valleyside woodland, bog, grassland and moor
Specialities:	Rare Arctic-Alpine plants

This reserve is relatively isolated on the peninsula of Morvern, to the north of Oban. Reached via the regular ferry over the Corran Narrows (south-west of Fort William) at the head of Loch Linnhe and thence on the A861 along Glen Tarbert, branching off on the A884 in the direction of Lochaline. A track leads north-west past the beautiful Loch Arienas to Kinloch. Alternatively, you can enter the reserve by walking up the Black Glen from Acharn (at the Post Office).

There is a well preserved mixed oak woodland on the north shore of Loch Arienas, with blanket bog and mountain grassland clothing much of the hills behind. The peaks of Beinn na h-Uamha (pronounced Ben-a-hoor) and Beinn Iadain, which rise up above the reserve are special because, like The Storr on Skye, they are of a base-rich volcanic rock which supports a rich and rare flora.

The wild plants include four species of saxifrage, Alpine Meadow Rue, Moss Campion, Northern Rock-cress, Norwegian Sandwort, Hairy Stonecrop, Three-flowered Rush and Holly Fern. Look out for the insectivorous Butterwort and both Round-leaved and Great Sundews in the blanket bogs nearby.

Greenshank and Red-Throated Diver breed on the marshy ground and lochans and it is always worth scanning the skies around for Peregrine and even the huge Golden Eagle.

Other important sites nearby: Sunart Woods at Ariundle, near Strontian (NM 8364) are fine, damp oakwoods with rich flora. The Isle of Mull is easily accessible via the ferry at Lochaline and is full of wild, exciting country, especially on the west coast. Golden Eagles breed on the island and are always worth watching for over the peaks. On Mull there is an interesting NTS coastal reserve at Burg on the Ardmeanach peninsula (NM 4226).

14 LOCH GRUINART (ISLAY)

Location:	In N of Islay (southern-most of Inner Hebrides)
Grid Reference:	NR 2767; L60
Visiting:	Regular ferries from Kennacraig; flights from Glasgow. Reserve is easily seen from adjacent roads (B8017 and minor road along W bank to Ardnave)
Terrain:	Pasture, saltmarsh, sea loch
Specialities:	Migrant Barnacle and Greenland White-fronted Geese in winter

Loch Gruinart is a small sea-loch lying about 8km north of Bowmore in the north-west of the Isle of Islay in Strathclyde. The flats at Loch Gruinart attract thousands of Barnacle and Greenland White-fronted Geese in October and November, and the whole island of Islay shelters up to 70 per cent of Greenland's Barnacle Geese and 25 per cent of its White-fronted Geese.

The track along the east side of the loch is also worth exploring. Here the moorland and patchy groves of birch often shelter Black Grouse.

Islay is good raptor country and Kestrel, Sparrowhawk, Merlin, Hen Harrier, Buzzard, Peregrine and Golden Eagle are all possible to spot here.

Great Northern Diver are quite common in the sea-lochs during the winter, and Loch Indaal has several hundred Scaup, along with Goldeneye, Eider, Common Scoter and Red-breasted Merganser.

Other important sites nearby: Loch Indaal to the south is an excellent site for winter birdwatching (especially sea ducks, geese and waders).

The west coast, around Lossit Point and Machir Bay is home to Peregrine and Choughs, also found on The Oa, a peninsula in the south of the island, which also has Golden Eagle.

The Rahoy Hills encompass a wide range of habitats, from valley oak and birch woods, through blanket bog, to mountain peaks.

15 ARGYLL FOREST PARK

Location:	N of Dunoon, from Holy Loch N to Lochs Goil and Long
Grid Reference:	From Kilmun (NS 1682) to Ardgartan (NN 2704); L56/63
Visiting:	Free access all year. Several walks through area; maps and information available from forest offices in Kilmun, Ardgartan and Glenbranter (NS 1198)
Terrain:	Huge area (240km²) encompassing shoreline, mountain, moorland, natural forest, plantation and streams
Specialities:	Arctic-Alpine flowers; Capercaillie, Black Grouse

This was the first forest park to be created in Britain and covers a large area, including part of Benmore Forest, Glenfinart Forest, Loch

Looking towards Ardtornish, from the east side of Lochaline, Morvern, Argyll. This small sea-loch still has resident Otters, and Red-breasted Merganser are frequent visitors. The hills of Morvern can be seen in the background.

Eck Forest, Glenbranter Forest and Ardgartan Forest, as well as several peaks such as Beinn Bheula, Beinn Dornich, Beinn Arthur and the highest mountain in the Park, Beinn Ime (about 6km north west of Arrochar) which tops 1,000m. It is within easy reach of the major population centres of Scotland and is therefore very accessible.

Large parts of the forest are coniferous plantation, but there are also smaller pockets of native mixed deciduous woodland. The birds of the plantations include Black Grouse, Capercaillie, Scottish Crossbill, Sparrowhawk and Siskin and the more natural oakwoods are home to Wood Warbler. Red Squirrel can sometimes be seen in these forests. These woods are very damp and support a rich moss and fern flora, including the delicate Oak and Beech Ferns and the strange and translucent Wilson's Filmy Fern (especially on wet rocks, often by waterfalls).

Loch Lomond is a popular spot, easily accessible by road. Much of its shoreline still supports well-grown oak woodland.

Above the forests, the open moorland has Red Grouse, Curlew, Twite, Stonechat, Buzzard, Raven and the occasional Hen Harrier. Higher still some of the peaks have small numbers of Ptarmigan and Golden Eagle.

In the higher areas, such as in the 'Arrochar Alps' north of Glen Croe, are Arctic-Alpine plants such as Alpine Lady's Mantle, Alpine Meadow-rue and Moss Campion, and patches of Dwarf Willow and Holly Fern.

The narrow sea-lochs have rich growths of seaweeds and a fascinating variety of marine molluscs and other invertebrates. They are often visited by Grey Seals, and it is worth watching here for Otter. Basking Shark are sometimes seen in the lochs.

16 LOCH LOMOND	
Location:	c. 7km N of Dumbarton
Grid Reference:	NS 4392 (Balmaha); L56
Visiting:	Permit required for most of reserve from Scottish Natural Heritage. Access from Balmaha on B837; car park here. May–July for flowers and breeding birds; October–December for wildfowl
Terrain:	Oak woodland, open freshwater loch with fringing swamp vegetation, and islands
Specialities:	Winter wildfowl

Loch Lomond is probably Scotland's most famous loch after Loch Ness. It is very beautiful, and also has the distinction of being the largest freshwater lake in Britain. It is within easy distance of many centres of population and is therefore very popular in the high holiday season.

The Scottish Natural Heritage reserve includes part of Endrick Water which flows into the loch at the south-east corner, as well as five small islands, the largest of which, Inchcailloch, can be visited by boat from Balmaha.

Inchcailloch has well established Sessile Oak woods, with Scots Pine on the drier rocky areas, and Alder and willows in the wetter parts. There is also a picnic area, a camp-site and a 3km nature trail on the island. There are both acid and alkaline soils on the island and corresponding variations in ground flora. Heather, Bilberry and Wavy Hairgrass are common on the acid soils, whilst the calcareous sites have species such as Dog's Mercury and Sanicle. The woodland birds here include such western species as Redstart and Wood Warbler along with Garden and Willow Warblers, Tree Pipit, Great Spotted Woodpecker and Jay.

The loch is perhaps best known for its large gatherings of winter wildfowl. These include up to 1,000 Greylag Geese, over 100 Greenland White-fronted Geese, and parties of Whooper Swans, along with ducks such as Tufted Duck, Pochard, Goldeneye, Shoveler, Mallard, Teal and Wigeon.

Other important sites nearby: Ben Lomond. Queen Elizabeth Forest Park occupies a large area immediately to the east of Loch Lomond, as far as Aberfoyle, taking in Ben Lomond, which rises to 973m. Ben Lomond has a rich Arctic-Alpine flora and birds such as Ptarmigan, Ring Ousel and Raven. Wild Cats are found within the forest park, but are notoriously difficult to spot.

3. EASTERN SCOTLAND AND HIGHLANDS

The Eastern Highlands contain the largest land mass over 600m in Britain and Ireland, most notably in the ancient dissected plateau of the Cairngorms, which contains some 150 square miles of uninhabited mountain country. Here, rocky outcrops are interspersed with open high moorland and grassland, and much of the surface is snow-covered during the winter months. The pattern of snow-melt strongly influences the vegetation which develops here.

The birds of the high plateaux are interesting, and include Snow Bunting, Dotterel, Golden Eagle and Ptarmigan.

Another important feature of this region are the remnants, some quite sizeable, of the original ancient forests of Scots Pine, with their associated special wildlife. These woods in the eastern highlands still support that magnificent giant gamebird the Capercaillie, along with Crested Tit, Siskin and Scottish Crossbill. The mammals include Red Deer and Pine Marten.

Certain lakes in the Spey Valley and elsewhere in this region, such as Loch Ruthven RSPB reserve, are the haunt of the rare Slavonian Grebe, which now numbers around sixty-five pairs in Scotland. The Spey Valley area is also the centre of the now thriving Osprey population (currently about fifty-five pairs).

Botanists know that granite has a poor flora, but nevertheless the Cairngorms region has its specialities. Nowhere else can the fascinating zonation around late snow-patches be seen so clearly, with abundant Alpine Lady's Mantle and Least Cudweed. The high corries also shelter a special flora, including Highland Saxifrage, Starwort Mouse-ear Chickweed, and some special hawkweeds.

In complete contrast are the mountains with softly-weathering mica-schist, of which the most famous is Ben Lawers. This mountain has the richest mountain flora in Britain and Ireland, with many special flowers some characteristic of Alpine habitats. Among these are Alpine Gentian, Drooping Saxifrage, Alpine Forget-me-not, and Rock Speedwell. The dwarf mountain willows are very attractive and include the Woolly Willow. Other characteristic plants of these mountains are Alpine Milk-vetch, Rock Whitlow-grass, Mountain Sandwort, and Snow and Alpine Pearlworts.

One of the highland region's more unusual mammals is the Reindeer (Rangifer tarandus), introduced here from Scandinavia.

Highland Saxifrage (Saxifraga rivularis), a rare mountain flower known from just a few sites in the highlands of Scotland.

17 RANNOCH MOOR

Location:	c. 15km E of Glen Coe
Grid Reference:	NN 3652; L41/42
Visiting:	Best April–July. Access from A82 or Rannoch Station at end of B846
Terrain:	Open blanket bog and lochs
Specialities:	Flowers, sedges and rushes

Rannoch Moor is one of the largest areas of blanket bog in the whole of Britain. It occupies part of a plateau in the Grampian Mountains south of Loch Laidon and straddles the border between Strathclyde and Tayside.

The moor has a rather desolate, wild appearance and can be very bleak and exposed in bad weather, so waterproof and windproof clothing is advised.

The pearls of the blanket bog are its wild flowers, which include many national rarities, such as the Rannoch-rush, for which this is the only British site. Insectivorous species such as sundews are well represented and in the pools all three bladderwort species

FIFTY INTERESTING SPECIES TO LOOK FOR

Black-throated Diver	Scottish Crossbill	Alpine Gentian	Woolly Willow
Buzzard	Siskin	Alpine Lady's Mantle	Dark-green Fritillary
Capercaillie	Slavonian Grebe	Alpine Milk-vetch	Large Heath
Crested Tit	Snow Bunting	Alpine Pearlwort	Mountain Ringlet
Dotterel	Wigeon	Drooping Saxifrage	Northern Brown
Golden Eagle	Mountain Hare	Highland Saxifrage	Argus
Golden Plover	Pine Marten	Least Cudweed	Pearl-bordered
Greenshank	Red Deer	Mountain Avens	Fritillary
Osprey	Red Squirrel	Mountain Sandwort	Scotch Argus
Peregrine	Reindeer	Rannoch-rush	Small Pearl-bordered
Ptarmigan	Wild Cat	Rock Speedwell	Fritillary
Purple Sandpiper	Alpine Bartsia	Rock Whitlow-grass	
Raven	Alpine Blue Sow-thistle	Snow Pearlwort	
Ring Ousel	Alpine Forget-me-not	Starwort Mouse-ear	

occur. Sedges are abundant and include White Sedge, Slender-leaved Sedge and Bog Sedge. Other interesting plants of the reserve are Bog Myrtle and Dwarf Birch.

The moorland also has several interesting breeding birds, including Golden Plover, Snipe, Dunlin, Greenshank and Black-throated Diver. The mammals include Red and Roe Deer.

Other important sites nearby: Black Wood of Rannoch (NN 5755) is a fine relict Scots Pine and birch forest, with Capercaillie and Black Grouse.

18 BEN LUI	
Location:	c. 12km W of Crianlarich
Grid Reference:	NN 2626; L50/56
Visiting:	June–July. Access from Forestry Commission car park in Glen Lochy (NN 238276), crossing over river and under railway, or following up River Cononish from A82 between Crian-larich and Tyndrum
Terrain:	Mountain, upland grass-land, rocky cliffs, crags
Specialities:	Mountain flowers

The main interest in this reserve lies in its rich collection of Arctic-Alpine flowers. These cluster on the crags on the northern side of the mountain, which reaches over 1,100m. What makes the cliffs so rich is the fact that the rocks are derived from mica schist and limestone, and the species include such plants as Starry, Yellow and Purple Sax-ifrages, Roseroot, Mountain Avens, Globe-flower and Alpine Bartsia.

Be very careful when approaching the crags and ledges, because they can be slip-pery, and in this part of country cloud and mist can descend with alarming rapidity. Also be sure not to uproot or disturb any of the Alpine flowers.

Other important sites nearby: Glen Fal-loch has a remnant Scots Pine forest with a good population of Red Squirrels.

19 BEN LAWERS	
Location:	c. 10km E of Killin, on N side of Loch Tay
Grid Reference:	NN 6138; L51
Visiting:	May–August
Terrain:	Upland grassland and high mountain scree and cliff-ledges
Specialities:	Mountain flowers

Ben Lawers, rising to a height of over 1,200m, is one of the jewels in the crown of Scottish mountain botany. It has high, cal-careous cliff-ledges where the brittle rock is constantly eroding, providing new sites for the plants to colonize.

As on Ben Lui, it is the Arctic-Alpine flowers which provide most interest. As well as mountain plants such as Alpine Lady's Mantle, Roseroot and Yellow Saxifrage, there are rarer flowers including Alpine Gentian, Drooping Saxifrage, Alpine Forget-me-not, Rock Speedwell, Alpine Cinquefoil and Alpine Saw-wort.

The birds include species such as Raven, Buzzard and the occasional Peregrine, and the open grassland provides breeding sites for Skylark and Meadow Pipit and Wheatear nest amongst rocks and scree. Watch out for Ring Ousels, particularly in rocky places. Red Grouse and Ptarmigan are also found on the reserve, though not in large numbers.

Brown Hare and Red Deer can be located on the mountian slopes, and, on the high tops, Mountain Hares are seen. Ben Lawers is also known for its unusual insects, including Emperor Moth, Northern Eggar and Fox Moth, and this region is the stronghold of the Small Mountain Ringlet.

20 TENTSMUIR POINT	
Location:	Between Dundee and St Andrews.
Grid Reference:	NO 5024; L54
Visiting:	Either spring, summer for flowers, or September–March for birds
Terrain:	Sand dunes, mudflats and sand banks
Specialities:	Flowers, butterflies, shorebirds

The pretty blue Alpine Forget-me-not (Myosotis alpestris) is an Alpine rarity, found at a few localities in Scotland and northern England.

This National Nature Reserve has a dual interest to the visiting naturalist. In the autumn and winter the shoreline itself and the offshore sand banks are home to vast flocks of waders, including Little Stint and Grey Plover as well as Sanderling, Dunlin and Oystercatcher. The wildfowl include fine flocks of both Pink-footed and Greylag Geese, as well as sea ducks such as Eider (up to 15,000), Common Scoter, Red-breasted Merganser, Long-tailed Duck and Scaup.

However, in the spring and summer this reserve is well worth visiting for its flowers and insects. The dune system is well developed, with all stages visible, from old dunes colonized by Alder, willow and birch scrub, through maritime heath, to open sand. Patches of grassland amongst the dunes support a rich growth of flowers, notably Grass-of-Parnassus, Purple Milk-vetch and Coralroot Orchid.

Grayling, Small Copper, Dark Green Fritillary and Ringlet can all be seen here, as can the Six-spot Burnet and Cinnabar Moth.

The grassy slopes and rocky outcrops of Ben Lawers hold many botanical treasures.

Watch out along the offshore sandbanks for hauled out Grey and Common Seals.

Other important sites nearby: Tentsmuir Forest, inland from the reserve, has Capercaillie, Crossbill and Red Squirrel.

The Eden Estuary just to the south, is famous for its winter concentrations of waders, wildfowl and sea ducks.

21 LOCH LEVEN

Location:	Just E of Kinross
Grid Reference:	NO 1303; L58
Visiting:	April–August (breeding duck); October–March (wintering wildfowl). Access at Kirkgate Park (north) or Findatie (south)
Terrain:	Large, rich lake with grassy margins
Specialities:	Breeding and wintering wildfowl

Loch Leven is undoubtedly one of the finest wildfowl refuges in Britain, and huge numbers of ducks, geese and swans gather here every winter. In the summer, watch out for Great Crested Grebes and breeding ducks such as Mallard, Tufted, Gadwall, Wigeon, Shoveler and Shelduck, especially around St Serf's Island, towards the south of the loch. Common Tern also breed on the island.

The main spectacle in winter is provided by the autumn arrival of large numbers (up to several thousand) Pink-footed Geese, joined later by hundreds or thousands of Greylags and Whooper Swans.

The shores of the loch also attract waders on passage, and these include Greenshank, Green Sandpiper and Ruff. The surrounding hills have Curlew and Red Grouse, and Tree Pipit in the woods.

Other important sites nearby: the RSPB educational reserve of Vane Farm lies on the southern margin of Loch Leven. Its man-made lagoons attract waterbirds. It is open year-round and has car parking and hides.

22 CAENLOCHAN

Location:	About 15km S of Braemar
Grid Reference:	NO 2070; L43
Visiting:	Apply to Scottish Natural Heritage for permit, June–October
Terrain:	Mountain, with cliffs and steep valleys
Specialities:	High Alpine plants

Caenlochan is a National Nature Reserve and one of Britain's finest localities for Arctic-Alpine flowers, rivalling Ben Lawers. As with the latter, it is the combination of high altitude with calcareous rock outcroppings that provide the conditions for many rare flowers.

The reserve includes over 3,600ha of high plateau to the north-east of Glenshee, just to the east of the Devil's Elbow. The highest point is the summit of Glas Maol, at 1,067m. Corries and steep cliffs provide much of the interest, but should be approached with great care. As with all highland sites, adequate clothing and stout footwear are highly recommended.

Flowers of the cliff-ledges and other high-altitude sites include Alpine Bistort, Alpine Meadow-rue, Highland Cudweed, Purple and Yellow Saxifrages, Northern Bedstraw, Three-leaved Rush, Moss Campion and Mountain Avens. Look out also for Holly and Parsley Ferns.

Birds to watch out for are Golden Eagle hunting over the hills, with Ring Ousel, Ptarmigan and Golden Plover elsewhere.

The waters of Loch Leven attract large numbers of visiting wildfowl during the winter months.

Mountain Hare can be located on the high plateaus, and Red Deer almost anywhere in the area.

Other important sites nearby: the Cairnwell chairlift, a short distance along the Braemar road, at NO 1478, also gives access to fine Alpine habitats, with a similar collection of unusual species.

23 SANDS OF FORVIE/ YTHAN ESTUARY	
Location:	c. 20km NE of Aberdeen
Grid Reference:	NK 0328; L38
Visiting:	Easy access by footpath from car-park. Permit needed away from paths
Terrain:	Dunes, maritime heath, saltmarsh
Specialities:	Waders, sea-ducks (especially Eider) and other wildfowl

This dune system is one of the best and least disturbed, and there is a gradation of habitats, from the sandy shore, through dunes of increasing age and plant cover, to maritime heath. There are also some cliffs in the north of the reserve, and small areas of saltmarsh provide further variety. The mussel beds at the mouth of the estuary are an important feeding-ground for Eider.

This stretch of coast holds good numbers of breeding seabirds, most notably a large population of Eider – around 2,000 pairs, making this the largest colony in Britain. They nest in amongst the dunes

Sea-watching can be worthwhile from the cliffs around Collieston, and species to watch

for include Kittiwake, Common and Velvet Scoters, Long-tailed Duck, Eider and even the occasional King Eider! Common, Arctic, Little and Sandwich Terns breed on the reserve and Great and Arctic Skuas are often seen over the sea.

In winter, this reserve plays host to huge numbers of wildfowl, including several thousand Pink-footed and Greylag Geese, and 200 or more Whooper Swans.

The reserve also has its botanical interest, mainly concentrated on the stable dunes, where the flowers include Heather, Crowberry, and Stag's Horn Clubmoss.

Golden Eagle *Aquila chrysaetos* L75–86, W190–230

When seen clearly, this is an unmistakable, large, dark, powerfully built bird of prey with a large bill and strong talons. The top of the head and neck are golden brown, and the wings long and relatively narrow. Its tail is quite long and broad. Juveniles are very dark, with large white patches on their wings, and a white tail with a broad black tip. Eagles are often seen soaring over hills and mountains. In soaring adults, the front and rear edges of the wings are almost parallel.

There are now approximately 450 pairs of Golden Eagle in Britain, nearly all in Scotland, with just a single pair in the Lake District (Haweswater). This represents about 20 per cent of the west European population. Eagles feed mainly on grouse, Hares and Rabbits.

24 CAIRNGORMS	
Location:	c. 10km SE of Aviemore
Grid Reference:	NJ 0101; L36
Visiting:	Best April–August. Certain areas off-limits during deer cull (August–October). Otherwise unrestricted access. Visitor centre at Loch an Eilein, off B970 between Inverdruie and Polchar
Terrain:	Varied; high mountain, moorland, bog, forest, rivers, lochs. Weather changes rapidly. For safety, always tell someone where you are walking on the hills
Specialities:	Mountain birds, Alpine plants, Reindeer, Scottish Crossbill

This huge reserve, Britain's largest, covers nearly 260km², and is one of the finest stretches of protected country in the whole of

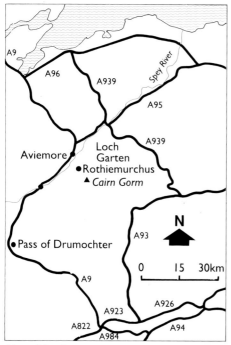

Map of the Cairngorms.

In flight, the Osprey (Pandion haliaetus) shows a characteristic black-and-white pattern, and angled wings.

Europe. It epitomizes wild Scotland and encompasses the whole variety of inland mountain habitat. Much of the reserve is at high altitude, with several mountains topping 1,200m, and it reaches its highest point at Ben Macdui (1,309m), Britain's second highest mountain.

Rothiemurchus Forest, which lies in the reserve, is the largest native Scots Pine forest remaining in the British Isles, and has a special significance. This unique ecosystem has specialities such as Scottish Crossbill, Capercaillie, Crested Tit, Black Grouse and Redpoll. In addition, it is always worth keeping an eye open for Red Squirrel or Roe Deer.

The plants of the forest are also rather special, with Creeping Lady's Tresses, Lesser Twayblade, and four species of wintergreen. With luck, or local knowledge, you may even spot Twinflower. An interesting forest invertebrate here is a large species of wood ant, which makes nest-mounds out of the fallen pine needles.

Up on the high plateaus, the scene is completely different, dominated by windswept moorland, cliffs and snow-bed plant communities with species such as Least Willow, Roseroot, Mountain Sorrel, Moss Campion and Three-leaved Rush. The birds here include Snow Bunting, Golden Eagle, Peregrine, Red Grouse, Ptarmigan, Dotterel and Ring Ousel. The mammals of the hills include Red Deer, Wild Cat and Mountain Hare.

Other important sites nearby: Craigellachie (NH 8812), a birch wood at the base of cliffs near Aviemore has fine woodland birds and Peregrine nesting nearby. It is also a good place to see Scotch Argus butterfly. Loch Garten (NH 9718), the famous RSPB Osprey reserve, has an observation hide.

4. SOUTHERN SCOTLAND AND BORDERS

Visitors to Scotland do not often linger in the Border Country and Lowlands, although this region is well worth a visit in its own right.

On the mainland, this is a land of rolling hills and moorland, with upland birds such as Hen Harrier, Merlin and Golden Plover well represented. However, there are impressive coastal habitats too, such as estuaries like Caelaverock, with its important concentrations of winter wildfowl and waders, or rocky headlands and islands such as St Abb's Head and Ailsa Craig with their huge colonies of seabirds.

Several plants, of which the Sticky Catchfly is perhaps the best known example, find habitats there on roadside rocks, and the lakes and pools provide good hunting-ground for some special aquatics, such as the curious Awlwort and the Eight-stamened Waterwort. One plant, Tufted Loosestrife, has its main British localities in South Scotland, especially around Glasgow. Other characterisic plants of this area are Holy Grass, Monk's Rhubarb and Scottish Dock.

The umbellifers are well represented here. In wet meadows, especially in Dumfries and

Small Copper (Lycaena phlaeas). This lively, brightly coloured butterfly can be seen almost anywhere throughout lowland Britain and Ireland. It is very territorial and flies up to attack other passing insects.

Galloway, the Whorled Caraway and the Spignel or Baldmoney can be found, whilst the delightful Sweet Cicely is common near houses throughout much of this region. Another umbellifer, Scots Lovage, a very

FIFTY INTERESTING SPECIES TO LOOK FOR

Barnacle Goose	Pink-footed Goose	Mountain Hare	Labrador Tea
Black Grouse	Purple Sandpiper	Red Deer	Monk's Rhubarb
Common Gull	Raven	Natterjack	Roseroot
Common Scoter	Red Grouse	Alpine Lady's Mantle	Scots Lovage
Dipper	Ring Ousel	Awlwort	Scottish Dock
Gannet	Rock Pipit	Baldmoney	Sticky Catchfly
Golden Plover	Scaup	Bog Rosemary	Sweet Cicely
Goosander	Shag	Cloudberry	Tufted Loosestrife
Grey Wagtail	Short-eared Owl	Cranberry	Whorled Caraway
Hen Harrier	Whimbrel	Eight-stamened	Dark-green Fritillary
Kittiwake	Whooper Swan	Waterwort	Large Heath
Merlin	Common Seal	Harebell	Scotch Argus
Peregrine	Grey Seal	Holy Grass	

Upland heather moors are the favoured habitat of the compact falcon, the Merlin (Falco columbarius), whose numbers have declined seriously in recent years.

special Scottish plant, is found on rocks around the west coast.

One of the best protected of all British bogs, Silver Flowe, is found in this area, and many characteristic bog plants, such as Bog Rosemary and Great Sundew, grow there. The doubtfully native Labrador Tea occurs in bogs near Stirling.

25 CAIRNSMORE OF FLEET	
Location:	c. 10km due E of Newton Stewart, Galloway
Grid Reference:	NX 5266; L83
Visiting:	June–September. Restricted access; apply to Scottish Natural Heritage in Creetown
Terrain:	Upland heather moor, grassland, cliffs and bog
Specialities:	Birds, butterflies, plants

This reserve consists of a large, rounded massif of upland moor, rising to a height of 710m at its summit. The hills rise gently on the west, but there are steep cliffs and scree slopes on the eastern flank.

Lower down, the vegetation is dominated by Heather and Purple Moorgrass, with flowers such as Great Sundew and Pale Butterwort in the boggy patches.

Red Deer are a feature of the reserve, but more unusual is a herd of feral goats (also found around Loch Trool, to the north). On the upper slopes watch out for Mountain Hares.

In addition to Red Grouse, Raven and Golden Plover, you may strike lucky and see a Merlin gliding over the heather moor, or even a passing Golden Eagle.

The butterflies are a particular feature of the reserve and amongst the more notable species are Scotch Argus, Large Heath and Pearl-bordered Fritillary.

Other important sites nearby: Galloway Forest Park, further north, is a large area of forest and moorland and is ideal country for the serious naturalist/hill walker. These hills are good for Short-eared Owls, Hen Harriers, and Black Grouse.

Silver Flowe to Merrick Kells: this reserve (at NX 4782) with a blanket bog of great botanical interest contains southern Scotland's least disturbed peatland.

26 CAERLAVEROCK

Location:	N side of Solway Firth, c. 10km S of Dumfries
Grid Reference:	NY 0365; L84/85
Visiting:	Best September–April. Access from roads or at Eastpark Wildfowl Trust Reserve which has hides and towers
Terrain:	Saltmarsh and mudflats
Comment:	The tides come in rapidly, making the marsh hazardous. Do not stray without permission
Specialities:	Natterjack; winter wildfowl

Caerlaverock is host to Spitsbergen's entire Barnacle Goose population in the winter, with flocks of 10,500 at peak times. The geese arrive about late September and depart in mid-April. There are also large flocks of Pink-footed Geese (maximum about 35,000), up to 350 Whooper Swans and some Bewick's Swans. The other wildfowl include Shelduck, Pintail, Wigeon, Scaup and Red-breasted Merganser.

Watch out for birds of prey hunting along the shore in winter: Peregrine, Merlin, Hen Harrier and Sparrowhawk.

Waders are another feature of the area as a whole. Sanderling pass through in large numbers, especially in May, and in the autumn, look out for Black-tailed Godwit, Whimbrel, Spotted Redshank, Curlew Sandpiper and Little Stint.

In the summer Redshank, Lapwing and Oystercatcher breed in the area.

Another notable wildlife feature is the colony of Natterjacks which are near their northerly limit here. They live in the pools which lie near the edge of the saltmarsh and can be quite noisy in the breeding season.

Other important sites nearby: Southerness Point, at the other side of the Nith Estuary, to the west, is a good vantage point for watching seaducks and divers.

27 GREY MARE'S TAIL

Location:	15km NE of Moffat
Grid Reference:	NT 1815; L78/79
Visiting:	Beware damp, slippery rocks which can be treacherous
Terrain:	Moorland, cliffs, loch, waterfall
Specialities:	Spectacular waterfall

This site is well worth a detour because it is so spectacular. The waterfall lies quite close to the main road (A708) and is easily reached by a track. The water here plunges 60m in a sheer drop from the lip of a hanging valley.

The rocky gullies and cliffs around the waterfall have a rich flora with woodland plants such as Dog's Mercury growing luxuriantly alongside other plants such as Roseroot, Heather, Harebell and Goldenrod. Higher up the hills behind there are mountain flowers such as Alpine Lady's Mantle, Cloudberry and saxifrages.

The streams and rivers have breeding Dipper and Grey Wagtail. Beyond the fall lies Loch Skeen, which has a colony of Common Gulls. Ravens are often to be seen in the skies around the nearby cliffs.

This is another site which has been colonized by feral goats.

Other important sites nearby: Castle and Hightae Lochs, Lochmaben, lie about 30km south. They both attract large numbers of geese in the winter months, particularly Pink-footed and Greylag.

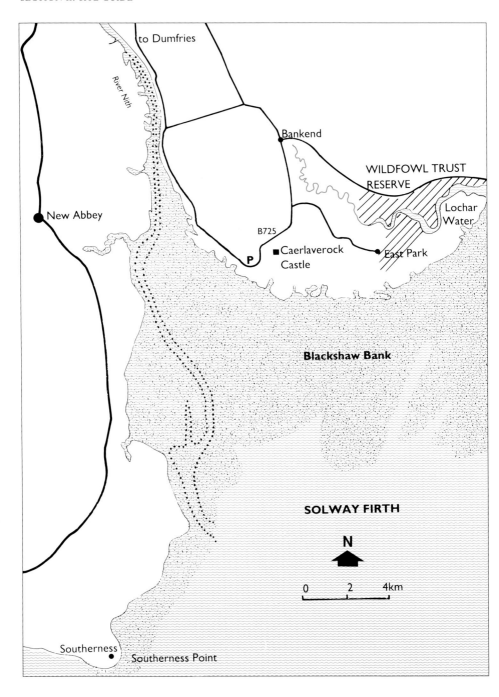

to Dumfries

River Nith

Bankend

WILDFOWL TRUST
RESERVE

Lochar
Water

New Abbey

B725

P ■Caerlaverock
Castle

East Park

Blackshaw Bank

SOLWAY FIRTH

N

0   2   4km

Southerness
Southerness Point

28 ST ABB'S HEAD

Location:	Between Dunbar and Berwick-on Tweed
Grid Reference:	NT 9269; L67
Visiting:	May–July (breeding birds); August–October (migration). Access by track from B 6438 near St Abb's village
Terrain:	Sea cliffs, maritime grassland, loch
Specialities:	Seabird colonies

This magnificent headland reserve juts out into the North Sea with cliffs rising to about 90m and it is a paradise for seabirds. St Abb's Head is justifiably famous for its huge colonies of Guillemot, which number about 10,000. There are also Razorbill and a few Puffin, as well as Fulmar, Kittiwake (several thousand), Herring Gull and Shag. Good views of the seabirds can be had from the track leading towards the lighthouse.

Watch the rocks for Rock Pipit, Turnstone and Purple Sandpiper in winter, and out to sea for passing flocks of Gannet, which breed on the Bass Rock further north.

In the autumn a seawatch will often reveal Arctic, Great and occasionally Pomarine Skuas, Manx and sometimes Sooty Shearwaters. The seas also have Red-throated Divers (occasionally Black-throated and Great Northern as well) and Eider and Common Scoter.

Migrant songbirds tend to concentrate in the bushes and scrub around Mire Loch during the spring and autumn. At this time the commoner species are sometimes joined by rarities such as Wryneck, Red-backed Shrike and Red-breasted Flycatcher.

Opposite: *map of Caerlaverock.*

The plants are also interesting, with Common Rock-rose, Purple Milk-vetch, Thyme, Thrift and Spring Sandwort adding their colour to the coastal grassland and rocky ledges.

The butterflies include Northern Brown Argus, Grayling and Small Copper.

Barnacle Goose *Branta leucopsis* L64
A medium-sized graceful goose with a small, black bill and white face, contrasting with the black neck. From a distance it looks black above and white below. The flight call is a soft barking and large flocks sound rather like small dogs.

Barnacle Geese breed mainly on inaccessible cliffs and rocky outcrops high above river valleys or fjords in Greenland, Spitzbergen and northern Russia. They are regular winter visitors from mid-October to mid-April to Scotland and Ireland (about 30 per cent of the total world population). In Scotland, the most important site is the island of Islay, where there may be more than 20,000 birds. In Ireland, the geese number about 7,500 and gather mainly on islands off the west coast, from Kerry to Donegal. Barnacle Geese feed on grasses, Eelgrass, algae and seedling crops.

29 AILSA CRAIG

Location:	c. 16km due W of Girvan in Firth of Clyde
Grid Reference:	NX 0399; L76
Visiting:	Permission required. Enquire Tourist Centre in Girvan. Access is by boat.
Terrain:	Rocky isolated island
Specialities:	Gannetry

The compact, rocky island of Ailsa Craig rises steeply from the sea about 20km due south of the Isle of Arran. The rounded mass is topped by rough grassland and the cliffs, some of which are 120m high, fall away to a rock-strewn coast.

The dominant feature of the site is the huge gannetry with over 20,000 pairs, one of the largest in Britain. The cliffs also house 10,000 Kittiwakes, several thousand Guillemots and Razorbills, and a few Puffins. Other breeding birds are Herring, Lesser and Great Black-backed Gulls, Fulmars, Eiders, Black Guillemots and Shags. Peregrines and Ravens are occasional, and the island has both Carrion and Hooded Crows. Other interesting birds of the island are Rock Pipit, Wheatear and Rock Dove.

Both Common and Grey Seals are often seen in the seas close to the island.

Part of the shoreline is accessible on foot, but check with the boatman, because there is a danger of being cut off by the tide.

Notable plants are Sea Spleenwort, Tree Mallow, Sea Campion, Thrift and Navelwort.

Scots Lovage *Ligusticum scoticum*
This attractive, bright green, shiny umbellifer is nearly confined in the British Isles to the Scottish and north Irish coasts, where it grows on rocks by the sea. Its continental distribution is the sea coast of north-west Europe, but it also occurs in the Faroes, Iceland, Greenland and in eastern North America. Like the true Lovage, which grows only in gardens in Britain, it was used as a pot-herb, but has not been cultivated. It is a stout perennial with flowering stems reaching nearly 1m.

30 GOATFELL, ARRAN

Location:	N of Brodick, Isle of Arran
Grid Reference:	NR 9941; L62/68/69
Visiting:	By ferry to Brodick from Ardrossan. Footpath from Brodick Country Park, or up Glen Sannox
Terrain:	Heather moor, upland grassland
Specialities:	Glaciated scenery

Goatfell, rising near the sea to almost 875m, is an impressive granite mountain which dominates the north of the island. It has classic geological glacial features such as corries, moraines and hanging valleys.

The high ground supports a fauna more typical of the highlands to the north, and birds such as Peregrine, Raven, Golden Plover and Ring Ousel can all be seen here. The mountain even has a breeding population of Ptarmigan – Britain's most southerly one - and Golden Eagles are sometimes seen.

The wet heaths and moorland are particularly noteworthy for their dragonflies, which include the Highland Darter and Four-spotted Chaser.

The plants of the moors include Heath Milkwort and Heath Spotted Orchid, whilst Starry Saxifrage, Mountain Sorrel and Alpine Buckler Fern can all be seen higher up.

Other important sites nearby: Brodick Country Park (NS 0238) has a fern-rich mixed deciduous woodland with rare whitebeams. The bird life is rich too, with Tawny and Barn Owls, Buzzards, Sparrowhawks, Woodcock and Scotland's largest population of Nightjars.

Glen Diomhan (NR 9246) is a mixed birch wood in a rocky gorge, also with rare native Arran whitebeams.

The peak of Goatfell towers over the northern part of the Isle of Arran.

31 ABERLADY BAY

Location:	c. 25km E of Edinburgh
Grid Reference:	NT 4681; L66
Visiting:	April–July; September–March. Access from roads by footpath
Terrain:	Sandy coast with dunes, saltmarsh and grassland
Specialities:	Coastal birds

Aberlady Bay has Eelgrass beds, with salt-marshes and also quite extensive dune systems. The stable grey dunes have a particularly rich flora and are well worth looking at in detail. Search for Autumn Gentian, Grass-of-Parnassus, marsh orchids and Moonwort.

This bay is however known primarily for its birds – both for its breeding ducks, and also for the excellent winter birdwatching it offers. The grebes are a particlular feature of these coastal waters and both Red-necked and Slavonian Grebes are regular visitors.

*Sweet Cicely (*Myrrhis odorata*) is common along roadsides in upland parts of England and Scotland.*

In winter, there are flocks of Pink-footed Geese in the area, as well as Whooper Swans, and sea ducks including Common and Velvet Scoter, Eider, Long-tailed Duck, Goldeneye and Red-breasted Merganser. Wigeon congregate to feed on the mudflats.

The spring and autumn migrations bring a good selection of waders, amongst which may be Curlew Sandpiper, Sanderling, Green Sandpiper and Black-tailed Godwit. In the autumn and winter there are usually large numbers of Bar-tailed Godwits, Knot, Dunlin and Grey Plover.s.

Other important sites nearby: Gullane Bay and Gullane Point lie a little further east. Both species of seal are regularly seen in Gullane Bay, as are Red-throated Divers in winter.

Bass Rock, an isolated rock off the coast near Berwick has a huge gannetry with over 20,000 pairs. Visit by boat from Berwick.

5. NORTH-WEST ENGLAND

The Lake District lies at the centre of this region (Cheshire, Merseyside, Greater Manchester, Lancashire and Cumbria) and has a good mountain flora and fauna, although with rather few specialities. Amongst plants, those few are Alpine Catchfly, with a small population in a rather secret locality. Another remarkable Lake District rarity can, however, be publicized with safety: on the vertiginous screes above Wastwater, and around the Pillar high level track can be found the only mountain populations in Britain and Ireland of the Shrubby Cinquefoil, otherwise confined to Teesdale and the Burren (Ireland).

The tops of Lake District mountains offer a typical wind-swept flora, including the Dwarf Willow, a diminutive 'tree' which shows only the new tips of its twigs above the rough stony surface. Small lakes and tarns provide good habitat for Water Lobelia and for the Quillwort.

Many upland birds, such as Buzzard, Peregrine and Raven are found in the Lake District, and this is also the only region in England in which Golden Eagle can still be found breeding.

The Isle of Man has one very special plant named after it, the Isle of Man Cabbage, which grows on sea-cliffs especially on the west coast from Lancashire to Ayrshire, and which is endemic to Britain. The island is also a stronghold of the Chough (with about fifty pairs), a rare bird which is dependent upon cliffs, combined with rough, traditional pasture.

Some other characteristic plant species of this region are Alpine Bartsia, Bird's-eye Primrose, English Sandwort and Round-leaved Wintergreen.

The active Bank Vole (Clethrionomys glareolus) *is a common rodent of woodlands and hedgerows in mainland Britain. It has reddish brown fur.*

32 LAKE DISTRICT NATIONAL PARK	
Location:	Centred on hills S of Keswick, Cumbria
Grid Reference:	NY 3015; L89/90/96/97
Visiting:	Best in spring or summer
Terrain:	Mixed: mountains to coastline
Comment:	Weather can be glorious, but this is a high rainfall area so waterproof clothing advisable. Always inform someone of your route when hillwalking
Specialities:	Dramatic scenery and excellent hillwalking

The Lake District National Park contains a mosaic of habitats, centred upon a compact range of hills, with picturesque valleys and freshwater lakes (meres). The park covers land from sea-level right up to England's highest peak at Scafell Pike (978m) and there is something here to fascinate every naturalist or outdoor enthusiast. It has some of the character of a miniature and condensed version of the Scottish highlands.

The beauty of this park lies in its accessibility, combined with its variety. In summer, the major tourist resorts, such as Ambleside, can become very congested with cars and caravans, but it is always possible to escape along footpaths and to enjoy the peaceful countryside.

Gouging by ice-sheets during glaciations was responsible for the dramatic scenery of the Lake District, and these hills abound with features such as hanging valleys, corries, moraines and other glacial phenomena.

The lakes mostly radiate outwards from the central core of higher ground and many are very deep. They tend to have fringing vegetation of reeds and tall flowers, notably Yellow Loosestrife, with floating patches of White Water Lily in the shallows.

SELECTION OF IMPORTANT SITES WITHIN THE LAKE DISTRICT NATIONAL PARK

Bassenthwaite Lake (NY 2030)

The fourth largest of the lakes with about

FIFTY INTERESTING SPECIES TO LOOK FOR

Bittern	Redstart	Bee Orchid	Round-leaved
Buzzard	Ringed Plover	Bird's-eye Primrose	Wintergreen
Chough	Shelduck	Dune Helleborine	Shrubby Cinquefoil
Common Sandpiper	Short-eared Owl	Dwarf Willow	Water Lobelia
Dipper	Tawny Owl	Early Marsh Orchid	Dark-green Fritillary
Golden Eagle	Tree Pipit	English Sandwort	High Brown Fritillary
Great Black-backed	Wood Warbler	Grass-of-Parnassus	Pearl-bordered
Gull	Pine Marten	Green-flowered	Fritillary
Great Spotted	Red Squirrel	Helleborine	Scotch Argus
Woodpecker	Natterjack	Interrupted Club-moss	Small Mountain Ringlet
Lesser Black-backed	Palmate Newt	Isle of Man Cabbage	Small Pearl-bordered
Gull	Smooth Newt	Lycopoduim inundatum	Fritillary
Oystercatcher	Warty Newt	Marsh Helleborine	
Pied Flycatcher	Alpine Bartsia	Pyramidal Orchid	
Pink-footed Goose	Alpine Catchfly	Quillwort	

seventy bird species breeding and thousands of duck in winter, and Whooper Swans. The southern edge has a large area of mire and reedbeds.

Borrowdale (NY 2618)

This valley is particularly rich in deciduous woodland. Mostly oak woods, but with a lot of birch as well. Some woods have elm and Ash mixed in the tree-layer. The main woods are:

Lodore-Troutdale Woods
Great Wood
Seatoller Wood
Johnny's Wood
Castlehead Wood
The Ings

Watch for Buzzard, Tawny Owl, Great Spotted Woodpecker, Tree pipit, Wood Warbler, Pied Flycatcher and Redstart. Some of the woods also have populations of Red Squirrel, and Pine Marten in the Dale Head area (NY 2215).

The woodland flowers here include Herb Robert, Alpine Enchanter's Nightshade and Small Cow-wheat, and the woods have a rich fern flora.

Rydal Water (NY 3606)

Easily reached and well worth a stop. A footpath circles the lake, passing woodland, and taking in the rich fen vegetation between Rydal Water and Grasmere.

Brockhole (NY 3901)

This is the Visitor Centre for the National Park (open daily late March–early November) and should be visited early for the information provided, useful in planning outings.

Looking down Broughton Mill Valley from Stickle Pike. The Lake District is a region of rolling, sheep-grazed hills and pockets of woodland.

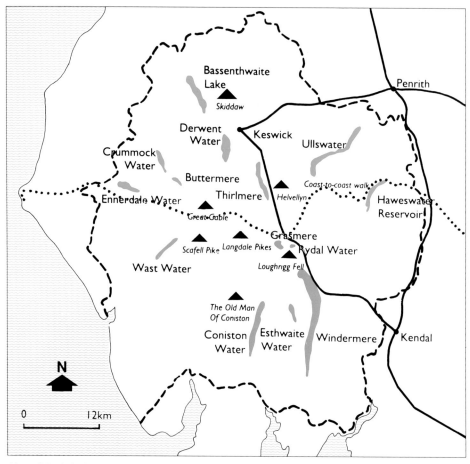

Map of the Lake District.

However, it is worth a visit in its own right as well. It is an attractive spot, with a frontage onto Windermere. Look out for Nuthatch, Pied Flycatcher and Buzzards overhead.

Haweswater (NY 4814)

In this area, which is somewhat remote, there is the chance that you might see one of England's very few Golden Eagles hunting over the hills near the lake. Only two pairs breed in England, both in the Lake District National Park. Beware, however, confusion with the much commoner Buzzard when no scale objects are present. Watch out also for Raven, Peregrine and Ring Ousel. Elsewhere Small Mountain Ringlet butterflies frequent the high ground; the Lake District is the only area where this species is found in England.

Duddon Estuary (SD 2385)

An important site for wildfowl and waders, and for hunting birds of prey in winter.

33 ESKMEALS DUNES AND DRIGG DUNES	
Location:	Near Ravenglass
Grid Reference:	SD 0897; L96
Visiting:	By permit only to both sites. Access to Eskmeals Dunes via Newbiggin near A595. To Drigg Dunes (closed last two weeks of May) via Drigg
Terrain:	Dunes and estuary
Specialities:	Waders, wildfowl, amphibians

34 SOUTH WALNEY	
Location:	Southern tip of Walney Island, just S of Barrow-in-Furness
Grid Reference:	SD 2262; L96
Visiting:	All year, but closed most Mondays
Terrain:	Maritime meadow, sand dunes, saltmarsh, mudflats
Specialities:	Large gull colony, autumn and spring migrants; shingle flowers

Eskmeals Dunes is a sandy spit offering excellent views over the saltmarsh and mudflats alongside the estuary. Banks of Sea Buckthorn grow amongst the dunes. This area is also excellent for ducks, waders and seabirds.

The dunes at Drigg have a large colony of gulls, with Black-headed, Herring and Lesser Black-backed Gulls, as well as nesting Common, Arctic, Sandwich and Little Terns. Watch out for Little Owl and Sparrowhawk near to the conifers close to the approach road. The mudflats of the Irt estuary are important feeding grounds for a variety of waders, including Green Sandpiper, Spotted Redshank, Greenshank, Grey Plover and Whimbrel.

This reserve boasts all six native amphibians, with colonies of Common Frog, Common and Natterjack Toads, as well as Great-crested, Palmate and Smooth Newts. Adders also breed here.

The flowers are also interesting, with Portland Spurge, Sea Spurge and Sea Bindweed amongst the dunes, and Glasswort and Sea Purslane in the saltmarsh. The shingle has the uncommon Isle of Man Cabbage.

This reserve occupies the southern tip of Walney Island at the mouth of Morecambe Bay. Although the dunes dominate, there is a wide variety of habitat here, from open water, through saltmarsh and mudflats, to shingle and both wet and dry meadows.

Breeding birds: include Eider (650 pairs) at the most southerly breeding ground, Herring and Lesser Black-backed Gulls (about 9,000 pairs of each), Great Black-backed Gull, Oystercatcher, Ringed Plover and Shelduck.

This is a prime birdwatching site for spring and autumn migrants and rarities are regularly recorded here, with such species as Red-breasted Flycatcher, Firecrest and Black Redstart. Skuas and shearwaters of several species are often seen at sea, particularly in the autumn.

Merlins and Peregrines are a regular feature in winter, as are Short-eared Owls.

The shingle flowers include Sea Beet, Sea Bindweed, Sea Campion, Sea Spurge, Sea Holly, Yellow Horned-poppy and Thrift. In the drier sites the heath has species such as Heather, Cross-leaved Heath, Tormentil, Gorse and Bracken.

35 AINSDALE DUNES

Location:	Between Southport and Formby
Grid Reference:	SD 2810; L108
Visiting:	Visitors Centre and footpaths. Permit needed off paths
Terrain:	Sand dunes
Specialities:	Flowers, amphibians, insects, birds

These dunes, a National Nature Reserve, are botanically some of the richest in the whole of Britain, and also some of the most extensive, stretching a distance of some 10km and about 1.5km wide.

Ainsdale Dunes have a very rich flora, and the Sea Buckthorn bushes attract migrant birds.

All stages in the dune succession are here, from shifting young dunes, through to stable dunes with a developed tree cover of alder and willow scrub. The patches of Sea Buckthorn attract migrant birds in the autumn and thrushes in the winter.

In places, the younger dunes have a very rich flora with Grass-of-Parnassus, and orchids such as Early Marsh Orchid, Bee Orchid, Pyramidal Orchid, Marsh Helleborine, Green-flowered Helleborine, and the rare Dune Helleborine.

Ainsdale is the most northerly known locality for the nationally rare Sand Lizard, and also holds one of the largest colonies of Natterjack Toads.

The planted Scots and Corsican Pines hold populations of Red Squirrels which are sometimes quite easy to spot.

The insects include Dark Green Fritillary and Oak Eggar moth, as well as sand wasps and Emperor Dragonfly.

36 MARTIN MERE

Location:	c. 8km NE of Ormskirk
Grid Reference:	SD 4315; L108
Visiting:	Open throughout year, but best in winter
Terrain:	Lake, marsh
Specialities:	Winter wildfowl

In the Wildfowl Trust tradition, this reserve has a fine collection of wildfowl from around the world, either penned or pinioned. This makes it an excellent educational centre and a good place to learn how to recognize ducks and geese.

However, the reserve also has real value as a wildlife site because it attracts large numbers of wild geese and ducks, as well as other birds, to its lake and flooded meadows.

The best time to visit is in early winter. At

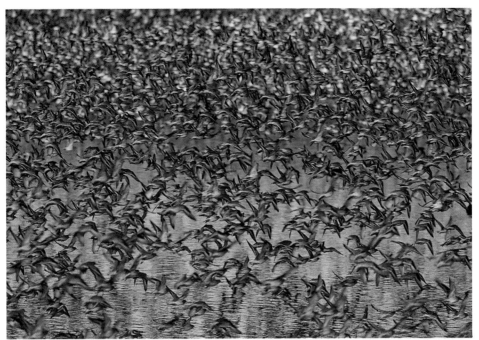

Knot (Calidris canutus) gather in huge flocks on coastal mudflats such as those of the Ribble estuary. When disturbed they remain in tight flocks as a protection against aerial predators, such as Peregrines.

37 RIBBLE ESTUARY	
Location:	Between Southport and Lytham St Anne's
Grid Reference:	SD 4024; L102/108
Visiting:	Winter for birds. Access along minor roads and embankments from A565
Terrain:	Saltmarsh, mudflats, wet pasture
Specialities:	Waders and seabirds

this time, the reserve comes alive with thousands of Pink-footed Geese (peak about 34,000), with a couple of hundred each of Bewick's and Whooper Swans.

Teal, Pintail, Gadwall, Shoveler, Tufted Ducks, Wigeon, Goldeneye and Goosander are often present in winter, as are predators such as Short-eared Owl, Hen Harrier and Merlin.

Waders are also attracted to Martin Mere and it holds the largest winter population of Ruff. Other waders regularly seen include Curlew, Redshank, Dunlin, Greenshank, Lapwing, Black and Bar-tailed Godwits, Golden and Grey Plovers.

This estuary covers a large area and has well developed saltmarsh as well as enormous sheets of mud which are exposed at low tide. This combination of habitats makes it ideal as a feeding ground for birds, especially in the winter.

The Ribble estuary is of international importance for its large gatherings of waders and wildfowl. Undoubtedly the biggest spectacle is provided by the large flocks of Pink-footed Geese which begin to arrive here in the late autumn and winter. There are also both Whooper and Bewick's Swans feeding on these marshes during the winter.

In addition to the geese, look out over the sea for Red-throated Diver, Red-breasted Merganser, Goldeneye and Common and Velvet Scoter.

The waders are very impressive here, with up to 70,000 Knot, in addition to more usual species such as Redshank, Dunlin, Sanderling and Golden Plovers. The estuary also attracts large numbers of Black-tailed Godwits.

A seawatch can be rewarding for the bird-watcher, especially after north-westerly gales, with the chance of Sooty as well as Manx Shearwater, Leach's Petrel, Kittiwakes and Little Gulls.

Other important sites nearby: St Anne's Dunes, near Blackpool Airport, is a small dune system with a fine flora, including many orchids, such as Bee Orchid, Early Marsh Orchid, and Marsh Helleborine.

38 GAIT BARROWS	
Location:	c. 7km NW of Carnforth
Grid Reference:	SD 4877; L97
Visiting:	Spring–summer. Easily accessible on footpaths from roads close to A6. Permit from NCC needed off footpaths.
Terrain:	Limestone pavement, woodland, grassland, lake
Specialities:	Rich limestone flora

This National Nature Reserve is dominated by the limestone pavement, perhaps the finest example of this rare and interesting habitat anywhere in Britain. Limestone pavement is pock-marked with holes, channels and gulleys, or grikes, in which the soil accumulates, creating a natural rock garden of great botanical value.

Here the plants, such as Bloody Cranesbill, Hemp Agrimony, Saw-wort and Tutsan can grow safe from grazing, and in the darker, damp gullys ferns like Rusty-back Fern,

Gait Barrows National Nature Reserve. The limestone pavement is riddled with clefts and gullies, forming a natural rock-garden full of flowers such as Bloody Cranesbill, Hemp Agrimony and Saw-wort.

South side of Arnside Knott. Low cliffs with oak woodland lead down to the saltmarsh at this coastal reserve.

Hart's-tongue and Hard Shield Fern come to the fore.

Many of the plants found growing here, such as Spindle, Dogwood and Small-leaved Lime, are at their northernmost limit in the country. In the scrub look for Lily-of-the-Valley, Dropwort, Deadly Nightshade, Pale St John's Wort and Dark-red Helleborine.

Around the lake, Little Hawes Water, there is an Alder carr woodland, with fen vegetation. The lake has bird interest as well, with Bittern and Water Rail both nesting and occasional visits from Marsh Harriers and migrating Ospreys.

Butterflies include the rare and local High Brown Fritillary and Duke of Burgundy. This is one of very few sites where the High Brown Fritillary is on the increase.

Other important sites nearby: There is another good limestone pavement reserve at Hutton Roof Crags, about 10km east, near Burton-in-Kendal.

Arnside Knott, about 3km west, is a fine limestone grassland site, with pavement remnants, sloping down to saltmarsh.

Warton Crag, just north of Carnforth, is pavement and limestone grassland, with a rich butterfly fauna. Species include Green

Hairstreak, Pearl-bordered, Small Pearl-bordered and High Brown Fritillaries.

39 LEIGHTON MOSS	
Location:	Silverdale, near Carnforth. Well signposted from A6
Grid Reference:	SD 4875; L97
Visiting:	By permit bought on site (closed Tuesdays), or along public footpaths. Free to RSPB members
Terrain:	Fine reedbeds, fen carr, woodland, saltmarsh
Specialities:	Breeding fenland birds, winter wildfowl

Leighton Moss is a fine reserve with a variety of habitats, dominated by very extensive reed-beds. The edges of the fen are wooded, and there is also a small area of heath. At the seaward side the land slopes down towards a saltmarsh with views out over Morecambe Bay.

The reserve is special as the main stronghold of Bittern, with around 20 per cent of the national population found here.

May–June is the best period to have a chance of seeing a Bittern. Bearded Tits also breed in the reedbeds, as do Water Rail, the rare Spotted Crake, and Marsh Harrier. Buzzard and Sparrowhawk also breed at Leighton Moss. Watch out for Hawfinches in the trees around Woodwell.

In winter this reserve attracts waders and wildfowl in large numbers.

Large tussocks of Tufted Sedge dominate part of the fen towards the northern end, with flowers such as Marsh Marigold, Meadowsweet, Purple Loosestrife, Great Willowherb, Water Mint and Ragged Robin. There are orchids too, such as Common Spotted Orchid and Southern Marsh Orchid. There is a gradation from fen carr,

A Bittern (Botaurus stellaris) lurks camouflaged at the edge of a reedbed.

dominated by Buckthorn and Alder Buckthorn to mature oak/Ash woodland.

The dragonflies of the reserve include Brown Hawker and damselflies. In addition to commoner butterflies such as Peacock, Small Tortoiseshell, Orange-tip and Small Copper, there are also Pearl-bordered, Small Pearl-bordered and High Brown Fritillaries, and a rich moth fauna with hawkmoths a feature.

The woods have Red Squirrels, and the fish-rich mere in the reserve also attracts Otters to feed here.

6. NORTH-EAST ENGLAND

This area encompasses a wide variety of scenery, from the rather sparsely populated uplands of Northumberland and Durham, through the rolling dales and moors of Yorkshire, south to the flat land of coastal Lincolnshire, where the landscape blends into the East Anglian fens.

Golden Plover, Red Grouse and Curlew breed on many of the uplands and moors, and their calls certainly help to create the atmosphere of these windswept habitats. Merlin may be seen gliding over the heather moor here, as may Short-eared Owl and Hen Harrier.

Northumberland National Park comprises over 113,000ha of hill country in the very north of England. It hangs down from the Scottish border between the Cheviot Hills in the north, which reach their highest point at the Cheviot (815m), and Hadrian's Wall in the south.

The main habitats here are woodlands and the farms of the valleys, rocky streams, lakes and bogs, and the open upland grassland and moorland of the higher areas, in places topped by crags and cliffs.

The huge brooding plantation of Kielder

Jacob's-ladder (Polemonium caeruleum) at Upper Lathkilldale, near Monyash, Derbyshire. This species is locally common on limestone in the north of England.

Forest dominates the western flank of the park, but there are also scattered natural deciduous woods in some of the valleys–oak on drier sites, and Alder in wetter places.

The heather moors of the hills are mainly managed as grouse moors and although much of the park is private land, rights of way and footpaths abound. The Pennine Way runs the length of the park, passing along part of Hadrian's Wall.

Curlew, Golden Plover and Red Grouse are common on the hills, with Blackcock, Short-eared Owl and Merlin ocurring in some of the heather moorland. Wheatear breed on the upland as well, often inside the many drystone walls.

Mammals of the park include Roe Deer, Fox, Badger, Brown Hare, Rabbit, Otter and Red Squirrel.

Lindisfarne and the Farne Islands provide excellent birdwatching, with important colonies of birds such as Puffin and Eider, and large concentrations of wintering wildfowl and waders. Further south, the splendid coastal reserve of Gibraltar Point is a great place to sample saltmarsh flora, as well as a prime site for migrant birds.

One of the best plant sites in this region is undoubtedly Upper Teesdale, a favourite with British botanists, offering a remarkable assemblage of rare and local species, among them the famous Spring Gentian. Other specialities are the Teesdale Violet and the Teesdale Sandwort, the latter only known from this area in Britain. Several other interesting plants can also be found in the vicinity of Teesdale, including the Hoary Rock-rose and Dwarf Milkwort, whilst the rich hay-meadows in this region have a fine flora with abundant Globeflower.

The moorland on the Durham–Yorkshire border produces the rare Yellow Marsh Saxifrage, and the Wood Stichwort is more common in the lowland parts of County Durham than anywhere else in Britain.

North York Moors National Park is centred upon an area of upland to the north and west of Scarborough on the Yorkshire coast, stretching west almost to Thirsk, and north to the border with Cleveland. It covers an area of nearly 144,000ha and includes valleys such as Brasdale and Rosedale in the southwest of the Park, and Eskdale in the north.

The gentle landscape of the river valleys contrasts with the rather bleak open plateaux of the hills, which reach a maximum height of 454m in the north-west.

The hills are mostly heather clad and have flowers such as Bell Heather and Bilberry, Crowberry, Cowberry, and Cloudberry in some places. On the boggy areas, there are cottongrasses, Cranberry, Bog Myrtle and a wide range of sedges. Other plants of the damp sites are Globeflower, Grass-of-Parnassus and Bird's-eye Primrose.

Yorkshire Dales National Park covers some 176,000ha in the northern Pennines, between Skipton in the south and Richmond in the north-east. Part of the famous Pennine Way walk runs through the centre of this park.

It contains some grand scenery, with high limestone and millstone grit peaks, upland grassland, limestone pavement, heather moor and gentle valleys such as Ribblesdale, Airedale and Wharfdale, which drain south, and Wensleydale and Swaledale, which drain east. The highest hills are mostly towards the western side of the park and include Pen-Y-Ghent (693m), Ingleborough (723m) and Whernside (737m). In some places, such as at Malham Cove and Gordale Scar, there are impressive limestone cliffs.

FIFTY INTERESTING SPECIES TO LOOK FOR

Black Grouse	Razorbill	Dark-red Helleborine	Northern Spike-rush
Common Scoter	Red Grouse	Dwarf Milkwort	Nottingham Catchfly
Curlew	Ring Ousel	Globeflower	Shady Horsetail
Eider	Short-eared Owl	Hoary Rock-rose	Shrubby Cinquefoil
Gannet	Wheatear	Hoary Whitlow Grass	Spring Cinquefoil
Golden Plover	Whinchat	Jacob's-ladder	Spring Gentian
Goosander	Whooper Swan	May Lily	Teesdale Sandwort
Goshawk	Grey Seal	Melancholy Thistle	Teesdale Violet
Guillemot	Red Squirrel	Mossy Saxifrage	Wood Stitchwort
Kittiwake	Alpine Bartsia	Mountain Avens	Yellow Marsh Saxifrage
Long-tailed Duck	Alpine Cinquefoil	Mountain Pansy	Large Heath
Merlin	Alpine Currant	Northern Bedstraw	
Puffin	Bird's-eye Primrose	Northern Hawksbeard	

The park has about half of Britain's limestone pavement and underground the porous rocks have been channelled into a huge complex of cave systems and underground rivers, streams and potholes.

Further south, the Derbyshire Dales have a rich limestone flora, with choice plants like Jacob's-ladder and Nottingham Catchfly, a flower first described in Britain from the walls of Nottingham Castle. Two pretty flowers of the grazed upland turf are Spring Cinquefoil and Mountain Pansy, the latter often abundant.

Other characteristic plant species of this region are: Northern Hawksbeard, Northern Spike-rush, Shady Horsetail, Melancholy Thistle, May Lily, Alpine Currant and Mossy Saxifrage.

40 HARBOTTLE CRAGS	
Location:	c. 12km west of Rothbury
Grid Reference:	NT 9305; L80
Visiting:	Best in summer. Park west of Harbottle village
Terrain:	Upland grassland and moor, farmland
Specialities:	Flowers, birds, insects

A fine example of heather moorland and upland grassland. Managed for Grouse shooting by regular cutting and burning.

One interesting feature of the reserve are the cliffs and crags which jut out above the moorland. Here, there are patches of well-grown Heather with Bilberry, Crowberry and Cowberry, as well as ferns.

Birds to watch out for here are Short-eared Owl, Kestrel and sometimes even Merlin. Both Black and Red Grouse can be seen, and there are also Ring Ousel, Wheatear and Whinchat.

The Melancholy Thistle (Ciroium Helenioides) is a spineless thistle which grows in damp pastures in upland Britain.

Lepidoptera include Small Heath, and Northern Eggar, Fox and Emperor Moths.

Hadrian's Wall is worth a visit in its own right, and the adjacent moorland has interesting wildlife too.

41 HADRIAN'S WALL/ BORDER LOUGHS

Location:	Near Haltwhistle, between Carlisle and Hexham
Grid Reference:	NY 7868; L86/87
Visiting:	Convenient park at Housesteads Fort
Terrain:	Upland grassland, farmland, lakes
Specialities:	Winter wildfowl, wetland plants

This site is well worth visiting for the chance to enter the world of Roman Britain by walking some of Hadrian's Wall and admiring the remains of the Roman Forts, such as Housesteads.

The wildlife is also of interest, however, and the string of lochs here attract good numbers of wildfowl in the winter. At Grindon Lough (NY 8268) Whooper Swan, Bean, Pink-footed and Grey-lag Geese can all be seen from the roadside, or even from the car. However, Greenlee Lough (NY 7869), the largest, is the best for Whoopers.

Crag Lough (NY 7767) is probably the best for seeing the typical vegetation of these border loughs. Here carr-like scrub grades into swampy fen vegetation dominated by Common Reed and sedges. Other flowers here are Marsh Marigold, Marsh Cinquefoil, Bogbean, Ragged Robin, Skullcap and Marsh Lousewort.

42 UPPER TEESDALE

Location:	c. 20km north west of Barnard Castle
Grid Reference:	NY 8628; L91/92
Visiting:	Best spring–summer. Rough walking over footpaths. Visitor centre at Bowlees
Terrain:	Upland grassland, heather moor
Specialities:	Arctic-Alpine flowers

This site is a favourite of keen botanists because of its unique collection of rare or local species. Two reserves are particularly noteworthy: Cronkley Fell (NY 8628) and Widdybank Fell and Cauldron Snout (NY 8328). Cronkley Fell can be reached by following the Pennine Way up from Holwick or by following the river upstream from Dale Chapel. The rocks here are a special kind of limestone, called sugar limestone because of its crumbly texture. The plants are a mixture of Arctic-Alpines, some of them rare, and more usual southern species. They include Thyme, Spring Sandwort and Northern Bedstraw. Alongside the river there are splendid stands of Juniper and also, in places, Shrubby Cinquefoil.

The hay meadows in this area (best late June) are very fine and unimproved, with a large array of flowers, including several species of lady's mantle, Yellow Rattle, Great Burnet, marsh orchids, Ragged Robin, Melancholy Thistle and Globeflower.

On Widdybank Fell, amongst the specialities are the beautiful blue Spring Gentian, Teesdale Violet, Scottish Asphodel and the

Cauldron Snout, Upper Teesdale, Durham. The fells near this fine waterfall are the habitat of the rare Spring Gentian and Teesdale Violet.

Teesdale Sandwort. Other flowers to look for are Alpine Penny-cress and Spring Sandwort.

Other important sites nearby: Moor House (NY 7729) lies further up the Tees valley towards the highest point of the Pennines at Cross Fell (893 m). Here there is splendid blanket bog and Alpines on rocky outcrops.

High Force waterfall (NY 8828) should certainly be visited. It is an impressive sight as it thunders over the rocks. There are Red Squirrels in the nearby woods.

43 LINDISFARNE (HOLY ISLAND)	
Location:	c. 16km south of Berwick-on-Tweed.
Grid Reference:	NU 1343; L75
Visiting:	Reached by causeway at low tide. Be sure to consult tide-tables!
Terrain:	Rocky islands, rock pools, mudflats, dunes
Specialities:	Seabirds

This is one of the north-east's best bird-watching sites, especially for wildfowl and waders in autumn and winter.

Red-throated Diver and Slavonian Grebe are fairly common in the nearby sea in the winter, and Black-throated Diver and Red-necked Grebe are also possible. The wintering wildfowl include pale-bellied Brent Geese (a speciality), Greylag Geese, sometimes with Pink-footed and Bean Geese as well, Whooper Swan, with the occasional Bewick's Swan, Wigeon, Shelduck, Teal, Eider, Common (and more rarely Velvet) Scoter, Long-tailed Duck and Scaup.

Predators such as Hen Harrier, Short-eared Owl, Peregrine and Merlin are all regular visitors in the winter.

The commonest waders are Dunlin, Knot and Bar-tailed Godwit, but rarer species are fairly likely too, including Purple Sandpiper and Greenshank.

The flowers of Lindisfarne are interesting too, especially in the dune areas (such as The Snook, and The Links). Look for Grass-of-Parnassus and orchids such as the Dune Helleborine. Below the castle, itself worth a detour, there are Thrift, Biting Stonecrop and Sea Campion.

Other important sites nearby: The Farne Islands (NU 2337) is a group of twenty-eight small islands, reached by a regular pleasure-boat service from Seahouses. There is a large colony of Eider, and thousands of Puffin, Kittiwake and terns (including a few Roseate). The islands are also a good habitat for Grey Seals, which can often be seen here.

44 LEVISHAM MOOR	
Location:	In Newton Dale about 10km north-east of Pickering.
Grid Reference:	SE 8594; L94/101
Visiting:	Spring–summer. Keep to footpaths
Terrain:	Heather moor, cliffs, woodland, plantation, pasture, and bog
Specialities:	Arctic-Alpine plants, moorland birds

Levisham Moor is a reserve with a range of habitats and is set in a scenic valley on the edge of the moorland plateau.

Watch out for moorland birds such as Golden Plover, Red Grouse, Curlew and Snipe, and also for Merlin, with Dippers on

Lindisfarne (Holy Island) castle stands proudly over the surrounding fields. Its walls have flowers such as Thrift and Sea Campion. This is one of the best birdwatching areas in the north-east, especially in the winter, when divers and grebes gather on the sea and the surrounding mudflats are alive with waders and Brent Geese

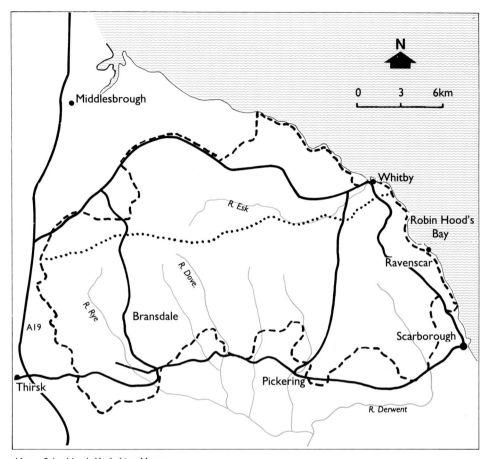

Map of the North Yorkshire Moors.

the streams. The reserve is famous for certain Arctic-Alpine plants such as Chickweed Wintergreen and Dwarf Cornel.

Other important sites nearby: Forge Valley Woods (SE 9986), about 7km west of Scarborough, are a fine example of relatively unspoiled woodland within the North Yorkshire Moors National Park. The woods grade from oak higher up, to communities with Ash and elms, and to Alder and willows in the lower, damper parts.

Robin Hood's Bay (NZ 9505) and Ravenscar (NZ 9803), both just south of Whitby, are fascinating coastal sites well worth a visit. The former has a fine platform coast with many rock pools, below fossil-rich cliffs with many ammonites. At Ravenscar the rocks are also very rich in fossils, and some even have dinosaur footprints.

Malham Cove, from the west side, Yorkshire. The cove, a limestone outcrop, lies just to the south of Malham Tarn. Its cliffs provide a natural breeding site for House Martins.

45 MALHAM TARN

Location:	c. 9km east of Settle
Grid Reference:	SD 8967; L98
Visiting:	Easy access by road and footpath from village of Malham. Permit required away from nature-trail or paths
Terrain:	Lake, fen, limestone pavement, grassland, scree, woodland, cliffs
Specialities:	Limestone plants, including Alpine species; birds

Malham Tarn is one of the most intensively studied sites in the country and has a FSC field centre. A Nature Trail leads around part of the lake and there are parking places conveniently close to the reserve.

This is a botanist's paradise, and the surroundings of the tarn have a rich flora of peatland species, some growing in alkaline fen conditions, others in the more acid raised bogs nearby. Bottle Sedge colonizes the open water, and there are many other sedge species in the fen vegetation, along with flowers such as Bog Bean, Marsh Cinquefoil and Valerian.

Yorkshire Milkwort is a rare species found growing here, and other interesting flowers in the reserve include Alpine Bartsia, Alpine Cinquefoil, Mountain Avens, Mountain Pansy, Bird's-eye Primrose, Hoary Whitlow Grass and Northern Bedstraw.

Birds to watch out for include Curlew, Golden Plover, Red Grouse, Wheatear and Ring Ousel on the high ground, Common Sandpipers on the lake, Dippers along the streams and Redstart in the woods.

Malhan Tarn is on the southern part of the Yorkshire Dales National Park where the countryside features cliffs and other outcroppings of limestone rock. Underground there is an extensive cave and river system.

46 FLAMBOROUGH HEAD	
Location:	Headland to N of Bridlington
Grid Reference:	TA 2571; L101
Visiting:	May–July (breeding birds); spring and autumn (migrants)
Terrain:	Rocky headland with cliffs, grassland and scrub
Specialities:	Breeding seabirds; seawatching

Flamborough Head is easily reached by road from Bridlington via the village of Flamborough and there are a number of car parks, including one at the lighthouse. Tracks then lead around the headland.

Although not as high as nearby Bempton Cliffs, the cliffs at Flamborough head are impressive and it is the breeding seabirds which provide the chief attraction to the naturalist. There are large numbers of Kittiwake, Guillemot, Razorbill, Puffin, Herring Gull and Fulmar, and a few Shags. Look out also for wild Rock Doves.

This is a good spot to watch groups of Gannet plunge-diving for fish and Manx Shearwater are also a fairly regular sight offshore, with occasional Sooty Shearwater as well in autumn. In the autumn also keep an eye out for Little Gull passing by, and for Great Skua.

In late spring and late autumn Flamborough is used as a refuge by migrating songbirds, especially after storms. Pied Flycatcher, Redstart, Ring Ousel, Whinchat, Wheatear and Wryneck are regular, with the chance of rarities such as Yellow-browed and Icterine Warblers.

Other important sites nearby: Bempton Cliffs (TA 1974) are the highest chalk cliffs in the country, rising to over 120m. They hold large seabird colonies, including Britain's only mainland gannetry (with about 650 pairs). There are also Kittiwake, Guillemot, Razorbill and Puffin. Visit May–July.

47 THE PEAK DISTRICT NATIONAL PARK	
Location:	On Pennine ridge from between Manchester and Sheffield, south to Ashbourne
Grid Reference:	L110, (118), 119
Visiting:	Spring and summer
Terrain:	Upland; sheltered valleys
Specialities:	Moorland birds and flowers; flower-rich dales

This National Park, the first to be created, in 1951, lies in a broad crescent astride the

Red Grouse *Lagopus lagopus* L38
A reddish-brown, plump gamebird, characteristic of upland heather moor, mainly in northern Britain and Ireland, but also found on Exmoor and very rarely on Dartmoor. Red Grouse fly up abruptly from the heather when startled, making loud laughing cackling calls. Many areas of upland are managed to encourage Red Grouse, which are then shot for sport. They eat heather shoots, insects and berries.

Pennines, from Macclesfield and Leek in the west, to Ashbourne and Matlock in the south and east, north to include the high ground between Sheffield and Manchester.

Although it includes much private land, most parts of the park are accessible by footpath, and the southern part of the Pennine Way starts here, at Edale.

The high moorland of the northern part, known as Dark Peak, forms a plateau rising to a height of over 630 m at Kinder Scout. Here the vegetation is mostly acid upland grassland, heather moor and eroded blanket bogs, or peat hags.

Further south, in the gentler, lower valleys and farmland of the White Peak, the soils are calcareous, and the flora reflects this difference. The valley sides sometimes have

The Edale valley in the Peak District National Park has fern-rich streams and Ash-dominated woodland.

semi-natural woodlands, mainly dominated by Ash, and there are some fine sites on exposed rocks and scree slopes with a rich flora. The fields margins are marked by picturesque drystone walls.

Important sites within the National Park: Kinder-Bleaklow Uplands (SK 0993). These are easily accessible from the A57 from Sheffield to Glossop. This area, which is crossed by the Pennine Way, has one of the best blanket bogs in the country. Hardly any bog is actively growing now, however, and erosion has cut through the layers of peat to the hard millstone grit rocks beneath. Bilberry, Crowberry and Cowberry grow on the moors, and in some places Cloudberry, here towards its southern limit. The birds of these moors include Curlew, Ring Ousel, Red Grouse, Golden Plover and the occasional Merlin.

48 LATHKILL DALE	
Location:	Over Haddon, near Bakewell
Grid Reference:	SK 2066; L119
Visiting:	Best spring and summer. Permit needed off footpaths
Terrain:	Woodland, streams, cliffs, scree, limestone grassland
Specialities:	Rich limestone flora

This reserve consists of woodland and limestone grassland in a beautiful valley setting. It also has one of the finest natural Ash woods, with woodland shrubs including Hazel, Guelder Rose, Rowan, Wych Elm, Field Maple, Hawthorn and Dogwood. On the woodland floor grow such species as Lily-of-the-Valley, Dog's Mercury and Red Campion, and even the rare Mezereon.

The Dark-red Helleborine (Epipactis atrorubens) is an orchid of limestone rocks, and occurs from Derbyshire northwards, and in the west of Ireland (notably in Connemara and the Burren).

The chalk grassland here is very rich, especially on southerly aspects, with flowers such as Bird's Foot Trefoil, Marjoram, Common Rock-Rose, Wild Thyme, Bloody Cranesbill, Fragrant Orchid, Globeflower and, in some places, the rare Jacob's Ladder. On stonier soils, look out for Dark Red Helleborine, Spring Cinquefoil and Mossy Saxifrage.

Birds breeding in this fine reserve include Redstart, Wood Warbler, Hawfinch, Grey Wagtail and Dipper.

Other important sites nearby: Monk's Dale (SK 1473), 10km north-west of Lathkill Dale, is more peaceful, and equally rich in flowers, with scree and flush communities

as well as grassland. Two other dale reserves lie close by – Cressbrook Dale (SK 1774) and Chee and Miller's Dale (SK 1473).

49 SPURN PENINSULA	
Location:	c. 10km south-east of Patrington, Humberside
Grid Reference:	TA 4215; L113
Visiting:	Car park near Kilnsea. Entry fee
Terrain:	Shingle, sand, saltmarsh, mudflats
Specialities:	Migrant birds

A narrow spit of shingle and sand stretching out into the Humber estuary. On the landward side there are large areas of mudflat, exposed at low tide.

The migrant birds are impressive here, both in the spring and in late summer and autumn. In March there are large numbers of common birds such as Lapwing and Starling, but also rarer species like Wryneck and Black Redstart.

But it is the late summer and autumn migration which brings the most interesting birds. Skuas are a regular feature, as are Sooty Shearwater, Little Gull and Little Auk. The waders include Spotted Redshank, Curlew Sandpiper and Little Stint, as well as commoner species such as Dunlin, Knot, Redshank, Oystercatcher and Turnstone. Large flocks of Fieldfare and Redwing feast on the berries of the Sea Buckthorn.

In late August and September, you may spot such rarities as Bluethroat, Red-backed Shrike, Icterine and Barred Warbler. Long-eared Owls are also regular as are wintering Great Grey Shrike and Snow Bunting.

The dunes contain Marram Grass, Sea Buckthorn and flowers such as Sea Holly, Sea Bindweed and Pyramidal Orchid.

50 SALTFLEETBY-THEDDLETHORPE DUNES

Location:	6km N of Mablethorpe
Grid Reference:	TF 4790; L113
Visiting:	Car parks available; open all year
Terrain:	Dunes, marsh, mudflats
Specialities:	Coastal birds and flowers, butterflies

This fine coastal reserve has much to offer the visitor. The sand and mudflats offshore are a good feeding ground for waders and wildfowl, whilst the saltmarsh and dune sysspecies. The reserve is especially good for butterflies.

The saltmarsh has Thrift, Annual Sea-blite, Common Sea Lavender and Sea Purslane. Other special plants of the reserve are the Marsh Pea, Autumn Gentian, Bog Pimpernel, Carline Thistle and Fairy Flax. There are also a number of orchids in and around the dunes. These include Bee, Pyramidal, and Early Marsh and Southern Marsh Orchids.

Marsh orchids (Dactylorhiza spp.) are impressive at Saltfleetby nature reserve in May and June in the dune slacks of this reserve.

Pools in the dune slacks offer ideal breeding conditions for the Natterjack, along with Common Frog, Common Toad and Smooth Newt.

This reserve is well known for its rich insect fauna too. In addition to dragonflies and damselflies, this is a good site for butterflies, including Green Hairstreak and Dark Green Fritillary.

Breeding birds include Oystercatcher, Redshank, Snipe and Shelduck.

Other important sites nearby: Tetney Marshes (TA 3604) is a good birdwatching site. It contains a large colony of Little Tern, with wintering Bar-tailed Godwit and Brent Geese.

Donna Nook and Saltfleet (TF 4299), also have good mudflats with waders and seals, as well as rich dune systems.

51 GIBRALTAR POINT	
Location:	c. 4km south of Skegness
Grid Reference:	TF 5658; L122
Visiting:	Parking at reserve; nature trails open all year
Terrain:	Saltmarsh, mudflats, dunes
Specialities:	Migrant birds, seabirds, flowers

This reserve is of equal interest to the birdwatcher and botanist. It has splendid saltmarsh communities and fine dunes, with scrub. Plants of the saltmarsh include Sea Purslane, Common Sea Lavender (which colours whole areas purple), annual Sea-blite and Sea Aster. This reserve is also possibly the most northerly site for Shrubby Seablite.

Dunes can be seen here at all stages of development, with a mixed scrub of Sea Buckthorn, Elder, Hawthorn, Privet and rose on the lee side of the older dunes. Look for Pyramidal Orchids in the dune grassland, along with Cowslip and Springbeauty.

The birds include a colony of Little Terns nesting on the shingle. Other notable species breeding on the reserve are Shelduck and Short-eared Owl.

Interesting migrant birds here are Snow Bunting, Twite and the occasional influx of Waxwings. In winter, Sparrowhawk, Merlin and Hen Harrier are regularly seen.

The Mere, which has a public hide, attracts gulls, waders and wildfowl, particularly in autumn and winter. On migration watch for Little Ringed Plover, Curlew and Wood Sandpipers, Little Stint and Spotted Redshank.

To the south of the reserve lies the expanse of the wash, one of Britain's finest wader sites in winter. Dunlin, Knot and Bar-tailed Godwit often gather here in large flocks.

7. EASTERN ENGLAND

This region is characterized by a continental climate having relatively low rainfall, cold winters and warm summers, and a range of contrasting soil types. Soils range from the dry, often acidic, sandy soils of the Breckland to the alkaline peat of the fens.

Three contrasting habitats stand out as particularly noteworthy in this region: the fens, the boulder-clay woods and the Breckland heaths. There is precious little fenland remaining now, but pockets such as Wicken Fen and the Norfolk Broads (the latter not strictly part of the true fenland, but having comparable wildlife) serve to remind of the riches of the past, and still retain special species and communities.

The Stone Curlew (Burhinus oedicnemus) is an unusual bird which is a Breckland speciality. The breeding population of this declining species is now down to about 150 pairs.

The peat fen flora, now largely destroyed by drainage or cultivation, still shows its special plants in the few fenland reserves. At Wicken Fen and in the Broads can be seen the handsome Marsh Pea and Milk Parsley, the latter the larval food-plant of the rare Swallowtail butterfly. Birds of the fens include Marsh Harrier, Bittern, Bearded Tit, and Reed, Sedge, Grasshopper, Savi's and Cetti's Warblers.

Several species of plants are largely or wholly confined to this part of the British Isles. Perhaps the best known of these, and certainly one of the most beautiful, is the Oxlip, a locally abundant spring-flowering relative of the widespread Cowslip and the Primrose. This flower can be seen in abundance in some semi-natural woodlands in the region, perhaps most notably at Hayley Wood, Cambridge.

In the Breckland of Norfolk and Suffolk the light, sandy soils also have a very special flora, of which the Spanish Catchfly is a famous example. It is related to a group of species widespread on the steppes of Eastern Europe, and is the sole representative of this group in Britain. Other Breckland species are Sickle Medick, Mossy Stonecrop and Spring Speedwell. Breckland has its special birds too, with Wood Lark, Nightjar, Hobby and Stone Curlew perhaps most noteworthy. In certain spots on the edge of Breckland and fen, the rare Golden Oriole is a recent and welcome addition to the bird life.

The North Norfolk Coast is a magnificent stretch of coastal habitats extending from Holme-next-the-Sea in the west to Salthouse in the east. Most of the strip has some form of protection, as a chain of individual reserves, and the whole area has Biosphere Reserve and Ramsar status, reflecting the international importance of the site.

The wildlife is varied, reflecting the multitude of habitats, which include open sea, shingle spits, shallow lagoons, mudflats, sand dunes, coastal woodland, heath, marsh, reedbeds and open freshwater.

A particular feature of the hedgerows in this area are the clumps of the tall bright-green umbellifer, Alexanders, which has yellow flower heads. It tends to take over from Queen Anne's Lace in the lanes and hedges near to the sea.

Corsican Pines and Silver Birch have colonized a long stretch of stable dunes at Wells/Holkam, providing a welcome habitat for migrant birds and occasional Red Squirrels.

52 HOLKHAM

Location:	2km east of Wells, North Norfolk
Grid Reference:	TF 8945; L132
Visiting:	All year. Parking along road opposite Holkham Hall entrance
Terrain:	Saltmarsh, dunes, mudflats, woodland
Specialities:	Waders, migrants, saltmarsh plants

The coast at Holkham is a fine reserve, easily accessible by footpath, from Wells or from the coast road. Coastal grazing land is protected from the sea by a high ridge of dunes, clad for much of their length by a well-grown plantation of Corsican and Scots Pines.

When the tide is out, the mud and sandflats along this coast are very extensive and attract good numbers of waders.

The fields immediately south of the pinewoods attract flocks of migrant geese during the winter. Watch out especially for White-fronted and Brent Geese, with some Pink-footed Geese. In addition, feral Egyptian Geese breed in this area and may be seen in the fields throughout the year.

FIFTY INTERESTING SPECIES TO LOOK FOR

Avocet	Lapland Bunting	Wood Lark	Spring Speedwell
Bearded Tit	Little Tern	Fallow Deer	Sulphur Clover
Bewick's Swan	Marsh Harrier	Roe Deer	Common Blue
Bittern	Nightingale	Alexanders	Dingy Skipper
Black-tailed Godwit	Nightjar	Cambridge Milk Parsley	Essex Skipper
Black Tern	Ruff	Fen Violet	Holly Blue
Brambling	Savi's Warbler	Marsh Pea	Large Copper
Brent Goose	Shorelark	Marsh Sow-thistle	Large Skipper
Cetti's Warbler	Snow Bunting	Milk Parsley	Purple Hairstreak
Egyptian Goose	Spoonbill	Mossy Stonecrop	Small Skipper
Garganey	Spotted Redshank	Oxlip	Swallowtail
Golden Oriole	Stone Curlew	Sickle Medick	
Hawfinch	Water Rail	Spanish Catchfly	

During the spring and autumn migrations, the woods and nearby scrub are attractive to songbirds and there are usually good numbers of warblers, flycatchers and Redstarts. Occasionally, rarer species like Wryneck and Ring Ousel turn up, or even Red-backed Shrike, Red-breasted Flycatcher or Barred Warbler.

Other important sites nearby: Holkham Hall (TF 8843) stands in very fine walled grounds which form a marvellous nature reserve in their own right. A public road and footpaths run through the estate. The lake has a Cormorant roost on the island. Hawfinches and Bramblings can occasionally be seen under the Beech trees.

---

53 CLEY AND SALTHOUSE MARSHES

Location:	Near Blakeney
Grid Reference:	TG 0545; L132
Visiting:	All year; best migrants in autumn. Good birding from banks and paths. Permit needed for reserve
Terrain:	Reedbeds, open water, coast
Specialities:	Migrant birds

This is possibly England's most famous birdwatching reserve, with over 325 species recorded. It is a mecca for 'twitchers', which makes it a reserve not to everyone's liking, and there is often the feeling of queing up to see something special. Nevertheless, it is well worth a visit, especially after gales or easterly winds between late July and October.

Map of Wells and Holkham.

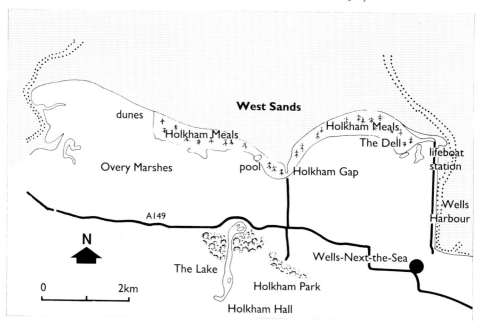

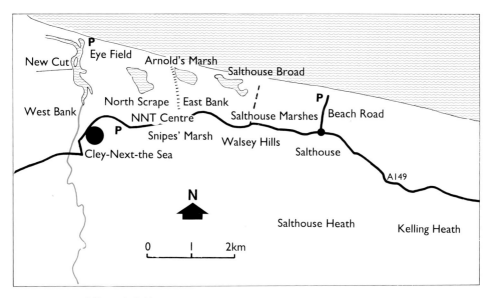

Above: *map of Cley with Salthouse.*
Below: *map of the Cley area showing Blakeney Point.*

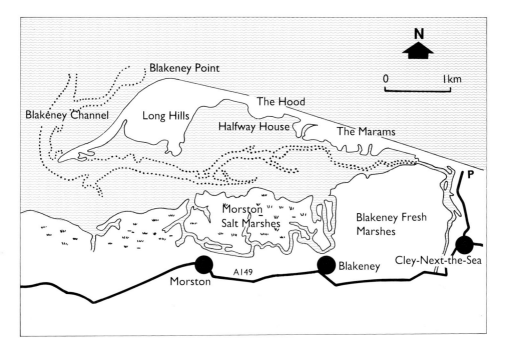

Cley Windmill and reedbeds. Cley is a splendid bird reserve, with a wide range of habitats, including reed beds, coastal shingle, lagoons and grazing marsh.

The habitats are reedbeds, open fresh and brackish water, pasture, shingle scrapes, and shingle beach.

This is one of the best reserves to see Avocets, which breed here and can be seen indulging in elaborate courtship in the spring and early summer. Other speciality breeders are Bittern (difficult to see but you may hear them booming) and the much more obvious Bearded Tits. The latter bound in small parties over the reeds making sharp, metallic 'pinging' contact calls. The damp meadows contain good numbers of Yellow Wagtails.

The woods and heaths to the south of Salthouse are good places to hear Nightjars and Nightingales in the summer, and if you are very lucky, a Great Grey Shrike in the winter.

But it is in the autumn that the reserve really pulls in the birders, with the famous East Bank regularly marched on by small groups scanning the marshes for waders. The list is a long one and includes Ruff, Black-tailed Godwit, Whimbrel, Spotted Redshank, Greenshank, Common, Green and Wood Sandpipers and Little Stint. Other visitors to the reserve are Garganey, Marsh Harrier, Black Tern and Spoonbill. The shingle bank and nearby fields sometimes have flocks of Shorelark and Snow or Lapland Buntings.

Other important sites nearby: Blakeney Point (TG 0046) is rightly famed for its colonies of terns (Sandwich, Common and Little). Boat trips from the harbour to see Common, and occasionally Grey, Seals hauled out at tip of point.

Blakeney Marshes and the associated pools attract large numbers of waders, including Avocet, which breed nearby.

54 HICKLING BROAD

Location:	c. 15km north-west of Great Yarmouth
Grid Reference:	TG 4322; L134
Visiting:	Best in summer. Closed Nov–March and Tuesdays. Access by public footpath. Permits needed for reserve
Terrain:	Reedbeds, open fresh water, grazed marsh, fen carr, woodland
Specialities:	Swallowtail butterfly, birds, flowers

Hickling is the largest and one of the most important of the Norfolk Broads. One of its main claims to fame is as one of very few sites where the rare Swallowtail butterfly still breeds and thrives.

The reserve has a wide range of wetland and fen plants, including Milk Parsley (the food plant of the Swallowtail), Water Violet, Purple Loosestrife, Marsh Pea and Common Spotted and Southern Marsh Orchids.

This is a good site for the rare Savi's Warbler, which has a similar song to a Grasshopper Warbler, but which prefers reedbeds. Grasshopper Warblers are also found here, in the bushy areas. Marsh Harriers breed, as do Bittern and Bearded Tit.

In the spring, the broad attracts passing migrants, including Osprey and Black Tern, and in winter, the ducks include Goldeneye, and the occasional Smew.

Other important sites nearby: Martham Broad (TG 4621) is much smaller, but it also has Swallowtails and a rich fen flora.

Upton Broad White Water-lilies, (Nymphaea alba), flourish in the still waters of this reed-fringed broad. Fen carr takes over on the landward side.

Winterton Dunes (TG 4921) has shallow dune ponds with breeding Natterjack Toads. Stonechat also breeds here.

Strumpshaw Fen (TG 3407) has a similar array of plants, birds and insects as Hickling Broad. This is a good site for Cetti's Warbler.

Swallowtail *Papilio machaon* W 64–100mm
Our most spectacular and beautiful butterfly is now only regularly found in the Norfolk Broads, where the caterpillar feeds on Milk Parsley. It also bred at Wicken Fen until relatively recently and attempts have been made to re-establish it there, but so far without lasting success. Sometimes the continental subspecies breeds in southern England, mainly in Dorset, Kent, Hampshire and the Isle of Wight. Its caterpillar feeds on a range of umbellifers, including Carrot.

55 MINSMERE	
Location:	Between Southwold and Aldeburgh
Grid Reference:	TM 4767; L156
Visiting:	Any time, but best May. Access via Eastbridge or Westleton. Public hide on beach. RSPB members free access to reserve (closed Tuesdays)
Terrain:	Reedbeds, open water, grazing land, woodland, heath
Specialities:	Avocet, Marsh Harrier

Minsmere is one of the RSPB's most famous reserves, and justifiably so, since it supports a splendid variety of wetland and coastal

The delightful Bearded Tit (Panurus biarmicus) spends almost all its time in amongst the reeds.

species and offers excellent views from well-sited hides.

The Scrape has breeding Common and Little Terns, but the star attraction is undoubtedly the colony of Avocets which can be seen from close quarters from various hides, from mid-March until September. Kingfishers regularly flash over the open water, or perch in overhanging branches.

The reedbeds have Bittern and Water Rail, as well as large numbers of Bearded Tits. It is well worth scanning regularly over the reeds for the sight of a Marsh Harrier, another regular breeder here.

Savi's Warbler breeds here sometimes, as well as the very common Reed and Sedge Warblers. At the edge of the marsh, where bush meets reedbed, listen for the distinctive song of Cetti's Warbler, or for the monotonous reeling of a Grasshopper Warbler.

The woods have all three woodpeckers, Tawny Owl (sometimes Long-eared Owl), Nightingale and Redstart.

Although taking second place to the birds, Minsmere's flowers are not without interest. The grassy ditches have Common Spotted Orchid and Southern Marsh Orchid, and the marsh edges have Water Dock, Hemp

Agrimony and Yellow Flag. The tall and rare Marsh Sow-thistle can also be found here. The heathland has Bell Heather and Gorse as well as Heather, and the adjacent mixed oak woods are also worth investigating.

Other important sites nearby: Sizewell Power Station, immediately south of Minsmere, has breeding Black Redstarts.

Walberswick has one of the finest areas of unbroken reedbeds in East Anglia, with many rare marsh birds, including Marsh Harriers, Bitterns and Bearded Tits.

Covehithe and Benacre Broad is an interesting site. The broad, which is very close to the sea, attracts wildfowl including Smew in the winter.

Havergate Island (TM 4247) has the largest colony of Avocets (about 100 pairs).

56 CAVENHAM HEATH

Location:	SE Mildenhall, Suffolk, between villages of Tuddenham and Icklingham.
Grid Reference:	TL 7673; L155
Visiting:	Good access from either village. Best to walk into reserve along road that runs through it. Permit required for most of reserve
Terrain:	Fine example of Breckland heath, with adjacent birch and alder woodland. Also areas of damp grazed grassland along banks of River Lark
Specialities:	Roe Deer, Brown Hare, Fox; Nightingale, Nightjar, Sparrowhawk, Little Owl, Stone Curlew; Adder

A very good example of Breckland heath, a habitat that used to be much more widespread, but which has been largely lost to the plough or to building developments.

Much of this gently undulating reserve supports heather and gorse, broken up by pockets of damp birch and alder woodland, patches of Bracken, and small areas of fen. Willow carr is well developed towards the river, where there are also sedge and reed beds, with flowers such as Yellow Flag and Purple Loosestrife. Some of the damp woodland has Marsh Fern in the undergrowth, and in sandy areas Sand Sedge spreads rapidly to colonize soil. Along the tracks look out for Mossy Stonecrop, one of Britain's smallest land flowering plant. As its name

suggests, this Breckland speciality looks just like moss from a distance.

If you are lucky you might hear the strange wailing call of the rare Stone Curlew, or possibly the Curlew, which now breeds nearby. Green Woodpeckers feed on anthills on the heath and grassland, and the air is often loud with the songs of Tree Pipits performing their parachute displays. Buzzing flocks of Redpolls are a feature, especially in the birch woods, and Snipe and Redshank breed in the damp, grazed fields.

The well-drained sandy soils dry out and warm up quickly, making this habitat ideal for reptiles. Adder, Grass Snake and Common Lizard are all found on the reserve. Adder can be a danger, especially early or late in the season when they are sluggish, so boots are recommended.

The butterflies and moths include Grayling, Small Heath, Small Copper, Emperor Moth and Yellow Underwing moth.

57 WICKEN FEN

Location:	c. 15km north east of Cambridge
Grid Reference:	TL 5670; L154
Visiting:	Best spring, summer. Car park near reserve. Free to NT members otherwise by permit from office at fen
Terrain:	Fen carr, sedge fen, open water, reedbeds, wet meadows
Specialities:	Fenland plants

This well-researched fenland remnant is of great importance and lies as an oasis of semi-natural fenland habitat in an otherwise very agricultural region. It is one of Britain's oldest reserves.

Water has to be pumped onto the reserve to keep it sufficiently wet for the fenland communities to survive, and the restored windpump, Wicken's symbol, is sometimes used for this purpose. The footpaths are well marked and a boardwalk gives good dry access (also for wheelchairs) to part of the Sedge Fen. A tower hide gives good views over the artificial mere on Adventurers' Fen.

If you are lucky, particularly in mid-May, you might see a Hobby delicately plucking dragonflies out of the air over the fen. Hobbies are now regular visitors to Wicken. Marsh Harriers are often seen over Adventurers' Fen in the summer, but seldom breed here.

The fen carr is dominated by Buckthorn and Alder Buckthorn and represents a stage in succession from sedge fen towards wet woodland. The local Marsh Fern grows under the wet carr.

Other interesting Wicken flowers are Milk Parsley, Great Fen Sedge, Yellow Rattle, Meadowsweet, Hemp Agrimony, Wild Angelica, Southern Marsh Orchid, Marsh Pea and the rare Fen Violet.

In the winter, Hen Harriers gather to roost in the fen. They can be spotted just before dusk, particularly in the area of the hide.

Other important sites nearby: Woodwalton Fen (TL 8385) is another fenland remnant. Like Wicken, it has an outstanding fen flora, but it is also important as the last refuge of the now extinct Large Copper butterfly. Woodwalton has a colony of Large Coppers introduced from Holland.

This reserve is also an excellent place to see dragonflies, including the Ruddy Darter.

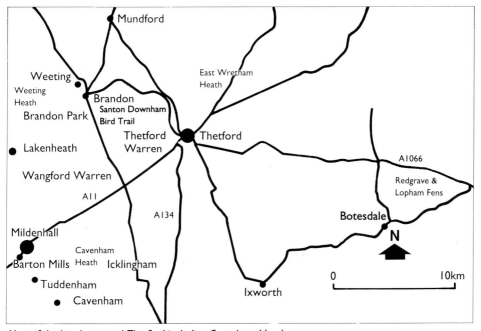

Map of the heaths around Thetford including Cavenham Heath.

Flooded Washes from Halfway Hide, near Welches Dam, Cambridgeshire. Flooded grazing land attracts huge numbers of wintering ducks and geese to the Ouse Washes. These include Wigeon, Pintail and Bewick's and Whooper Swans. In winter, the banks and fields attract Short-eared and Barn Owls, and Merlin, Peregrine and Hen Harrier may also be spotted hunting in the area.

58 OUSE WASHES	
Location:	c. 14km N of Ely
Grid Reference:	TL 5595; L143
Visiting:	Follow road through Purl's Bridge to Welch's Dam (car park)
Terrain:	Open damp grazing land, flooded in winter
Specialities:	Huge concentrations of wildfowl in winter

The Ouse Washes are the finest inland site for wildfowl in the whole region. These fertile grasslands are grazed in the summer, but are allowed to flood during the winter, providing ideal feeding conditions for swans and ducks. Observation is easy, using the numerous hides strategically placed half hidden by the levees at the edge of the flooded area.

The commonest ducks overwintering are Wigeon, Pintail, Shoveler, Pochard, Mallard and Teal. There are also occasional Goldeneye and Smew. However, the star attraction is undoubtedly the huge flocks of Bewick's Swans which gather on the reserve. These may number 2,000, with perhaps a couple of hundred Whooper Swans as well.

In summer, the washes take on a different appearance, with pools and ditches now revealed amongst the lush grassland pasture. Now is the time to watch for displaying Ruff and Black-tailed Godwit, both of which breed here. The fields are also the ideal habitat for Yellow Wagtail. Black Terns and Little Gulls are regular visitors; both have bred, and could do so again.

The washes are not without botanical interest too. The deeper water of the rivers and ditches may hold Fringed and Yellow

Wild geese find wide stretches of safe feeding grounds at Welney, on the Ouse Washes. These are Grey-lag Geese (Anser anser) coming in to land.

Water Lilies and Frogbit, with Comfrey, Meadowsweet, Yellow Flag and Purple Loosestrife at the margins.

Other important sites nearby: Welney Wildfowl Refuge (Wildfowl and Wetlands Trust) is the best spot from which to watch the Bewick's Swans gathering to feed.

Open water near the hide, and supplemental feeding pull in swans from a wide area.

59 REDGRAVE/LOPHAM FENS	
Location:	On Norfolk/Suffolk border, 7km west of Diss
Grid Reference:	TM 5078; L144
Visiting:	Car park at fen entrance
Terrain:	Fen, carr, oak/birch woods, reedbeds
Specialities:	Fenland plants and invertebrates

This reserve has become famous as one of the few sites in the region where the rare Fen Raft Spider occurs. It is a fine remnant of a rare habitat; fenland developed in a river valley –

in this case the upper valley of the Waveney and the Little Ouse. The rivers flood the fen with pure, calcareous water.

The interest of the reserve is enhanced by ridges of sandy, acid soil which support heath vegetation.

The fen communities are dominated by Reed and Purple Moor-grass, with Saw Sedge coming to the fore in some areas. There are many interesting fenland flowers here, including Meadow-sweet, Hemp Agrimony, Valerian, Marsh Valerian, Angelica and Marsh Bedstraw.

In the more acid areas affected by the sandy soils, there are species of heath and bog, including Heather, Cross-leaved Heath and sundews.

The reedbeds provide ideal breeding conditions for both Reed and Sedge Warblers.

Other important sites nearby: Knettishall Heath (TL 9580) is about 8km further west, towards Thetford. It is a typical Breckland heath, with dry grassland and woodland as well. Brandon Country Park (TL 7985) is an interesting area of Breakland, with picnic sites and trails through plantations. Crossbill and Red Squirrels occur here.

60 THERFIELD HEATH

Location:	3km south west of Royston
Grid Reference:	TL 3440; L154
Visiting:	Car park and footpaths
Terrain:	Hillside with chalk grassland and Beech woods
Specialities:	Chalk grassland flowers; butterflies

Chalk grassland is, perhaps surprisingly, rare in East Anglia, and Therfield Heath is one of the finest remaining examples of a once much more widespread habitat. The reserve also has fine mature Beech woods, developed on the well-drained soils of the hill top.

The landscape here is sloping and undulating, providing important differences of aspect; cooler, north-facing slopes, and much warmer and drier south and west-facing slopes.

This is a great place to learn about the flora of chalk downland and to see species such as Cowslip, Common Milkwort, Common Rock-rose, Salad Burnet, Wild Thyme, Clustered Bellflower, Wild Mignonette, Purple Milk-vetch, Dropwort and Horseshoe Vetch. Other flowers to keep an eye open for include Wild Candytuft, Bastard Toadflax, Spotted Cat's-ear, Field Fleawort, and Bee and Fragrant Orchids.

There is one rare species, however, for which this reserve is famed, and that is the magnificent Pasqueflower. Therfield is one of only a few sites where this beautiful plant still thrives. The Pasqueflower is at its most showy in April and May.

The butterflies are also of note and the range of plants provides food for several local species. The blues are well represented, with Common, Holly and Chalkhill Blue all breeding here. It would be worth watching for Small Blue as well since the conditions are suitable. Other species include Brown Argus, and Dingy, Large, Essex and Small Skipper.

The 'heath' provides nesting and hunting sites for birds such as Skylark, Meadow Pipit, Corn Bunting and Kestrel, and in or near the woods there are both Wood and Grasshopper Warblers.

Other important sites nearby: Fox Covert and Fordhams Wood (TL 3440) lie just to the south. They are fine woods, containing many flowers, including White Helleborine.

Hayley Wood, Cambridgeshire. Old oaks near the entrance to the reserve, in early spring.

61 HAYLEY WOOD

Location:	c. 16km west of Cambridge
Grid Reference:	TL 2954; L153
Visiting:	By permit from Wildlife Trust for Bedfordshire and Cambridgeshire
Terrain:	Ancient woodland
Specialities:	Flowers

Hayley Wood is one of the best studied of all our woodland reserves. It is an ancient community which has been managed intermittently for hundreds of years, partly as standard-with coppice.

The main trees are Pedunculate Oak and Ash, but there are other species such as Field Maple, Aspen, Elm, Hazel and Hawthorn in a mixed community.

Hayley has magnificent displays of woodland flowers in the spring, and is perhaps best known for its rare Oxlip (one of the largest populations) and for the sheets of Bluebells which appear every year in April and May. Oliver Rackham has estimated the population of Oxlip here at well over 1 million plants! Other woodland flowers here are Herb Paris, Dog's Mercury, Wood Anemone, Yellow Archangel, Enchanter's Nightshade, Lesser Celandine, Early Purple and Common Spotted Orchid, and both Common and Early Dog-violet. The careful observer may even spot the strange Bird's-nest Orchid, inconspicuous amongst the leaf litter of the woodland floor.

Hayley has abundant bird life too, including Great and Lesser Spotted Woodpecker, Treecreeper, Nightingale, Blackcap, Willow Warbler, Chiffchaff, Long-tailed, Blue, Great, Willow and Marsh Tit.

Other important sites nearby: Buff Wood (TL 2752) also has fine Oxlip, as well as

The beautiful Oxlip (Primula elatior) is more impressive than either the Primrose or Cowslip. It can only be found in the damp boulder-clay woods of East Anglia, as here at Hayley Wood.

many Primrose, and hybrids between the two.

Gamlingay Wood (TL 2554) is a new reserve. It provides a fascinating contrast to Hayley and Buff, being partly on acid greensand. It also has Oxlip and Bluebell, as well as the rare Wild Service Tree.

62 THE NAZE/NAZE POINT

Location:	Just north of Walton on the Naze
Grid Reference:	TM 2724; L169
Visiting:	Car park at site
Terrain:	Saltmarsh, mudflats, low cliffs, grassland and scrub
Specialities:	Migrant birds, such as Black Redstart, Ring Ousel, Pied Flycatcher; Brent Goose; Strawberry Clover

Hamford Water, which lies due west of the reserve at Naze Point, is a complex network of mudflats, saltmarsh and sea and is a major area for waders and wildfowl, especially during the winter months. In addition, the scrub and grassland of the Naze give shelter and food to many thousands of migrating birds every year.

A nature trail leads to Naze Point reserve and from it the visitor can get good views of the marshes and mudflats. The cliffs are composed of red crag, which contains many fossils.

Ringed Plover, Oystercatcher and Little Terns breed at Naze Point, and the flowers here include Slender Thistle, Pepper Saxifrage and Strawberry Clover.

In winter, thousands of Brent Geese gather in Hamford Water and it is possible to see Goldeneye, Eider, Red-breasted Merganser and Great Crested Grebe offshore or in Walton Channel.

Migrants are good here in spring and autumn. In autumn, Curlew Sandpiper are regular, and Redstart, Black Redstart, Ring Ousel, Pied Flycatcher and Firecrest are all regular visitors.

63 COLNE ESTUARY

Location:	12km south of Colchester
Grid Reference:	TM 0816; L168
Visiting:	All year
Terrain:	Shingle, saltmarsh, mudflats
Specialities:	Coastal plants and birds

This splendid estuary offers fine views of waterbirds and migrants, as well as the opportunity of seeing many coastal flowers.

In the summer, the saltmarshes are tinged with the delicate purple and pink of Sea Lavender, Sea Aster and Thrift. Other plants found here are Glasswort, Sea Purslane, Golden Samphire, Annual Sea-blite and Sea Arrowgrass.

On the sand and shingle the species include Yellow Horned Poppy, Sea Holly, Sea Bindweed, Sea Beet, Sea Wormwood and Shrubby Sea-blite.

Brent Geese flock to feed on the mudflats in winter and other wildfowl include Mallard, Goldeneye, Shelduck, Pintail, Teal and Wigeon.

Among the waders taking advantage of the rich pickings of the tidal mud are Curlew, Bar-tailed Godwit, Knot, Dunlin, Golden, Grey and Ringed Plovers, Redshank and Turnstone. On migration, other species turn up here, including Whimbrel and Greenshank.

Other important sites nearby: Abberton Reservoir (TM 9619) best known for its wintering duck and other waterbirds, which include occasional Smew, Goosander, and Red-necked, Black-necked and Slavonian Grebes.

Abberton has an unusual colony of Cormorants nesting in trees close to the water.

64 EPPING FOREST	
Location:	West of Loughton, North London
Grid Reference:	TQ 4298; L167/177
Visiting:	Many car parks and footpaths
Terrain:	Open mixed woodland, pasture, ponds
Specialities:	Ancient woodland, insects

As a tract of ancient woodland close to the capital city and surrounded by built-up areas, Epping Forest provides a valuable amenity. Here it is possible to escape the crowded city and sample the atmosphere of a truly old forest.

Beech, Sessile Oak, Hornbeam and Silver Birch are the major trees of the forest here and the area is a patchwork of woodland, open rides, ponds and heathy grassland. In some places, Holly forms a dark lower storey in the forest, and Wild Service Tree can also be found. Some of the open areas have been invaded by scrub of Hawthorn and Blackthorn, or groves of Silver Birch.

Epping has a very rich insect fauna, boasting almost 1,400 species of beetle alone. The butterflies include Purple Hairstreak, Holly and Common Blue, and Large, Small, Essex and Dingy Skipper, the latter a declining species.

Woodland birds include all three woodpeckers, Nuthatch, Treecreeper and Redpoll as well as less widespread species such as Redstart and Hawfinch.

Other important sites nearby: Rye House Marsh (TL 3910) educational reserve is a riverside marsh in the Lea Valley, with waterbirds, including nesting Common Tern. It has good hides.

*The Curlew (*Numenius arquata*) is a common winter visitor to the coastal mudflats and estuaries of south-east England.*

8. SOUTH-EAST ENGLAND

The chalk slopes of the North and South Downs provide special habitats for some southern species not able to grow much further north in Britain. Perhaps this is because the dry soils and short vegetation allow rapid heating of the surface during sunny weather, especially on south-facing slopes. This effect seems partly to determine the distribution of certain species of butterfly, such as the rare Adonis Blue, as well as a number of plants.

There are also some fine wetlands in this region, such as Pagham Harbour, with its expanses of mudflat and saltmarsh, and the marshes and wet meadows of Stodmarsh. At Dungeness there are almost desert-like conditions in the huge expanses of shingle which create an almost unique habitat.

One famous southern plant is the Box tree, which as a native plant gave its name to Box Hill. Among wild flowers, Ground Pine finds its best British home on the chalk of the south-east. There are also several special orchids, the most characteristic of which is the Lady Orchid, almost confined to open woodland on the chalk downs of Kent (where it is still, happily, not infrequent) and in Surrey, where it grows at its northern limit in Europe. The autumn-flowering Cyclamen, another mainly South European plant often grown in gardens, is a doubtful native anywhere in England, but in certain localities in Kent and Sussex, where it has been known for a long time, it has a good claim to native status.

Along the Kent and Sussex coasts are some other special British rarities, among them the Clove-scented Broomrape, one of a group of parasitic flowering plants which have no green colour. This species uses a bedstraw as host.

Other plant species are: Monkey Orchid, Early and Late Spider Orchids, Starry Clover, Spiked Rampion and Italian Catchfly.

The elegant White Admiral (Ladoga camilla) has its stronghold in the woods and forests of southern England. It has spread in recent years.

65 DUNGENESS

Location:	c. 3km south-east of Lydd, Kent
Grid Reference:	TR 0620; L189
Visiting:	RSPB reserve is a small part of the overall area and is open every day except Tuesday. Charge to non-members
Terrain:	Shingle, ponds, scrub
Specialities:	Coastal birds and flowers

The vast shingle banks at Dungeness have interesting plants such as Sea-kale.

Dungeness is a huge desert-like expanse of shingle which provides a habitat for many specialist coastal plants and birds.

Breeding birds include Common and Sandwich Terns, Black headed Gull, Herring Gull, and even a few Common Gull. Great Crested and Little Grebe also breed here. About 6 pairs of Black Redstart breed around the nuclear power station - watch out for them perching on the fence.

Dungeness is one of the finest places for watching the movements of passing seabirds. A favoured piece of sea is that close to the outflow from the power station, called 'The Patch'. In spring, both Little and Mediterranean Gulls and Roseate Terns are regular visitors. In autumn, Gannet, Great Skua and Little Gull may be seen, as well as Sandwich, Arctic and Black Tern. In the winter, look for divers and grebes.

FIFTY INTERESTING SPECIES TO LOOK FOR

Barn Owl	Little Owl	Shelduck	Lady Orchid
Bearded Tit	Little Ringed Plover	Smew	Late Spider Orchid
Black Redstart	Little Tern	Sparrowhawk	Monkey Orchid
Black-tailed Godwit	Mandarin	Water Rail	Adonis Blue
Brent Goose	Mediterranean Gull	Fallow Deer	Brown Argus
Cetti's Warbler	Oystercatcher	Roe Deer	Chalkhill Blue
Common Tern	Pintail	Box	Essex Skipper
Curlew	Reed Bunting	Clove-scented Broomrape	Heath Fritillary
Firecrest	Ring-necked Parakeet	*Cyclamen hederifolium*	Purple Emperor
Goldeneye	Ringed Plover	Early Spider Orchid	Purple Hairstreak
Grey Heron	Ruddy Duck	Ground Pine	Silver-studded Blue
Kestrel	Sandwich Tern	Italian Catchfly	White Admiral
Kingfisher	Savi's Warbler		

In the summer, the loud croaks of Marsh Frog can often be heard, colonists from nearby Romney Marsh. Grass Snake and Common Lizard are also found here.

66 KINGLEY VALE	
Location:	c. 8km north-west of Chichester
Grid Reference:	SU 8209; L197
Visiting:	By road from village of West Stoke
Terrain:	Yew forest, chalk down
Specialities:	Almost unique Yew community

Kingley Vale is a mysterious, dark forest of Yew occupying a hill-top site on the southern flanks of the South Downs. It is certainly the finest Yew wood in Britain, and one of the best in Europe.

The best time for a visit is in spring or summer, particularly on a warm day when the dry, open downs and the cool, shady wood provide the starkest contrasts. This is also the best time to see butterflies.

Intermediate betwen the chalk grassland and closed forest are areas of scrub, with Hawthorn, Blackthorn, Juniper, Spindle, Wayfaring Tree, Traveller's Joy and White Bryony.

The chalk grassland here is rich, with species such as Horseshoe and Kidney Vetch, Bird's-foot Trefoil, Common Rock-rose, Harebell, Clustered Bellfower and Round-headed Rampion. Amongst the orchids to watch for are Fly, Bee, Frog, Fragrant and Pyramidal Orchids and Autumn Lady's Tresses.

In addition to commoner species, the butterflies include Chalkhill Blue, Adonis Blue, Silver-washed Fritillary and the magnificent Purple Emperor.

Other important sites nearby: Levin Down (SU 8913) has fine Juniper scrub, and chalk downland with butterflies and flowers.

67 SEVEN SISTERS COUNTRY PARK

Location:	c. 3km east of Seaford, East Sussex
Grid Reference:	TV 5299; L199
Visiting:	Spring, summer. Car park and footpaths
Terrain:	Spectacular chalk cliffs, downland, shingle, marsh, ponds
Specialities:	Coastal plants and birds

This Country Park lies at the mouth of the Cuckmere River, just to the west of Beachy Head.

The shingle bank at the mouth of the river provides a habitat for Yellow Horned-poppy, Sea Beet and Sea Kale. By contrast, the rolling chalk grassland behind the Seven Sisters cliffs is very rich in flowers, among which are several species of orchid, including Early-purple, Pyramidal, Common Spotted, and Burnt, and the pretty blue Autumn Gentian. Other special flowers of nearby sites are Moon Carrot, and the rare Small Hare's Ear.

The cliffs provide breeding sites for Fulmar, Herring Gull and Jackdaw, and Ringed Plover and Common Tern nest on the shingle and nearby lagoons.

On the western side of the river there are patches of scrub which hold many migrant birds in spring and autumn. Ring Ousel, Pied Flycatcher and Redstart are regular

Opposite: The magnificent brilliant-white chalk cliffs of Beachy Head offer a landmark to seafarers, and probably to migrant birds too, since this is one of the finest sites for rarities in spring and autumn, especially after strong winds. Redstart, Pied Flycatcher and Ring Ousel are regular visitors, with occasional rarer species such as Serin.

migrants. Rarer species which might be seen include Bluethroat, Hoopoe and Wryneck.

Other important sites nearby. The first three are excellent chalk downland:

Castle Hill (TQ 3807) for butterflies and orchids (permit needed from English Nature).

Cissbury Ring (TQ 1409).

Ditchling Beacon (TQ 3313) for glow-worms and Marbled White.

Beachy Head (TV 5796): butterflies include Marbled White, Chalkhill Blue and Grizzled Skipper.

Also: Lullington Heath National Nature Reserve (TQ 5502) chalk heath.

68 PAGHAM HARBOUR

Location:	c. 7km south of Chichester
Grid Reference:	SZ 8697; L197
Visiting:	Car parks and footpaths; information centre
Terrain:	Mudflats, shingle, scrub
Specialities:	Sea and shore birds

This Local Nature Reserve is one of the best places on the south coast to see waders and wildfowl, particularly during the winter.

There is a thriving colony of Little Tern breeding on the shingle, along with Oystercatcher and Ringed Plover. Shelduck also breed in the vicinity. It is worth keeping an eye open for owls, as both Little and Barn Owl breed in this area.

The harbour attracts hundreds of Brent Geese in winter, and the ducks include Pintail, Goldeneye and the occasional Smew. Along with the commoner species, the waders to watch out for during the migrations are Curlew, Green and Wood Sandpiper, Little Stint, and Black-tailed Godwit.

The seas nearby usually have Red-throated Diver, Eider, Red-breasted Merganser and

Brent Geese (Branta bernicla) are a speciality of Pagham Harbour and nearby saltmarshes. In winter they arrive in such large numbers that they have become a problem to local farmers when they feed on local fields of winter corn.

Common Scoter in winter, and generally Slavonian Grebe.

The saltmarsh has plants such as Cord Grass, Glasswort and Sea Purslane, and the shingle to the seaward side of Church Norton is the habitat of Sea Kale, Yellow Horned-poppy and Sea Campion. It is also the only remaining site in England for Childling Pink.

69 ARUNDEL WILDFOWL RESERVE	
Location:	c. 12km west of Worthing, West Sussex
Grid Reference:	TQ 0208; L197
Visiting:	Open all year; fee to non-members
Terrain:	Pools, river, reedbeds
Specialities:	Wildfowl

This reserve occupies part of the flood-plain of the River Arun and it is fed by clear spring water, rising from the chalk hills nearby. The water has been artificially channelled to create a variety of pools and wetland habitats for a large collection of captive waterfowl, but also for wild birds.

There is an excellent information building with educational displays and comfortable viewing facilities, together with easily accessible walkways through the reserve, providing good views of tame and wild birds, predominantly waterfowl. This reserve is a splendid place to visit to learn about British (and other) ducks and geese and to see them at close quarters. Amongst wild species visiting Arundel are Bewick's Swan, Pochard, Tufted Duck and Teal.

Birds of the reedbeds include Water Rail, Reed Bunting (winter), Reed and Sedge Warblers, and, in winter, the occasional Bittern, Cetti's Warbler and Bearded Tit.

Other breeding birds of the reserve include all three woodpeckers, Nuthatch, Marsh Tit, Sparrowhawk, Tawny and Barn Owls, Cuckoo, Kingfisher, Grey Heron, Mute Swan, Ruddy Duck and Mandarin.

The Scrape Hide gives good views of waders such as Redshank, Snipe, Greenshank and Common and Green Sandpiper. Teal can often be seen from here as well.

The edges of the reedbeds are bright with flowers such as Hemp Agrimony, Great Willowherb, Purple Loosestrife and Meadowsweet.

70 STODMARSH	
Location:	c. 7km north-east of Canterbury
Grid Reference:	TR 2261; L179
Visiting:	Car park
Terrain:	Open water, ditches, grazed meadows, reedbeds
Specialities:	Wetland birds and flowers

Stodmarsh National Nature Reserve is a large tract of reedbeds and lagoons, which is particularly good for warblers, including the rare Savi's Warbler. The whole wetland area, one of the best in southern England, has been formed by the subsidence of old mine workings.

Stodmarsh is a splendid wetland National Nature Reserve and is arguably one of the best examples of this habitat in southern England. Access is easy along a flood barrier called the Lampen Wall, which gives good views over the nearby water and reedbeds.

In spring, the reserve is loud with bird song. Small numbers of Bearded Tit are usually present in the reeds – listen for their 'pinging' calls. Along with Reed and Sedge Warbler, Stodmarsh also boasts the much rarer Savi's and Cetti's Warblers. Savi's may be heard in the reedbeds, but Cetti's, which overwinters, favours the scrub and carr. Grasshopper Warblers breed in the drier sites, so this reserve potentially provides the opportunity to compare the similar songs of

Grasshopper and Savi's Warbler. Nightingales can also be heard here.

The meadows are home to Yellow Wagtails, Lapwing, Snipe, Redshank, Shoveler, Teal and the occasional Garganey. Marsh Harriers are regular visitors and may breed.

In winter, the reserve occasionally has a Great Grey Shrike in residence, but Hen Harrier, Merlin and Golden Plover are more regular.

The water plants include Bogbean, Greater Spearwort, Water Forget-me-not, Flowering Rush, Marsh Cinquefoil, Marsh Stitchwort and Frogbit.

Cetti's Warbler *Cettia cetti* L 14
This rather rare, skulking warbler lives in fen carr and at the edges of reedbeds in southern England and Wales. Often it is only detected by its sudden loud burst of song – *chetti-chetti-chetti*. A recent colonist from the warmer climes of Mediterranean Europe, Cetti's Warblers first bred in the early 1970s and have gradually spread, with occasional setbacks in hard winters (a problem also afflicting populations of another resident warbler, the Dartford Warbler).

71 QUEENDOWN WARREN	
Location:	c. 6km SE of Gillingham, Kent
Grid Reference:	TQ 8363; L178
Visiting:	Open access. Car park
Terrain:	Chalk grassland, woodland, scrub
Specialities:	Woodland and chalk flowers, especially orchids

This small reserve is centred on an ancient area of chalk grassland which used to be a managed rabbit warren as long ago as the reign of Henry III! Centuries of grazing have kept the grassland community intact and has resulted in a rich community with a good chalkland flora. The main area of interest is a large sloping meadow which affords good drainage. This is surrounding by a mixed woodland.

In addition to typical chalk grassland species such as Thyme, Common Milkwort, Marjoram, Common Rock-rose and Bird's-foot Trefoil, there are Horseshoe Vetch and several orchids, including Bee, Fly, Burnt, Green-winged, Man, Fragrant and Early Spider. Butterflies are also well represented with blues and skippers in particular.

There are also interesting areas of scrub composed of plants such as Hawthorn, Elder, Ash, Dogwood and Hazel, with plenty of Traveller's Joy clambering amongst them. This gives cover for birds such as Blackcap, Whitethroat and tits.

Mature woodland is also represented here, in the form of Beech stands, mixed in places with oaks, Hornbeam, birch, Wild Cherry and Sweet Chestnut. Flowers of woodland and scrub include Bluebell, Yellow Archangel, Honeysuckle, and both White and Broad-leaved Helleborines.

72 ELMLEY MARSHES

Location:	c. 8km North of Sittingbourne, Kent
Grid Reference:	TQ 9370; L178
Visiting:	All year, closed Tuesdays. Charge for non-members. Car park
Terrain:	Saltmarsh, mudflats, grazed marsh, lagoons
Specialities:	Wildfowl and waders; wetland flowers

Elmley is a network of regularly grazed marsh and wide 'fleets' of freshwater. There are also interesting areas of saltmarsh bordering the Swale, which is tidal.

The reserve has breeding Lapwing, Redshank, Oystercatcher, Ringed Plover, Avocet, Common and Little Terns, Mallard, Shoveler, Gadwall, Pochard, Tufted Duck, Shelduck and Yellow Wagtail.

Autumn brings migrant waders such as Curlew, Black-tailed Godwit, Greenshank, Golden Plover, Spotted Redshank, Ruff, Snipe, Green, Wood and Curlew Sandpipers, as well as Hen Harrier and Short-eared Owl. The birds can be watched quite easily from a series of hides overlooking flooded ground (three on the marshes and lagoons, and two on the Swale).

The reserve also attracts considerable numbers of wildfowl and waders in winter, with flocks of Brent and White-fronted Geese, Pintail, Red-breasted Merganser, Grey Plover, Turnstone, Knot and Dunlin.

Flowers to look for on the saltmarsh are Sea Lavender, Sea Aster, Thrift, Sea Purslane, Glasswort and Golden Samphire.

There are Common and Marsh Frog, Grass Snake and Slow-worm on the reserve.

73 THURSLEY COMMON

Location:	8km south-west of Godalming, Surrey
Grid Reference:	SU 9040; L186
Visiting:	From Thursley village; car park at Moat
Terrain:	Heath, bog, woodland
Specialities:	Heathland birds; insects

Thursley Common National Nature Reserve is a fine example of lowland heath, now a highly threatened habitat. As well as pure dry heath, the reserve has many gradations to

Intricate channels, edged by Glasswort, drain the saltmarsh at the wetland reserve of Elmley.

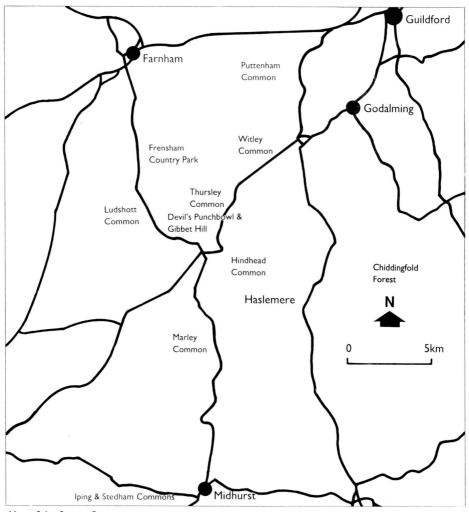

Map of the Surrey Commons.

wetter communities as well, including wet heath and bog. There is also a considerable amount of woodland, mostly birch and pine.

The dry heath is dominated by Heather, Gorse, Dwarf Gorse and Bell Heather, and the wet heath has Purple Moor-grass and Cross-leaved Heath. The boggy sites have many interesting plants, including both Round-leaved Sundew and the rarer Oblong-leaved Sundew, Common Cotton-grass, Bog Asphodel and Bladderwort.

The heath is a prime bird site with the star attraction provided by the Hobby, a species which breeds here and which can often be spotted circling and feeding on dragonflies or small birds. Sparrowhawk also breed in the

The Downy Emerald (Cordulia aenea) is a local dragonfly, mainly found in southern England.

Headley Heath (TQ 2054) for heath, wood, chalk grassland.

Box Hill Country Park (TQ 1851) chalk grassland, mixed woodland. Butterflies include Purple and Green Hairstreaks, Large, Essex, Dingy and Grizzled Skippers, Marbled White and Chalkhill Blue.

74 ASHDOWN FOREST	
Location:	c. 8km south of East Grinstead
Grid Reference:	TQ 4332; L187
Visiting:	Many car parks
Terrain:	Heath, woodland, bog
Specialities:	Heathland birds, flowers and insects

reserve. Other heathland birds here are Wood Lark, Tree Pipit, and Dartford Warbler (a small population). All three woodpeckers may be seen, as may Nightingale, Redstart and Stonechat. In winter, a Great Grey Shrike often take's up residence on the heath.

The entomologist is also extremely well catered for at Thursley. The heath is especially noted for its rich dragonfly fauna, with twenty-six species recorded, including the Small Red Damselfly, and the rare Brilliant Emerald and White-faced Darter dragonflies. The butterflies include Grayling and Silver-studded Blue (a declining species nationally).

Adders are common on the heath, so stout shoes are recommended.

Other important sites nearby: Frensham Country Park (SU 8541) also has Hobby and Dartford Warbler.

Witley Common (SU 9441) for heathland.

The remnants of an earlier hunting forest, Ashdown Forest preserves an intricate mixture of related habitats, including woodland, heath and bog. The whole area is provided with stopping places and footpaths.

The woodland is very varied, with Scots Pine, birch and oak, and areas where Beech is dominant. Wetter sites support Alder groves, with Alder Buckthorn in the shrub layer.

As at Thursley, there is both dry and wet heath here, the latter grading into true bog. Heather, Bell Heather, Gorse and Dwarf Gorse are found in the dry heath, with Cross-leaved Heath in damper places. The bogs, with their bogmosses (*Sphagnum*) also have Common Cottongrass, Bog Asphodel and sundews.

The mammals here are quite numerous and there are good populations of Fallow Deer, Badger, Fox, Stoat, Weasel and Wood Mice.

The birds include Nightingale, Tree Pipit, Stonechat, Nightjar, Kestrel, Sparrowhawk and Hobby.

The antlers of the Fallow Deer (Dama Dama) are distinctly flattened towards the tip. This species has a wide distribution in Britain and Ireland, particularly in lowland parkland.

Ashdown Forest is also a good site to see insects. It has many dragonflies, and the butterflies include such interesting species as Grayling, Silver-studded Blue, and Dark Green, Pearl-bordered, Small Pearl-bordered and Silver-washed Fritillaries. Watch out for the impressive Emperor Moth on the heath in April.

75 CHIDDINGFOLD FOREST	
Location:	Near Chiddingfold, Surrey
Grid Reference:	SU 9835; L186
Visiting:	Best in spring or summer
Terrain:	Mixed woodland, with conifer plantations
Specialities:	Butterflies, such as Purple Emperor and White Admiral

This area consists of a group of woods, pastures and small farms set in a rather well wooded part of the Surrey countryside close to the border with West Sussex. These woods are some of the best butterfly sites in the whole of Britain and Ireland and with patience, good weather, and visits at the right time of year, dozens of species can be seen here, including several which are relatively rare elsewhere. In fact these woods are also rich in woodland birds and flowers, and they therefore score very high for their general natural history.

Amongst the more interesting species of butterfly to be found here is the Wood White, rather scarce in this region generally, and on the wing in late May and June. Silver-washed Fritillaries are attracted to Bramble blossom along the woodland rides and these woods are also home to White Admiral and to the rare and magical Purple Emperor. In addition to commoner woodland and hedgerow species such as Brimstone, Peacock, Orange Tip and Comma, the woods also have Small, Large, Grizzled and Dingy Skippers and both Pearl-bordered and Small Pearl-bordered Fritillaries. It is also possible to see four out of the five species of Hairstreak here: Green, Purple, White-letter and Brown.

The woods also have a good flora, with species such as Primrose, violets, Woodruff, Marsh Thistle, and Common Spotted and Greater Butterfly Orchids.

The birds also deserve a mention. The thick undergrowth suits woodland warblers, such as Blackcap, Garden Warbler, Whitethroat and Lesser Whitethroat, Willow Warbler and Chiffchaff, and Nightingale. Sparrowhawks also breed here, and the plantations have Firecrest as well as the commoner Goldcrest.

Roe Deer are frequent, and the woods have many Adders as well as Grass Snakes.

76 STAINES RESERVOIRS	
Location:	Immediately south-west of Heathrow Airport
Grid Reference:	TQ 0673; L176
Visiting:	From A3044. Access limited to causeway
Terrain:	Open water
Specialities:	Wintering waterbirds

The best known and one of the most accessible of London's reservoirs, Staines is something of a favourite with birdwatchers, particularly in autumn and winter.

In the winter, ducks and other birds such as grebes, gulls and terns gather to feed and roost on the reservoir and can be watched relatively easily from the central causeway. A telescope is recommended for getting good views, as the birds may be some distance away.

When the water level is low, or when a reservoir is drained, large expanses of mud are exposed. At these times, many waders can be found, with occasional rarities.

The commonest ducks are Tufted Ducks and Pochard, but other species, including Goldeneye, Goosander and sometimes Smew do show up here. This is one of the best places to see Black-necked Grebe, especially in the autumn.

The migrants include Common, Arctic and Black Terns, and Little Gulls.

9. SOUTHERN ENGLAND

The most impressive features of this region are the chalk downland of Wiltshire and the New Forest heathland region of Hampshire, with very contrasting flora and fauna.

The inroads of modern agriculture have much reduced the flower-rich, original chalk turf of the Downs, but there are still some areas, mostly now protected in nature reserves, where the characteristic chalk plants, such as Horseshoe Vetch, can still be found in plenty, together with some more local specialities. Among chalk plants with their headquarters on southern chalk grassland, one of the most distinguished is the Round-headed Rampion, a remarkable relative of the bellfowers, with a tight head of blue flowers.

The downs are also rich in butterflies, with several species of skippers and blues a particular feature. Reserves such as Compton Down and Martin Down still have healthy populations of butterflies which were once much more widespread.

The New Forest is a wonderful mosaic of forest and heath with a very rich wildlife, including unusual birds such as Hobby, Nightjar and Honey Buzzard. Some of the heaths here and further south also have Dartford Warbler and the rare reptiles, Smooth Snake and Sand Lizard.

In the New Forest, the special plants tend to be restricted to two very characteristic habitats: the valley bogs, and the shallow pools with grazed margins. Some of the bogs still have marvellous shows in summer of the Marsh Gentian, with its large blue, trumpet-shaped flowers. Another speciality is the Bog Orchid, now extinct over most of England, although still not uncommon in western Scotland.

The winter-wet hollows and margins of pools on the acid, sandy soils have a very special flora, including Slender Marsh Bedstraw and the unique Hampshire Purslane.

A brightly coloured male Sand Lizard (Lacerta agilis) suns itself on a log. This attractive lizard is a speciality of southern heathlands.

77 NEW FOREST

Location:	Between Bournemouth and Southampton
Grid Reference:	L184/195/196
Visiting:	May–June best. Access easy
Terrain:	Heath, woodland, wetland
Specialities:	Heathland birds, flowers and insects

The New Forest is a huge area with many interconnected or separated tracts of heathland and forest, and occasional ponds, streams and bogs. It is the most important stretch of old lowland woodland in southern England and, because it has a mild climate, it is also home to many southern rarities. The more accessible parks and picnic areas throng with visitors in the summer, but it is always possible to escape the crowds by walking and seeking out more remote areas.

The mature woods are dominated by oaks, Beech, birches, with occasional Ash, Sweet Chestnut and Scots Pine. Holly is often conspicuous in the understorey, as are Bramble and Bracken. The Heather-

Typical lowland heathland near Beaulieu Road Station with Heather and stands of pine.

FIFTY INTERESTING SPECIES TO LOOK FOR

Barn Owl	Stonechat	Galingale	Dingy Skipper
Black Tern	Tree Pipit	Hampshire Purslane	Duke of Burgundy
Cirl Bunting	Wood Lark	Heath Lobelia	Glanville Fritillary
Dartford Warbler	Wryneck	Horseshoe Vetch	Grizzled Skipper
Firecrest	Common Dormouse	Marsh Gentian	Marbled White
Garganey	Fallow Deer	Round-headed	Purple Emperor
Hawfinch	Harvest Mouse	Rampion	Purple Hairstreak
Hobby	Lesser White-toothed	Small Fleabane	Silver-spotted Skipper
Honey Buzzard	Shrew	Wild Gladiolus	Silver-studded Blue
Little Gull	Red Squirrel	Wood Calamint	Small Blue
Nightingale	White-toothed Shrew	Adonis Blue	White Admiral
Nightjar	Yellow-necked Mouse	Brown Argus	
Short-toed	Bog Orchid	Chalkhill Blue	
Treecreeper	Field Eryngo	Clouded Yellow	

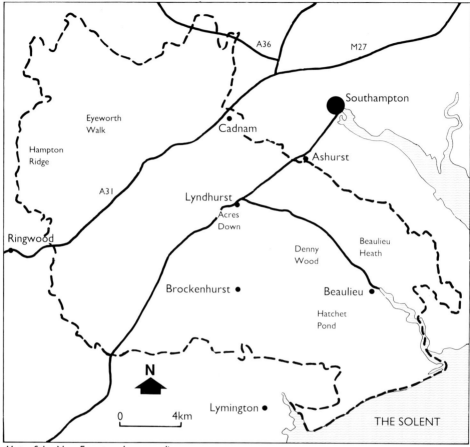

Map of the New Forest and surrounding areas.

dominated heaths form a mosaic with patches of grassland – Bristle Bent on dry soil, and Purple Moor-grass on wetter sites, and with Bracken.

There are acid bogs, but also mires in which the water is more mineral-rich, fed by streams. This gives a wide range of conditions and makes for a rich flora. All three sundews grow here, as do Bog Myrtle, the tiny rare Bog Orchid and local specialities such as the Hampshire Purslane and the handsome Wild Gladiolus.

The birds of the New Forest are also special. Curlew, Snipe and Redshank breed here, as do Stonechat, Tree Pipit, Wood Lark, Crossbill, Redstart, Wood Warbler, Hawfinch, Dartford Warbler and Nightjar. The birds of prey are particularly noteworthy, with Buzzard, Kestrel and Sparrowhawk frequent. The Hobby has increased markedly and is regularly seen, whilst the patient or lucky birdwatcher might spot a Goshawk or the summer-visiting Honey Buzzard soaring over the forest.

The invertebrate fauna is extremely rich, and shows connections with that of continental Europe. This is the sole locality for Britain's only cicada, and there are many dragonfly and beetle species.

Particularly good sites within the New Forest: Hatchet Pond (SU 3602) for the rare Hampshire Purslane.

Acres Down (SU 2808) for birds of prey, including Honey Buzzard, Hobby and Goshawk.

Bishop's Dyke/Denny Wood (SU 3405) for Hobby, Wood Lark and Honey Buzzard.

Hampton Ridge (SU 1714) for good heath with Dartford Warbler.

Beaulieu Heath (SU 4005).

Eyeworth Walk (SU 2414).

Nightjar *Caprimulgus europaeus* L 28
This ghostly nocturnal bird mainly inhabits lowland heathland, especially in southern England and East Anglia. It is often difficult to spot, but its strange mechanical churring song carries a long distance. Nightjars are best observed just after sunset on summer evenings, when they emerge to feed on moths and other night-flying insects. The Breckland and New Forest heaths are still good sites for Nightjars.

78 COMPTON DOWN	
Location:	c. 6km SE of Totland (Isle of Wight)
Grid Reference:	SZ 3785; L196
Visiting:	Car park
Terrain:	Chalk down, scrub
Specialities:	Chalk flowers and butterflies

This splendid stretch of chalk downland faces mainly towards the south-west over the Channel. This aspect makes for high temperatures in the spring and summer, giving ideal conditions for the development of butterflies. The sward is also rich in chalk-loving flowers, amongst them many brightly coloured species, including orchids.

In spring, the down has flowering Early Gentian, Cowslip, Early Purple and Green-winged Orchids. These are followed later in the season by eyebrights, Harebell, Wild Thyme, Horseshoe and Kidney Vetches, Clustered Bellflower and Bee Orchid.

The butterflies of the down include Common, Chalkhill, Adonis and Small Blue's, Marbled White and Dark Green Fritillary. However, undoubtedly the star turn is provided by the rare Glanville Fritillary, now restricted to the southern shores of the Isle of Wight and to the Channel Islands. Glanvilles sometimes feed on the down, but are more likely to be seen on the undercliffs at nearby Compton Bay, where they breed. Compton Down also attracts migrant butterflies, which stop by to use its flowers as a re-fuelling station. Regular migrants here include Clouded and Berger's Clouded Yellows.

Other important sites nearby: St Catherine's Point (SZ 4977) for Great Green Bush Cricket and Glanville Fritillary

The Needles/Tennyson Down (SZ 3084). Chalk down with splendid views.

79 PENNINGTON/KEYHAVEN MARSHES	
Location:	c. 5km south-west of Lymington
Grid Reference:	SZ 3293; L196
Visiting:	All year; keep to rights of way
Terrain:	Coastal marsh, shingle
Specialities:	Coastal plants, seabirds and waders

80 PEWSEY DOWNS	
Location:	10km south-west of Marlborough
Grid Reference:	SU 1264; L173
Visiting:	All year. Best in summer. Access on bridlepaths
Terrain:	Chalk downland
Specialities:	Flowers, butterflies

The edge of the saltmarsh here has plants such as Glasswort, Sea Aster, Sea Plantain and Annual Sea-blite, and the adjacent grassy swards, particularly around Hurst Castle, support Common Sea Lavender, Thrift, Sea Campion, Golden Samphire, Sea Kale and Yellow Horned-poppy.

However, the reserve is probably better known for its bird life. The winter concentrations of wildfowl can be spectacular, with hundreds of Brent Geese flighting in to feed on the Eelgrass, along with Shelduck, Teal, Mallard, Wigeon, Goldeneye and Long-tailed Duck. Waders also gather here, as do Red-breasted Merganser, Goosander and the occasional Slavonian Grebe. In the spring it is possible to see Little Gull and Black Tern, as well as divers and skuas over the sea.

Other important sites nearby: Langstone Harbour (SU 6804) also has excellent wild-fowl and waders. It is perhaps the key estuary for wintering birds along the southern coast. The islands in the harbour (part of an RSPB reserve) hold important colonies of Little and Common Tern. In winter, over 7,000 Brent Geese gather here, along with Wigeon, Teal and Shelduck, and thousands of waders.

Chalk downland is often restricted, as here, to steeper hillsides, or specific reserves.

The main grassland type is a mixture of Red and Sheep's Fescues, with Upright Brome. Other plants found here include Glaucous Sedge, Salad Burnet, Dwarf Thistle, Bastard Toadflax, Field Fleawort, Chalk Milkwort,

Horseshoe Vetch, Clustered Bellflower and Wild Thyme.

Like many other downland sites, Pewsey is rich in orchids. Look out for Burnt, Common Spotted, Bee, Frog, Fragrant, Green-winged and Pyramidal Orchids. Other flowers of particular interest are Round-headed Rampion, Betony, Devil's Bit Scabious and Tuberous Thistle.

Butterflies abound, especially the blues, with Common, Chalkhill, Small Blue and Brown Argus. The presence of its food plant, Devil's Bit Scabious, allows the Marsh Fritillary to survive here as well.

The reserve lies on the ancient Ridgeway track, popular with distance walkers, and close to the Wansdyke. There is also a famous landmark, a white horse, carved into the chalky flank of Milk Hill.

Other important sites nearby: North Meadow (SU 0994) is a fine ancient meadow with the largest population of Snake's-head Fritillary in the country.

81 MARTIN DOWN	
Location:	c. 12km south-west of Salisbury
Grid Reference:	SU 0519; L184
Visiting:	Open access
Terrain:	Chalk grassland, heath and scrub
Specialities:	Chalk flowers and butterflies

Martin Down is a large reserve with carefully managed chalk grassland, some areas cropped short, and others with a taller growth. There are also patches of chalk heath and scrub, which add to the overall diversity and interest.

The scrub is composed mainly of Ash, Buckthorn, Dogwood, Hawthorn, Privet,

Spindle and Wayfaring Tree, and Heather and Gorse dominate on the chalk heath.

Martin Down is a good reserve to visit to obtain an introduction to common, and not so common, flowers of the chalk. Here one can see species such as Horseshoe Vetch, Chalk Milkwort, Bastard Toadflax and Field Fleawort, along with a fine array of orchids. The following orchids can all be found here: Burnt, Bee, Fly, Frog, Pyramidal, Fragrant, Greater Butterfly, Southern Marsh, Common Spotted, and Man.

The other main attraction must be the butterflies, an amazing forty-three species having been recorded here! Chalkhill, Common and Small Blues are all common, as is the Brown Argus. Adonis Blue, Duke of Burgundy and Silver-spotted Skipper are also found on the reserve. Dark Green Fritillary is common in the taller grassland, and Silver-washed Fritillary can be seen in the wooded areas, along with White Admiral. It is also possible to see the rather local Marsh Fritillary here, even though there is no marsh. This reserve also boasts a large population of Glow-worms.

Birds include Barn Owl, Nightingale, Nightjar, and the mammals include Harvest Mouse and Common Dormouse.

82 PAMBER FOREST	
Location:	c. 10km North of Basingstoke
Grid Reference:	SU 6262; L175
Visiting:	Approach via Tadley; footpaths
Terrain:	Broadleaved woodland
Specialities:	Woodland flowers' butterflies

One of the best preserved mature woods in North Hampshire, with well-grown oaks.

Purple Emperor *Apatura iris* W 62–74
This is a rather rare and elusive species, with secretive habits. Its strongholds are the mature oak woods of Hampshire and Sussex, where they glide and dash over the canopy, usually attracted by a particular tall tree. They sometimes come down to the ground to drink from puddles, especially early in the mornings in hot, dry weather, but are otherwise hard to observe at close quarters.

Part of the wood has been coppiced and this encourages the growth of spring flowers, including Wood Anemone, Wood Sorrel, Early Purple Orchid and Common Twayblade.

The wood contains many mammals, including Roe Deer, Fox, Dormouse and Yellow-necked Mouse.

One beautiful insect found here is the splendid Purple Emperor butterfly, a large, powerful flier which is, however, difficult to spot because it tends to keep to the tree canopy. The Purple Emperor is something of a Hampshire speciality and is still found in many woods in the county. The White Admiral and Silver-washed Fritillary are also found here.

*Wild Daffodils (*Narcissus pseudonarcissus*) in Pamber Forest. The true Wild Daffodil is a scattered flower of damp southern and western woods in England and Wales.*

Other important sites nearby: Silchester Common which is adjacent to Pamber Forest has heath and bog habitats.

83 THATCHAM REEDBEDS	
Location:	c. 3km East of Newbury
Grid Reference:	SU 5067; L174
Visiting:	Some parking at Thatcham station; footpaths
Terrain:	Reedbeds, lake, carr
Specialities:	Waterbirds, plants, insects

This reserve protects part of one of the largest areas of reedbed in southern England. The uniqueness of the habitat is reflected in the diversity of insects and plants found here.

Amongst the wetland flowers are Yellow Flag, Great Willowherb, Wild Angelica, Tufted Vetch, Butterbur, Yellow Loosestrife, Hemp Agrimony, Comfrey and Common Meadow-rue.

The insects of the reserve have been well studied, and several rare moths live here, amongst them the Scarlet Tiger, Scarce Burnished Brass and Dentated Pug. There are also several species of dragonfly and damselfly, including Banded Demoiselle, Broad-tailed Chaser and Common Blue Damselfly.

Thatcham Reedbeds are a welcome refuge for migrant birds in both spring and autumn, and the species breeding here include Reed, Sedge and Grasshopper Warblers, Nightingale, Tufted Duck, Great Crested and Little Grebes, and Water Rail.

Other important sites nearby: The Kennet and Avon Canal runs close by. It has interesting wetland flowers and dragonflies.

Edible Dormouse *Glis glis*
L 130–190mm (head and body)
This charming rodent is only found in a small area of Chiltern woods, having spread only a short distance from the site of its introduction in 1902 at Tring in Hertfordshire. It looks rather like a small Grey Squirrel but is rarely seen by day, being strictly nocturnal. Its preferred habitats are woods and suburban gardens and it occasionally visits sheds and houses, sometimes scuttling about in lofts. Edible Dormice hibernate, often in small groups, from September to April.

84 WINDSOR GREAT PARK	
Location:	Immediately south of Windsor, Berkshire
Grid Reference:	SU 9674; L176
Visiting:	Best spring and early summer. Car parks and walks
Terrain:	Open parkland, lake, oak/Beech woods
Specialities:	Birds, mammals, insects

This park occupies what used to be an ancient hunting forest, and many of the oaks here are several centuries old. In many ways it resembles the New Forest in Hampshire. Like the New Forest, it has partly an open, park-like structure, with old trees set in grassy meadows, as well as areas of closed woodland

and scrub. Lakes add to the overall diversity of habitat, providing food and cover for a wide range of wildlife. In the south there is an area of lowland heath with a rather different set of animals and plants.

The birdlife here is typical of lowland woodland and parkland, with species such as Sparrowhawk, Little Owl, all three woodpeckers, Nuthatch, Treecreeper, warblers, tits, Spotted Flycatcher, Redpoll and Redstart. The heathy areas have Nightjar, Wood Lark, Stonechat and Hobby.

The insect life of the park is very rich indeed, with over 2,000 different species of beetle alone. The butterflies include White Admiral, Painted Lady, five species of skipper, Holly Blue and that heathland speciality the Silver-studded Blue, a species which has declined recently and which is now mainly found in parts of Dorset and New Forest. The damselflies include the rare Scarce Blue-tailed Damselfly, Southern Damselfly and Small Red Damselfly.

Deer are common here, with Red, Fallow, Roe and Muntjac all present.

Other important sites: Virginia Water (SU 9769) is a pretty lake at the south end of Windsor Great Park. It has wild breeding Mandarin ducks, which can be seen throughout the year. Look for them particularly at the east end of the lake, and just north of the car park. This is also a good place to spot Hawfinches, a rather local and elusive species. Hawfinches like Hornbeams, of which there are many well-grown specimens here.

Les Quennervais, Les Mielles, Jersey. This reserve has a fine system of sand dunes with flowers, such as Sand Crocus and Dune Pansy, and the rare Green Lizard.

85 CHANNEL ISLANDS

Location:	West of Cherbourg Peninsula, France
Specialities:	
Flowers:	Jersey Buttercup, Purple Spurge, Hare's Tail Grass, Galingale, Jersey Toadflax, Loose-flowered Orchid, Purple Viper's Bulgoss, Blue Romulea, Great Sea Stock
Birds:	Dartford Warbler, Wryneck, Kentish Plover, Cirl Bunting, Gannet, Puffin, Garganey
Mammals:	White-toothed and Lesser White-toothed Shrews, Red Squirrel
Reptiles/ Amphibians:	Green Lizard, Wall Lizard, Agile Frog

The Channel Islands are, from the natural history viewpoint, essentially a piece of France. They lie just a few kilometres from the French coast, and share many species with the nearby mainland. The mild winters here allow many frost-sensitive species to thrive, and several animals and plants which are rare elsewhere in the British Isles may be seen here. In addition, there are also specialities found on the Channel Islands which do not appear on mainland Britain.

SELECTED SITES OF THE CHANNEL ISLANDS

Jersey: Les Mieilles, near St Brelade in the south-west, contains a number of interesting sites. St Ouen's Pond is a wetland nature reserve with breeding Garganey and Cetti's Warbler. Nearby dunes have the Jersey Orchid. Les Quennevais is an area of sand dunes with flowers such as Dwarf Pansy, Sand Crocus and Jersey Thrift. There are also Green Lizards here, a species which is not found elsewere in the British Isles.

At the other end of the island, Noir Mont Headland gives good seawatching opportunities. The scrub here has Dartford Warbler. Flowers to look out for include Jersey Forget-me-not, Spotted Rock-rose and Autumn Squill.

Guernsey: Pleinmont Point at the south-western tip is worth a visit. The scrub here has breeding Dartford Warbler.

Herm is a charming island easily reached by boat from St Peter Port. Fine views of seabirds can be had on the journey, particularly Puffin. Visit the beautiful shell beach (with tiny cowries) and look out for Sand Crocus in the dunes.

Alderney: This is the most northerly island and has good seabird cliffs and breeding Wryneck, a rare bird on mainland Britain. The offshore stacks of Les Etacq and Ortac have about 4,000 pairs of Gannet.

The small island of Burhou, off Alderney's north-west coast has colonies of Puffin, Guillemot, Razorbill, British Storm-petrel and Shag.

10. MIDLANDS AND WELSH BORDERS

This region stretches from Northampton-shire and Buckinghamshire across to Here-ford and Staffordshire. The region, which avoids the extremes of the British climate, has fewer specialities than most. However, the limestone of the Cotswolds has a rich flora, including the rare Downy Woundwort, probably now extinct elsewhere in England. Other Cotswold species are the beautiful blue Meadow Clary and the Green Hound's-tongue. Some of the best localities for the truly wild Monkshood are to be found in damp wooded valleys on the Welsh borders, and in similar places grows the Alternate-leaved Golden Saxifrage, a much rarer flower than the Opposite-leaved Golden Saxifrage. In places within Cotswold coun-try, the two local bitter-cresses, the Large and the Narrow-leaved, may be found together.

Finally, one special Midlands flower de-serves a mention. A visit to a pond reserve owned by the Gloucestershire Naturalists Trust can show you the very rare Adder's-tongue Spearwort, now extinct in its earlier Dorset locality.

The birds include a trio of woodland species which are much commoner in this region, and in Wales, than further east. These are the beautiful Redstart and Pied Fly-catcher, and the rather inconspicuous Wood Warbler. These three species are characteris-tic of oak-dominated mixed woodland and can be seen at sites such as the Forest of Dean and Wyre Forest.

Wetlands of this region include the splen-did wildfowl reserve of Slimbridge, on the River Severn, and the huge freshwater reser-voir of Rutland Water.

Opposite: *Waxwings (Bombycilla garrulus) are rare winter visitors that can turn up anywhere, but particularly in the north and east of the region.* **Above:** *this dainty damselfly, the Banded Demoiselle (Calopteryx splendens) is common in Wales and southern England.*

The Great Spotted Woodpecker (Dendrocopus major) is the commonest of Britain's three species of woodpecker.

86 FOREST OF DEAN	
Location:	Between Monmouth and upper Severn estuary
Grid Reference:	SO 6410; L162
Visiting:	Best spring and summer
Terrain:	Mixed woodland
Specialities:	Woodland birds, such as woodpeckers, insects and flowers

This is one of the ancient royal hunting forests, developed over centuries on hills between the valleys of the Wye and Severn. There are large areas which still support a semi-natural woodland, mainly of Sessile Oak and Beech, although some parts have been planted with conifers such as Larch and Spruce. Ash, Wych Elm, Lime, Sweet Chestnut, Rowan and Holly are also common trees here.

One reason why the Forest of Dean has so much to offer to the botanist is that its soils encompass a range of different types, from acid to limestone, with corresponding changes in the flora. There are also streams, pools and small areas of bog which can repay a visit.

FIFTY INTERESTING SPECIES TO LOOK FOR

Buzzard	Woodcock	Alternate-leaved	Narrow-leaved Bitter-
Dipper	Wood Warbler	Golden Saxifrage	cress
Goldcrest	Badger	Autumn Crocus	Stinking Hellebore
Goosander (winter)	Dormouse	Bird's-nest Orchid	White Helleborine
Grasshopper Warbler	Fallow Deer	Candytuft	Duke of Burgundy
Marsh Warbler	Fox	Chiltern Gentian	High Brown Fritillary
Nightjar	Muntjac	Downy Woundwort	Marsh Fritillary
Nuthatch	Otter	Green Hound's-tongue	Pearl-bordered
Pied Flycatcher	Polecat	Herb Paris	Fritillary
Raven	Sika Deer	Large Bitter-cress	Purple Hairstreak
Redstart	Stoat	Martagon Lily	Silver-washed Fritillary
Siskin	Weasel	Meadow Clary	Small Blue
Sparrowhawk	Adder's-tongue	Mezereon	
Treecreeper	Spearwort	Monkshood	

Flowers of the forest include Autumn Crocus, Herb Paris, Bird's-nest Orchid, Stinking Hellebore, White Helleborine, and the spectacular Martagon Lily with its large pink-purple nodding flowers.

Birds of this area include Buzzard, Sparrowhawk, Raven, Woodcock, Pied Flycatcher, Redstart, Wood Warbler, Goldcrest, Siskin, Hawfinch, Crossbill, Dipper, Kingfisher, all three woodpeckers, Nuthatch and Treecreeper.

Mammals such as Fallow Deer, Fox, Badger, Dormouse, Stoat, Weasel, Otter and Polecat can be seen.

Insects to watch out for are White Admiral, Silver-washed, Dark Green, High Brown, Pearl-bordered and Small Pearl-bordered Fritillary, Holly Blue, Brown Argus and Grayling.

Other important sites nearby: Nagshead (SO 6108), within the forest, is an RSPB reserve with woodland nature walks.

Symonds Yat Rock (SO 5616) gives outstanding views over the Wye valley. It is the best place to view breeding Peregrines.

87 SLIMBRIDGE WILDFOWL AND WETLANDS TRUST	
Location:	About 7km north-west of Dursley, Gloucestershire
Grid Reference:	SO 7405; L162
Visiting:	Best in winter. Entrance fee for non-members; car park
Terrain:	Open coastal pasture, marsh, pools
Specialities:	Winter wildfowl

Slimbridge is one of the major birdwatching sites in this region. It is best known for the large numbers of wildfowl which gather to feed on the marshes and pasture in the autumn and winter.

Hides offer sweeping views over the marshes, and the chance to see large flocks of White-fronted Geese, with smaller numbers of Pink-footed and Bean Geese. The White-fronts peak after Christmas, but have all gone by March. Occasionally, there is a visit by Lesser White-fronted or Red-breasted Goose as well.

In addition to the geese, hundreds of Bewick's Swans also winter here. They can be seen from very close range. Ducks are well represented too, with large numbers of Wigeon, along with Mallard, Teal, Pintail, Shoveler and Gadwall.

River Wye from Symonds Yat Rock, Gloucestershire. A lookout gives fine views over surrounding woodland, river and fields.

Bewick's Swans (Cygnus columbianus) can be seen at several southern wetland reserves, such as Slimbridge. They can be very vocal.

Like Arundel, and other reserves of the Wildfowl and Wetlands Trust, Slimbridge is a great place to learn about the world's wildfowl, or brush up on identification at close range. Slimbridge has the world's largest collection of tame geese and ducks.

It is always worth scanning the marshes and nearby prominent trees or other perches for wintering Peregrines, which are often around, feeding on waders. Other predators to look for are Merlin, Sparrowhawk and Short-eared Owl.

There are also muddy pools which may attract waders such as Greenshank, Ruff, Spotted Redshank on passage and Black-tailed Godwit.

Little Owls breed in the willows towards the marsh and a hunting Barn Owl is a fairly regular sight, particularly towards dusk.

88 RODBOROUGH COMMON	
Location:	Just south of Stroud
Grid Reference:	SO 8503; L162
Visiting:	Spring, summer
Terrain:	Limestone grassland
Specialities:	Flowers of limestone

Rodborough Common is one of the best places to appreciate the riches of limestone grassland. It occupies a plateau where the soil is generally fairly deep, but on the slopes at the edges, the soil is much shallower, giving interesting variety to the flora. On the thinner soils, and even on loose limestone screes, can be found such flowers as Carline Thistle, Herb Robert, Yellow-wort and Common Restharrow.In the coarser grassland there are species such as Yellow Rattle, Greater

*The Pyramidal Orchid (*Anacamptis pyramidalis) *is often found on chalk grassland and scrub in England, Wales and Ireland.*

89 BUCKHOLT WOOD

Location:	Just north of Cranham
Grid Reference:	SO 8913; L162/163
Visiting:	Best in spring and summer
Terrain:	Beech woodland
Specialities:	Woodland plants

Buckholt Wood is one of the best mature Beech woods in Britain. It is developed over Cotswold limestone and forms a belt of

Harvest Mouse *Micromys minutus*
L 60–75mm (head and body)
This tiny mouse, Britain's smallest rodent, lives in long grassland and hedgerows in the southern half of Britain, notably around the Welsh borders. Harvest Mice have reddish fur (particularly on the rump) and a long, thin prehensile tail. Although traditionally associated with wheatfields, they tend to prefer overgrown field margins as well as reedbeds and damp meadows with rushes. They build round nests of grass stems, woven around a vertical stalk, and these can occasionally be found, especially in the autumn.

Knapweed, Kidney Vetch and Common Spotted Orchid, whilst Harebell, Bird's Foot Trefoil, Eyebright, Cowslip, Common Milkwort, Wild Thyme, Autumn Gentian and Rock-rose prefer the shorter sward. On some of the slopes, particularly where soil creep has created terraces, there are Marjoram, Horseshoe Vetch and Clustered Bellflower. Bee, Early Purple, Green-winged, Fragrant and Pyramidal Orchids also grow on the reserve, as well as two rather local species, Pasqueflower and Wild Liquorice.

The butterflies found here include blues and Marbled White.

Other important sites nearby: Minchinhampton Common (SO8502) is another fine limestone grassland with orchids.

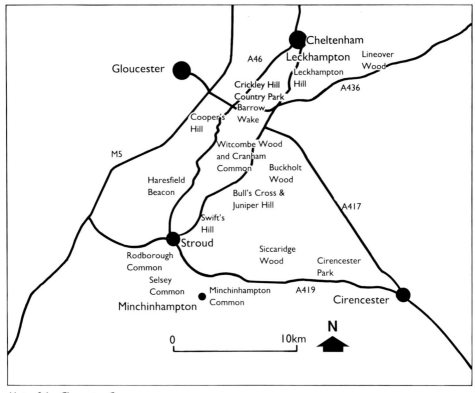

Map of the Gloucester Commons.

woodland with other nearby woods such as Witcombe Wood.

The tree-layer is dominated by tall, well-grown Beech trees, beneath which grow sapling Beech, along with Whitebeam, Wych Elm, Ash, oak, and in damper places, Alder and willows. Other shrubs of the undergrowth are Hawthorn, Hazel, Wayfaring Tree, Holly, Wild Cherry, Yew, Sycamore, Bramble and Wild Rose.

These woods which have been here, under various types of woodland management, for centuries still retain a rich flora, with many interesting woodland flowers. Dog's Mercury, Enchanter's Nightshade, Primrose, Sanicle, Woodruff and Wood Spurge are common, with occasional clumps of Green Hellebore on lime-rich soil.

Other notable plants found here are both Red and White Helleborines, Columbine, Lily-of-the-valley, Common Wintergreen, Bird's Nest Orchid, Greater Butterfly Orchid, Yellow Bird's-nest, and Narrow-lipped and Green-flowered Helleborines.

Other important sites nearby: Cranham Common, just to the south, has rich limestone grassland with many orchids and Moonwort. Witcombe Wood has a similar flora to Buckholt Wood, with Mezereon. Frith Wood (SO 8809) is another fine Beech wood. Painswick Hill (SO 8713) has rich chalk grassland with many orchids.

90 BURNHAM BEECHES	
Location:	About 4km north-west of Slough
Grid Reference:	SU 9485; L175/176
Visiting:	Best spring, summer, car park
Terrain:	Beech and mixed ancient woodland, scrub, grassland
Specialities:	Woodland flowers, such as Marsh St John's Wort, and birds, such as Redstart

91 ASTON ROWANT	
Location:	About 8km south of Thame
Grid Reference:	SP 7497; L 165
Visiting:	Best in summer
Terrain:	Chalk grassland, scrub, woodland
Specialities:	Flowers and butterflies

Burnham Beeches is a famous ancient woodland, established on acid soil. It occupies a low plateau which has a number of small valleys. The habitat is quite diverse for a woodland, with a mixture of ancient, mature woodland interspersed with coppice, scrub, and clearings with grassy vegetation.

The main dominant tree is Beech, but there are a good many other species too, including Pedunculate Oak, Holly, Hornbeam, birch, Rowan and Wild Cherry.

Much of the wood is on well-drained rather dry soil, but there are wetter areas which tend to have a richer ground flora. Species to look out for here include Marsh St John's Wort, Lesser Skullcap, Juniper, Orpine, Bladderseed, Round-leaved Sundew, Bog Asphodel, Hoary Cinquefoil and Wood Horsetail.

The birds are also of note, with all three woodpeckers, Nuthatch, Woodcock, Hawfinch, Redstart, Tree Pipit, Wood Warbler and Sparrowhawk all breeding here.

Other important sites nearby: Church Wood (SU 9787), an RSPB reserve, lies close by. It has woodland birds, and also Muntjac Deer, White Admiral and Purple and White-letter Hairstreaks.

This splendid reserve has a large area of chalk downland with a very rich flora. It is sited on a fairly steep chalk slope at the edge of the Chiltern Hills and there are wide vistas across the Vale of Aylesbury. In places, the open grazed turf of the grassland gives way to scrub, and this in turn grades into fully developed Beech woodland, mainly at the crest of the hill.

Some of the scrub here contains Juniper, often mixed with more familiar species such as Blackthorn, Bramble, Hawthorn and Dogwood. In some places there is also quite a lot of Yew, recalling sites like Kingley Vale further south.

Flowers of the woodland here include Sanicle, Woodrush, Yellow Archangel, and orchids such as White and Violet Helleborine. Species to look for on the open grassland include Common Rock-rose, Wild Thyme, Eyebright, Common Milkwort, Horseshoe Vetch, Bird's-foot Trefoil, Common Centaury, Oxeye Daisy, Marjoram, and Common Spotted Orchid. Two Chiltern specialities also grow here, Chiltern Gentian and Candytuft. Deadly Nightshade is frequent in the scrub close to the Beech woods.

The butterflies of this reserve are also worthy of note. In addition to commoner species, there are also Dark Green Fritillary, Chalkhill Blue, Small Blue, Brown Argus, Green Hairstreak, and Dingy and Grizzled

Autumn colours in the Wyre Forest, an oak wood on sloping ground.

92 WYRE FOREST

Location:	West of Bewdley, Hereford and Worcester
Grid Reference:	SO 7677; L138
Visiting:	Best spring and summer
Terrain:	Mixed woodland
Specialities:	Woodland birds, flowers and insects

A fine remnant of ancient woodland, with the added benefit of being adjacent to the River Severn and being bisected by a clear stream, the Dowles Brook. In this reserve there is a great variety of habitat, from acid oakwood, through neutral woods on clay to wet Ash/elm woodland, meadows, woodland glades and rich riverside communities. There are also patches of afforestation.

In the acid woods, Sessile Oak and birch dominate, with species such as Bilberry, Heather and Bracken below. These woods also have Lily-of-the Valley. Pedunculate Oak is also common here, but on the more clay-rich soils. Amongst the more interesting woodland flowers are Intermediate Wintergreen, Bloody and Wood Cranesbills, Columbine and Narrow-leaved Helleborine.

Glades on more alkaline sites have flowers such as Betony, Harebell, Yellow Rattle, Wild Thyme, and the rarer Green-winged Orchid and Adder's Tongue.

The forest also has good numbers of Fallow Deer, as well as typical woodland mammals such as mice, voles, shrews, Weasel, Stoat, Badger and Fox. Otters occur along the Severn. The bird interest is certainly enhanced by the stream which attracts Kingfisher, Dipper and Grey Wagtail. Elsewhere in the forest can be found all three woodpeckers, Nuthatch, Wood Warbler, Pied Flycatcher, Redstart and Hawfinch.

Skippers. However, pride of place must go to two rather special and local butterflies: Silver-spotted Skipper and Duke of Burgundy.

The woods have Sparrowhawk, woodpeckers and Hawfinch.

Other important sites nearby: Ivinghoe Beacon (SP 9617) also has fine chalk grassland habitat, with Pasqueflower and Duke of Burgundy.

The variety of habitat makes for a rich insect life too. The list of butterflies for Wyre Forest is long and includes Speckled Wood, Orange Tip, Purple Hairstreak, Brimstone, Comma, Peacock, Wood White and High Brown, Small Pearl-bordered, Pearl-bordered and Silver-washed Fritillaries. The Beautiful Demoiselle and White-legged Damselfly both occur here; look for them alongside the rivers. The dragonflies include the Club-tailed Dragonfly and Southern Hawker.

93 CASTOR HANGLANDS	
Location:	4km west of Peterborough
Grid Reference:	TF 1202; L142
Visiting:	Best spring or early summer. Park in Ailsworth. Bridle path; no access off right of way
Terrain:	Woodland, grassland, wetland
Specialities:	Flowers, insects, amphibians

This is a fine example of an old wood, earlier under coppice management. The presence of Wild Service Tree and the rich ground flora both point to the ancient nature of this wood. In places, grassland now occupies sites which were once also under woodland cover. Some of the grassy areas are acid with a heath-like cover, whilst other areas are more akin to chalk grassland. There are also wetland sites within the reserve, in the form of a series of ponds which add further to the wildlife richness.

Common woodland flowers here are Dog's Mercury, Bluebell, Primrose, Wood Anemone, Ramsons, Herb Paris and Wood Sorrel. Interesting species of the wet sites are Yellow Flag, Marsh Valerian, and Common Spotted, Early Marsh and Pyramidal Orchids.

The pools have breeding colonies of Common Toad and all three newt species and they also attract dragonflies and damselflies in good numbers.

Amongst the birds breeding here are Long-eared Owl, Woodcock and Sparrowhawk, with warblers including Grasshopper Warbler and Nightingale, particularly in the scrub areas.

Other important sites nearby: Nene Washes (TL 2899) has wet meadows, flooded in winter. It has a similar selection of birds to the Ouse Washes.

Monkshood *Aconitum napellus*
Monkshood, aptly named for its cowl- or helmet-like flowers, is a familiar garden plant. In parts of south-west England and south Wales the truly native plant can be found growing on damp, shady streamsides. Its flowers are a bluish-mauve in colour, slightly paler than the garden forms. Like many members of the buttercup family, Monkshood is **poisonous**. It may have been used in herbal medicine, perhaps by monks in the Dark Ages.

94 RUTLAND WATER

Location:	Just east of Oakham
Grid Reference:	SK 9006; L141
Visiting:	All year. Reserves near Lyndon and Egleton with parking and hides. Access by permit
Terrain:	Reservoir, reedbeds, lagoons, meadow, scrub
Specialities:	Water birds, such as Ruddy Duck and Garganey

Rutland Water is the second largest artificial lake in England, with a shoreline that stretches some 40km. It is now well established as a major gathering point for migrating birds, particularly for wildfowl and waders. The western end is protected and managed for the wildlife, and it is here that the two reserves of Egleton and Lyndon are sited. The water can also be viewed from other spots such as at Manton Bridge or near Edith Weston, and at Whitwell (Nature Trail) and Barnsdale.

Many waterbirds breed here, including Great Crested and Little Grebes, Mute Swan, Mallard, Gadwall, Pochard, Shoveler, Tufted Duck, Shelduck, Coot and Moorhen, as well as rarer species such as Ruddy Duck and Garganey.

Waders breed here too – Redshank,

Little Ringed Plover (Charadrius dubius) The bright-yellow eye-ring distinguishes this species from the commoner Ringed Plover. It often nests at gravel pits and reservoirs, such as Rutland Water, and has increased steadily over the last thirty years.

Snipe, Lapwing, Ringed and Little Ringed Plover and Oystercatcher.

Other important sites nearby: Eyebrook Reservoir (SP 8595) has a similar selection of wildfowl, and annual Osprey visits, as does Pitsford Reservoir (SP 7670) and Grafham Water (TL 1568).

95 THE LONG MYND	
Location:	Just west of Church Stretton, Shropshire
Grid Reference:	SO 4395; L137
Visiting:	Park in Cardingmill Valley
Terrain:	Heather moor
Specialities:	Upland birds and moor and bog plants

This reserve covers part of a plateau rising up from the plain. The curved mass of the Long Mynd is cut by several deep valleys which serve to break up the landscape and add to the diversity of habitat. The highest point lies at 517m and there are excellent views in clear weather, across to nearby Wenlock Edge and Stiperstones, and further as far as the Brecon Beacons and Cadair Idris in Wales.

The ridge, once forested like so much of England, now carries mainly heather moor which is managed to encourage Red Grouse, like much of the moorland further north in Britain. It is reminiscent in general appearance of parts of Dartmoor and Exmoor, with its gently rolling foothills and numerous valleys.

Long Mynd is a fine spot to see moorland shrubs such as Heather, Bilberry and Bracken, and flowers like Tormentil, Heath Bedstraw, Shepherd's Cress and Navelwort. The boggy sites can be found in places where springs rise at the plateau's edge. Here, flush communities carry such flowers as Common Butterwort, sundews, Bog Pimpernel, Marsh

Lousewort and Marsh Pennywort.

The birds here include Buzzard, Raven, Red Grouse, Dipper, Grey Wagtail, Wheatear, Whinchat, and Ring Ousel. Wood Warbler, Redstart and Pied Flycatcher breed in the pockets of woodland on the lower slopes.

Other important sites nearby: Wenlock Edge (SO 4888) is a much more wooded ridge, with pockets of orchid-rich chalk grassland. It is one of the most famous landmarks in the region.

Stiperstones (SO 3798) is mainly upland heather moor and bog. Its flowers include Mountain Pansy.

Wem Moss (SJ 4734) is a splendid raised bog with many bog plants. The bog also has Adders and is one of the most southerly sites for the local Large Heath butterfly.

96 CANNOCK CHASE	
Location:	About 10km south-east of Stafford
Grid Reference:	SJ 9715; L127/128
Visiting:	Best spring, summer. Many car parks and trails through Country Park
Terrain:	Woodland, heath and bog
Specialities:	Very good all round

This fine area of mixed habitats encompasses deciduous woodland, coniferous plantation, open heath, wet valleys and streams and upland moor. The Chase, as its name implies, was an earlier Royal hunting forest, but most of the original woodland has now been removed, replaced either by heath and moorland, or by plantations. Nevertheless, some remnants of mixed woodland do persist, mainly dominated by Sessile Oak and birch. The damper valleys have stands of Alder and willows.

Plants of the heath include Heather, Bell Heather, Bilberry, Crowberry and Cowberry. A rather special feature here is the population of hybrids between Bilberry and Cowberry, for which Cannock Chase is one of only a few sites. In the valley mires and more acid bogs can be found such species as Bogbean, Marsh Cinquefoil, Grass-of-Parnassus, Cross-leaved Heath, Bog Asphodel, Cranberry, Bog Pimpernel, Marsh Pennywort, Common Butterwort, both Round-leaved and Great Sundews, Marsh Valerian and Marsh Violet.

Amongst the birds of the plantations are Crossbill (winter), Coal Tit, Goldcrest, Long-eared Owl and Sparrowhawk, whilst the deciduous woods hold Redstart, Wood Warbler and Hawfinch. The heath has a good population of Nightjars, and also Grasshopper Warblers.

Butterflies are well represented too, with Green Hairstreak, Dingy Skipper and Small Pearl-bordered Fritillary, in addition to commoner species.

Deer are plentiful, with Muntjac, Red, Roe and Sika, and the commoner Fallow.

97 DOVEDALE	
Location:	About 10km north of Ashbourne
Grid Reference:	SK 1455; L119
Visiting:	Car park and plenty of footpaths
Terrain:	Woodland, cliffs, scree, limestone grassland
Specialities:	Flowers, insects, birds

Dovedale is a beautiful valley created by the river Dove as it cuts deep into the Staffordshire limestone. The area, which is well supplied with footpaths, is excellent for wandering through and offers a range of habitats including valley woodland and large sweeps of calcareous grassland, with associated flowers and butterflies, in addition to the clear, rushing waters of the river itself.

The woods are mostly dominated by Ash, with oaks, Beech, whitebeams and Rowan and they are home to many woodland birds, including Buzzard, Wood Warbler and Redstart. Kingfisher, Dipper and Grey Wagtail breed along the river.

The composition of the grasslands varies according to slope, humidity and aspect. They, and the nearby cliffs and rocky areas are rich in species, including Nottingham Catchfly, Orpine, Mossy Saxifrage, Dark-red Helleborine and Spring Sandwort.

Amongst the butterflies found here are Dingy and Grizzled Skippers, Brown Argus and Green and White-letter Hairstreaks.

Other important sites nearby: Manifold Valley (SK 1054) has a similar mix of habitats. Plants include Mezereon, Jacob's-ladder, Greater Butterfly and Green-winged Orchids and Sweet Cicelly.

98 SWITHLAND WOOD	
Location:	About 9km north of Leicester
Grid Reference:	SK 5413; L129/140
Visiting:	Car park and footpaths
Terrain:	Woodland
Specialities:	Flowers

Swithland Wood is part of the ancient Charnwood Forest which used to cover a large area here but which is now mostly represented by patches of grassland and heath. The wood is largely mixed deciduous, with oaks, Small-leaved Lime, birch, Hazel, and Alder and Ash in wetter sites.

Flowers of this reserve include woodland species such as Enchanter's Nightshade, Wood Sage and Bluebell, and acid indicators like Foxglove and Rose-bay Willowherb.

The diversity is increased by the presence of disused and flooded slate quarries, and by pasture, which has flowers such as Common Spotted Orchid, Betony, Adder's Tongue and Saw-wort.

Other important sites nearby: adjacent Bradgate Park has grassland and heath having Tormentil and Harebell, with Whinchat and Common Lizard and a herd of Fallow Deer.

Cropston Reservoir, just to the south, has Ruddy Duck, and passage waders.

*The Common Lizard (*Lacerta vivipara*) is particularly fond of dry, heathy habitats. However, like most reptiles, it is difficult to spot as it tends to slip away when disturbed.*

11. SOUTH-WEST ENGLAND

The south-west of England from the Avon south and south-west to the tip of Cornwall has a mild climate and a fairly high rainfall as well. It is well wooded, and the agriculture is biased towards pasture and grazing, quite unlike the intensively arable east. This means that the woods are interspersed with green fields and meadows with grazing livestock. This is probably one reason why large predatory birds such as Buzzard and Sparrowhawk are so common here; the woods provide secure nesting sites and the fields offer good numbers of small mammals as prey.

Cetti's Warbler and Cirl Bunting are two rather rare species which can be seen in this region. They are both at the northern limit of their European range and are badly affected by hard winter weather.

The south-west peninsula contains many botanical specialities, some of which are fortunately quite common. For example, in the Kingsbridge region of South Devon, the luxuriant lane banks will produce in summer the Balm-leaved Figwort, with the very handsome Yellow Bartsia in damp field margins.

The Lizard Peninsula is famous for many rarities and special plants, ranging from the locally common Cornish Heath, to the Ciliate Rupture-wort, and some small clovers.

Coastal limestone rocks in the south-west have their special plants too, such as the famous Cheddar Pink, and the White Rock-rose. Among the weedy flora, the fumitories are noteworthy, with Western Ramping Fumitory. On islands, the famous Peony, long naturalized on Steep Holm, has a special interest, but botanically more remarkable is the endemic Lundy Cabbage, which grows only on the island of Lundy and nowhere else in the world.

Dorset has one of the richest butterfly faunas of all counties, and the sheltered downland habitats are some of the best sites in the whole of Britain and Ireland to see many species, particularly blues and skippers.

The Exe estuary is the finest habitat for waders and wildfowl in the region, and the Isles of Scilly are visited regularly by both birdwatchers (mainly for the rare migrants) and botanists for the unusual flora.

Ringlets (Aphantopus hyperantus) mating. The Ringlet is a common, but rather unobtrusive butterfly found in hedgerows, damp grassland and woodland edges.

The Bluebell (Hyacinthoides non-scripta), a common species of woodland throughout Britain.

99 AVON GORGE/LEIGH WOODS	
Location:	Bristol
Grid Reference:	ST 5573; L172
Visiting:	Best spring, early summer. Nature trail
Terrain:	Rocky gorge with steep woods
Specialities:	Rare plants

The Avon Gorge holds a mixture of sheer cliffs, scree slopes and gentler gradients on which soil can develop. The climate is damp and the undergrowth often lush, with ferns such as Hart's Tongue abundant. On the flatter land towards the top of the gorge are the ancient Leigh Woods, with oaks, Ash, Beech and Small-leaved Lime mixed with Hawthorn, Spindle, Dogwood and Hazel, and in places the dark shade of Holly and Yew. In places there are twisting lianes of Old Man's Beard and a thick growth of Ivy.

A very special feature of these woods is the rare whitebeams which include the endemic Bristol Whitebeam, a tree only known from this locality. Other notable plants are Bristol

FIFTY INTERESTING SPECIES TO LOOK FOR

Buzzard	Mink	Peony	Large Blue
Cetti's Warbler	Muntjac	Purple Gromwell	Lulworth Skipper
Cirl Bunting	Otter	Round-headed Leek	Marbled White
Grey Wagtail	Red Deer	Sea Knotgrass	Marsh Fritillary
Raven	Slow-worm	Sea Stock	Pearl-bordered
Redstart	Balm-leaved Figwort	Strapwort	Fritillary
Ring Ousel	Bristol Rock-cress	Western Ramping	Purple Hairstreak
Ruddy Duck	Carrot Broomrape	Fumitory	Silver-washed Fritillary
Sparrowhawk	Cheddar Pink	White Rock-rose	Small Pearl-bordered
Stonechat	Ciliate Rupture-wort	Yellow Bartsia	Fritillary
Wheatear	Cornish Heath	Brown Hairstreak	White Admiral
Whinchat	Hairy Greenweed	Dark Green Fritillary	
Wood Warbler	Lundy Cabbage	Heath Fritillary	
Grey Seal	Pennyroyal	High Brown Fritillary	

Cheddar Gorge is a splendid limestone feature and a site for the famous Cheddar Pink.

Other important sites nearby: Steep Holm (ST 2361) is an island reserve in the Bristol Channel (by boat from Weston-super-Mare). It is famous for its wild Peony and Wild Leek. It has Cormorant, Herring, Lesser and Great Black-backed Gulls, Raven and Peregrine. There are also Slow-worms on the island, and Muntjac Deer.

100 CHEW VALLEY LAKE	
Location:	About 12km south of Bristol
Grid Reference:	ST 5760; L172/182
Visiting:	Good views from roads; permits for hides
Terrain:	Open water, reedbed, mudbanks, scrub
Specialities:	Water birds, notably Ruddy Duck

Chew Valley lake is a shallow reservoir which is best known for the large populations of duck and other wildfowl which it attracts.

Many species of duck breed here, including Mallard, Gadwall, Pochard, Tufted Duck, Shelduck, Shoveler, Garganey, and the star bird, the rather local Ruddy Duck (their first breeding site in Britain). Great Crested and Little Grebes also nest here, as do Kingfisher.

On passage, the mud and banks attract waders such as Black-tailed Godwit, Spotted Redshank and Curlew Sandpiper, and Osprey and Marsh Harrier are not infrequently seen.

In winter, the ranks of wildfowl are swelled by Bewick's Swans, Wigeon, Pintail, Goldeneye, Smew and Goosander.

Other important sites nearby: Blagdon Lake (ST 5260) is clearer, with a more interesting flora, but tends not to attract as wide a variety of birds.

Rock-cress, Round-headed Leek, Hutchinsia, Honewort and Spiked Speedwell. There is also Yellow Corydalis, Herb-Robert, Bluebell, Wood Sage, Columbine, Green Hellebore, Toothwort and Bird's-nest Orchid, and on the open scrubby areas, Small Scabious, Common Rock-rose, Salad Burnet, Spring Cinquefoil and Autumn Squill.

101 EBBOR GORGE

Location:	About 5km north-west of Wells
Grid Reference:	ST 5248; L182
Visiting:	Best spring, summer; permit off paths
Terrain:	Limestone gorge with woodland
Specialities:	Flowers, butterflies

This deep valley has rough limestone slopes, many of which are wooded with a mixed community of oaks, Ash, Wych elms, whitebeams and, locally, Small-leaved Lime. The woods are shady and in the damper areas have a rich moss and fern flora, including Hart's Tongue, Bladder Fern, Maidenhair Spleenwort, Polypody, Rustyback, Wall-rue, and Tunbridge Filmy-fern. Flowers of these habitats include Shining Cranesbill and Wall Lettuce.

Higher up the slopes there are remnants of limestone grassland and heath with flowers such as Salad Burnet, Marjoram, Common Rock-rose, Wild Thyme, Horseshoe Vetch, Betony and eyebrights.

In some places there are damp meadows with Marsh Marigold, Meadowsweet, Lesser Spearwort and Ragged Robin. In the drier woodland, there are carpets of Bluebells, Wood Anemone, Lesser Celandine and Primrose and many other flowers such as Goldilocks, Bugle, Early Dog-violet, Wood Sorrel, Broad-leaved Helleborine, Nettle-leaved Bellflower and Purple Gromwell.

The woodland birds here include Buzzard, Sparrowhawk, Tawny Owl, Kestrel, woodpeckers and Nuthatch, with Grey Wagtail along the streams. In the scrub there are Grasshopper Warblers.

The varied habitats and rich flora support many species of butterfly. Woodland species here are White Admiral, Silver-washed and High Brown Fritillaries, and Purple and White-letter Hairstreaks. In more open sites, look out for Common, Chalkhill and even Silver-studded Blue, Brown Argus, Marbled White and Dark Green Fritillary.

Other important sites nearby: Cheddar Gorge (ST 4854) has limestone cliffs with interesting plants including the rare Cheddar Pink, with Rock-rose, Green-winged Orchid and stonecrops.

Cheddar Pink *Dianthus gratianopolitanus*
This very beautiful rock plant has been known in Cheddar Gorge for more than two centuries. Elsewhere in Europe it occurs in similar habitats, usually on limestone rocks. It is related to the familiar garden pinks and has been cultivated for many years. It is a clump or mat-forming plant, covering rocks with its pretty grey-green foliage. The sweet-scented flowers are usually borne singly on short stalks in May and June. They are about 2cm across, with five toothed pink petals. Cheddar Pink has been over-collected in the Cheddar Gorge for many years and it has now largely retreated on to the inaccessible parts of the steep cliffs, where neither human beings nor grazing animals can reach it.

102 LUNDY

Location:	About 20km north of Hartland Point, north Devon
Grid Reference:	SS 1444; L180
Visiting:	Regular boat trips from Ilfracombe on the north Devon coast
Terrain:	Rocky island
Specialities:	Seabirds, including Manx Shearwater and British Storm-petrel; shore-life; Lundy Cabbage

Lundy is a long, narrow rocky island surrounded by cliffs and stony coves. Inland it is mostly bare moorland. The waters around Lundy are now a Marine Nature Reserve.

The flowers include typical cliff and coastal species such as Thrift, but the island is most famous for the Lundy Cabbage, which grows nowhere else.

However, the main interest of the island, and the reason why many people visit it, is provided by its large seabird colonies. Birds breeding here include Puffin, Guillemot, Razorbill, Fulmar, Kittiwake, Shag, Herring, Lesser and Great Black-backed Gulls, Manx Shearwater and a few British Storm-petrel.

In addition, Lundy is a prime spot for migrant birds and many rarities have been seen here, and also more regular migrants such as Firecrest, Black Redstart, Ring Ousel, Pied Flycatcher, Dotterel and Ortolan and Lapland Buntings. It is also in a good position to attract migrants from North America.

Grey Seals breed in the coves and sea caves around the island and may sometimes be spotted in the water.

103 BRAUNTON BURROWS

Location:	10km west of Barnstaple
Grid Reference:	SS 4635; L180
Visiting:	Car parks provided. Open access. Military area occasionally closed
Terrain:	Saltmarsh, sand dunes, dune slacks
Specialities:	Excellent wetland and dune plants

Braunton Burrows is a huge dune system, one of the largest in northern Europe. It covers about 1,000ha and some of the dunes are huge – up to 30m. Its uniqueness has led to its international designation as a Biosphere Reserve.

Dunes in all stages of development and age can be seen here, with their corresponding differences in vegetation. The chemistry of the sand is also important in determining the plants to be found here, and this is a lime-rich shell-sand which results in a very rich flora indeed.

Flowers such as Yellow Rattle, Evening Primrose, Marsh Helleborine, Viper's Bugloss, Wild Pansy, storksbills, Thyme and Bird's-foot Trefoil put on a colourful display, with fine stands of Yellow Flag in the slacks. Other species found here include Sea Holly, Sea Bindweed, Round-leaved Wintergreen, Sea Spurge and Sea Rocket. Amongst the rarer flowers are Sand Toadflax, Sea Stock, Clustered Club-rush, Water Germander and Fen Orchid.

The range of insects is good too, with fourteen species of dragonfly, many butterflies, including Small Blue and Dark-green Fritillary and abundant grasshoppers. Glow-worms are also found here.

Other important sites nearby: Hartland Point (SS 2427) with its coastal cliffs, scrub and grassland is an excellent look-out point for seabirds.

104 BRIDGWATER BAY	
Location:	10km north of Bridgwater
Grid Reference:	ST 2746; L182
Visiting:	Keep to footpaths and hides
Terrain:	Estuary, saltmarsh, lagoons
Specialities:	Wildfowl and waders

Bridgwater Bay, and in particular the more sheltered waters and mudflats of the Parrett Estuary, offer safe feeding and roosting sites for thousands of waders and wildfowl, and these are the principal attraction of the reserve. The birds are at their most interesting and varied during the spring and autumn migrations and during the winter.

One of the best areas for birdwatching is around Stert Point. Here there are good views over the Parrett and out to sea, with hides. Waders include Dunlin, Oystercatcher, Redshank, Black-tailed and Bar-tailed Godwits, Knot, Grey Plover and Turnstone. This is also a good place to see Whimbrel on their northward spring migration.

Bridgwater Bay has a special claim to fame as a traditional moulting ground for thousands of Shelduck which gather here for this purpose in July. In winter, the wildfowl include hundreds of Wigeon and Mallard, as well as Teal, Pintail and Shoveler.

The flowers are also of interest, with species such as Yellow Horned Poppy, Knotted, Sea Clover and Henbane.

Do not stray out onto the mudflats. This disturbs the birds and can be dangerous, since the surface is treacherously soft in places and the tides rise rapidly.

Other important sites nearby: Berrow Dunes (ST 2954) have interesting flowers, with orchids. Brean Down (ST 2959) is good for migrant birds and also has a fascinating limestone and coastal flora, with Dwarf Sedge, Somerset Hair-grass and White Rock-rose. The butterflies include Painted Lady, Marbled White and Grayling.

Cormorants (Phalacrocorax carbo) are frequently seen around Britain's coasts and estuaries diving for fish.

105 DARTMOOR NATIONAL PARK	
Location:	Large area about 20km north-east of Plymouth
Grid reference:	L191/202
Visiting:	Many car parks and footpaths
Terrain:	Moorland, granite outcrops, wooded valleys, rivers
Specialities:	Moorland plants and birds

Dartmoor is a great mass of granite upland which rises to its highest point at around 620m at High Willhays and Yes Tor, about 5km south of Okehampton. The whole area has National Park status and is well supplied with information points, car parks, footpaths and maps.

The high rolling uplands are largely dominated by poor grassland (Bristle-bent and Mat-grass) or by heather moor, with flowers such as Tormentil, Bilberry and Bell Heather. In wetter spots Cross-leaved Heath and Purple Moor-grass appear and there are also extensive areas of bog with *Sphagnum*, sundews and cottongrasses.

Whilst the main expanse is windswept and tree-less, the sheltered valleys do retain important woodland remnants, as for example in the Dart and Bovey valleys. Certain strange gnarled woods can also be found higher up, in sites where grazing is difficult, as at Wistman's Wood. This confirms the view that Dartmoor is not naturally without trees. Flowers of the wooded valleys include Wild Daffodil, Wood Anemone, Bluebell and Ramsons.

Buzzards are common on Dartmoor, either wheeling over their woodland breeding grounds, or hunting above the open

A relatively high rainfall feeds Dartmoor's bogs and streams. This photograph was taken near Burrator, in the south of the moor.

A female Sparrowhawk (Accipiter nisus) with young in the nest. This fine hawk has made a dramatic recovery in recent years.

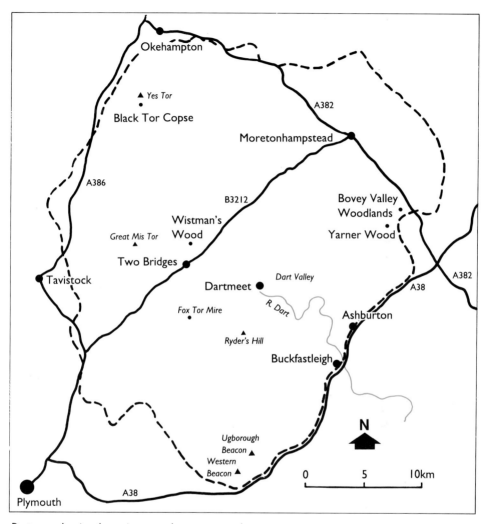

Dartmoor showing the main tors and routes across the moor.

moor. Other birds of the open moor are Ring Ousel, Wheatear, Stonechat, Whinchat and Raven.

The woodlands provide nesting opportunities for Kestrel, Sparrowhawk, Tawny Owl, all three woodpeckers, Treecreeper, Nuthatch, Redstart, Pied Flycatcher and Wood Warbler.

Along the rivers watch for Kingfisher, Grey Wagtail, Dipper and Grey Heron. If you are very lucky you might even spot a feral Mink or Otter silently slipping into the water or making its way steadily along the river.

The rare and declining High Brown Fritillary can still be found in certain places on Dartmoor.

Some important sites within the National Park:

Wistman's Wood   About 4km northeast of Princetown (SX 6177). An unusual wood of twisted ancient oaks growing amongst boulders. Very damp with rich moss and fern epiphyte flora.

Bovey Valley Woodlands   (SX 7980). Fern and moss-rich oak woods; also valley bog. Redstart, Pied Flycatcher, Wood Warbler, Dipper and Grey Wagtail. Royal Fern.

Yarner Wood   (SX 7979). Mainly Sessile Oak wood with Birch and Holly. Wood Warbler, Pied Flycatcher. White Admiral and Purple and Green Hairstreaks.

Dart Valley (SX 6773–7070) Wooded riverside with patches of heath. Woods vary from Alder at river's edge to mixed oak, with Holly, birch and Beech on drier ground.

Yarner Wood, Devon. Note the rich, damp undergrowth with Hard Fern and Hart's-tongue Fern, and the epiphytes on the tree trunks.

106	EXMOOR NATIONAL PARK	
Location:	Large area, mainly south and west of Minehead	
Grid Reference:	L180/181	
Visiting:	Best spring, summer. Many car parks and footpaths	
Terrain:	Moorland, valleys, woods, coast	
Specialities:	Moorland birds, Redstart, Pied Flycatcher, Buzzard; moorland flowers; Red Deer, Otter	

The mix of habitats on Exmoor is similar to that of Dartmoor, but the Exmoor National Park includes some 20km of spectacular rugged coastline, providing an extra element and increased wildlife diversity.

The heather-dominated high moorland has the expected mix of species with Bilberry, Bracken, Gorse, with Western Gorse and Bell Heather towards the coast. Wet heath and bog has Cross-leaved Heath, Purple Moor-grass,   Deergrass,   cottongrasses, sundews, Bog Asphodel and both Common and Pale Butterworts.

The coastal beauties of Exmoor are perhaps best sampled from the Somerset and North Devon Coast Path. This stretches from County Gate in the west, along the coast to Minehead in the east. Sometimes the path is at sea-level, in other parts it rises with the land to give excellent panoramic views out across the sea.

Many of the streams and rivers of Exmoor support Otters, and Red Deer roam across the open moorland, descending to the shelter of woodland in bad weather. The famous Exmoor ponies also range widely on the hills.

The highest point on Exmoor is at the splendid viewpoint of Dunkery Beacon, south of Porlock, which reaches 519m.

Important sites within or close to the National Park:

Horner Wood (SS 9045) is an ancient valley woodland with typical Exmoor woodland wildlife. The main dominant trees are Sessile Oaks, with Holly, Hazel, Rowan and birch below. Flowers here include Goldenrod, Cornish Moneywort, Wood Spurge and Ivy-leaved Bellflower. At the upper slopes the wood grades into heath, and eventually open moorland. The birds include Redstart, Wood Warbler and Pied Flycatcher, with Grey Wagtail and Dipper along the streams. Horner Wood is also one of the favoured wintering grounds for the Red Deer of Exmoor.

Lyn Valley Woodlands (SS 7548) has a nature walk which takes you through a range of interesting habitats. These include rocky clear streams with Dippers and Grey Wagtails, through mixed oak woodland with Pied Flycatchers, Redstart, Buzzard and Sparrowhawk, to heather moor, and down to the cliffs and rocks of the coast. The flowers include Welsh Poppy.

107 SLAPTON LEY	
Location:	About 10km south-west of Dartmouth, South Devon
Grid Reference:	SX 8344; L202
Visiting:	Permit needed for woodland
Terrain:	Shingle, lagoon, reedbeds, woodland
Specialities:	Shingle plants, migrant birds

The shingle bank which separates the large shallow lagoon from the sea is the most south-westerly in Britain, and the lagoon itself is one of the biggest areas of fresh water in the region.

The shingle has plants such as Yellow Horned Poppy, Ray's Knotgrass, Shore Dock, and Sea Radish. Plants of the lagoon include White Water Lily, Spiked Water Milfoil, Shoreweed, and the rare Strapwort for which this is the only British sites.

Slapton has a rich bird life, with Buzzard, Sparrowhawk and Raven around the woodland, and Great Crested Grebe breeding on the lagoon. Sedge and Reed Warblers and Water Rail are found in the reedbeds and the scrub also holds a good population of Cetti's Warbler, a species which overwinters. A South Devon speciality is the Cirl Bunting which can be seen in the valley leading inland from the reserve.

But it is for its migrant and winter birds that Slapton is best known. Great Northern Diver and Slavonian Grebe are regular winter visitors offshore, with all three divers occurring in the spring. Wintering ducks include occasional Smew, Goosander, Long-tailed Duck and Ruddy Duck, in addition to the commoner species such as Pintail, Pochard, Tufted Duck and Shoveler. Other

151

birds seen regularly here on passage are Garganey, Black Tern and Arctic Skua.

Other important sites nearby: Start Point (SX 8436) and Prawle Point (SX 7735). The bushes in these areas have Cirl Bunting. There is excellent seawatching from the points themselves.

108 WEST SEDGEMOOR	
Location:	Between Taunton and Langport, Somerset
Grid Reference:	ST 3624; L193
Visiting:	Car park, footpaths, hides and visitor centre
Terrain:	Wet meadows, ditches, woodland
Specialities:	Birds and flowers of flooded meadows

The once extensive flooded fields and fens of Sedgemoor are now largely drained and converted to agricultural land. However, pockets remain, such as this attractive reserve. The meadows are mostly flooded in the winter months, but dry out again in the spring. They are either cut for hay or grazed by cattle.

The meadows provide nesting sites for several waders such as Lapwing, Snipe, Redshank, Curlew and Black-tailed Godwit and large numbers of Whimbrel use the reserve as a staging post on their spring migration north. In winter there are large numbers of Lapwing, joined by Golden Plover.

Wildfowl which regularly visit include Bewick's Swan, Teal and Wigeon.

Swell Wood has breeding Buzzard, Marsh Tit and Nightingale and in addition boasts one of Britian's largest heronries, with around seventy pairs.

Flowers include Marsh Marigold, Ragged Robin, marsh orchids and Water Violet.

Other important sites nearby: Weston Moor (AWT) is the last reedbed left in the Gordano Valley. It has Reed, Sedge and Grasshopper Warbler and rich fen vegetation.

109 EXE ESTUARY	
Location:	Near Exmouth, South Devon
Grid Reference:	SX 9884; L192
Visiting:	Keep to footpaths
Terrain:	Mudflats, dunes
Specialities:	Sea and shore birds

This is the south-west region's largest and most important estuary, attracting huge numbers of waders and wildfowl every winter. The specialities include Brent Geese, Avocets and Black-tailed Godwits.

Seawatching can be good from Langstone Rock and from Exmouth, which has sandstone cliffs at Orcombe. Birds to watch for

Avocet (Recurvirostra avosetta). This beautiful wader regularly winters in good numbers on the Exe Estuary.

on the sea in winter are Slavonian Grebe, Red-throated Diver, Eider, Common Scoter and occasional Velvet Scoter.

The Brent Geese often number around 2,000 and are joined in the estuary by thousands of Wigeon, with Mallard, Gadwall, Teal and Pintail. There are also regular small numbers of Red-breasted Merganser and Goldeneye. All three species of swan may also be seen on the estuary.

There are large numbers of wintering Avocet, 500–600 Black-tailed Godwits, Dunlin, Curlew, Redshank, Golden Plover, Grey Plover, Oystercatcher, Turnstone and Ruff. The rocks at Langstone and beneath the cliffs at Orcombe sometimes yield Purple Sandpipers.

Breeding birds include Shelduck, Lapwing, with Reed and Sedge Warbler and Reed Bunting in the reedbeds. There is a heronry at Powderham on the western shore.

The rare and local Cirl Bunting breeds in this area too, good areas being the hedges near Langstone and Exminster.

Other important sites nearby: Dawlish Warren (SX 9878) is an area of dunes, saltmarsh and scrub, with excellent plants. This is one of the few remaining sites outside the Channel Isles for the Sand Crocus.

*This small, active finch, the Redpoll (*Carduelis flammea*) is often seen in damp birch and Alder woodland, and in conifer plantations.*

110 STUDLAND HEATH	
Location:	5km north of Swanage, Dorset
Grid Reference:	SZ 0384; L195
Visiting:	Open access with car parks and trails
Terrain:	Lowland heath, woods, lakes, sand and mudflats
Specialities:	Heathland birds, flowers, insects

Studland Heath is one of the finest remaining areas of lowland heath, itself an internationally rare community, and is a National Nature Reserve. The star bird species here is undoubtedly the Dartford Warbler, for which this is one of the prime sites. These lively birds breed in gorse on the heath, but they can be tricky to spot, especially in windy weather when they keep well hidden.

Other birds breeding here include Nightjar, Hobby, Sparrowhawk and Green and Great Spotted Woodpecker.

In winter, the sea attracts divers, grebes and sea-ducks in large numbers, with Black-necked and Slavonian Grebes a regular feature. The more sheltered waters of Poole Harbour have Brent Goose, Pintail and Goldeneye, and the mudflats encourage large numbers of waders to stop and feed, amongst them Black-tailed Godwit and Avocet.

Studland Heath also has a rich insect fauna, with many dragonflies and butterflies. It also has the distinction of housing all six British reptiles, including the rare Smooth Snake and Sand Lizard.

Other important sites nearby: Arne (SY 9788) is an RSPB reserve with Dartford Warbler, Stonechat and Nightjar. It also has all six reptiles, and over twenty species of dragonfly, and Roe and Sika Deer. The local Dorset Heath also grows here.

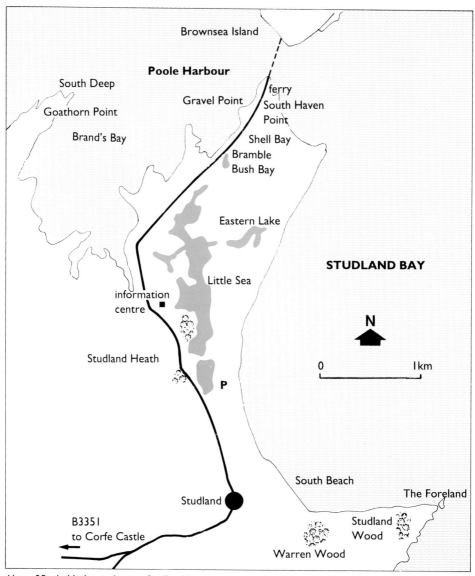

Map of Poole Harbour, showing Studland heath.

Brownsea Island (SZ 0388) has Grey Herons, Common and Sandwich Terns, waders, Red Squirrel, Sika Deer, Speckled Wood, Marbled White and Grayling.

111 AXMOUTH/LYME REGIS UNDERCLIFFS	
Location:	About 5km east of Seaton, South Devon
Grid Reference:	SY 2790; L192/193
Visiting:	Keep to paths. Dangerous rocks
Terrain:	Cliffs, rocky woods, coast
Specialities:	Flowers, ferns

This reserve protects what is essentially an unstable ecosystem, caused by a series of landslips from the chalk and sandstone cliffs above. The result is an almost unique habitat, with rich damp woodland rising up from a jumble of rocks and boulders, partly protected from the sea by larger chunks of rock. The reserve is closed from time to time because of the danger of fresh landslips.

The natural woodland which has developed here is dominated by Ash, with Field Maple, Hazel, Blackthorn, Dogwood, Spindle and other shrubs. Long lianes of Ivy, Traveller's Joy and Honeysuckle clamber over the rocks and trees and the undergrowth has a rich growth of ferns and flowers. These include Hart's Tongue, Male Fern, Soft Shield Fern, Broad Buckler Fern, Wood Spurge, Herb Robert, Dog's Mercury and Yellow Archangel.

The wet sites have a fascinating flora which includes Purple Loosestrife, Great Horsetail, Bog Pimpernel and Water Mint.

The breeding birds include some odd companions, such as Herring Gull and Nightingale, Goldcrest and Rock Pipit.

The undercliffs are an important habitat for the small and delicate Wood White, a rather scarce butterfly in Britain.

Other important sites nearby: Black Ven and the Spittles (SY 3593) is a similar site with orchids and Great Green Bush Cricket.

112 CHESIL BEACH/THE FLEET	
Location:	About 5km west of Weymouth, Dorset
Grid Reference:	SY 6480; L194
Visiting:	Car parks at Ferrybridge and Abbotsbury. Parts of beach closed in nesting season
Terrain:	Long, shingle bank, with tidal lagoon behind
Specialities:	Waders and wildfowl

Chesil Beach is a remarkable geological phenomenon in its own right, leaving aside for a moment the considerable biological interest. Here one of Europe's largest shingle banks stretches some 25km straight along the coast, joining the 'Isle' of Portland to the mainland and sheltering behind it a shallow lagoon, The Fleet, from the ravages of the sea.

Along the shingle one may hope to see plants such as Yellow Horned-poppy, Sea-Kale, Rock Samphire, Rough Clover, Shrubby Seablite and Sea Pea and the lagoon is well supplied with Eel-grass. This area is a breeding site for both Common Tern and the rarer Little Tern.

At the western end of The Fleet is Abbotsbury Swannery, a traditional breeding ground for semi-domesticated Mute Swans which gather in large numbers here, particularly in winter. The swans are joined by other wildfowl such as Brent Goose, Mallard, Wigeon, Gadwall, Goldeneye, Pintail, Coot,

The pretty Sea Pea (Lathyrus Japonicus) grows on coastal shingle, particularly in the south, as here at Chesil Beach.

and Pochard. The Fleet also attracts Shelduck, Shoveler, Tufted Duck, Teal and Red-breasted Merganser.

Mud around the Fleet provides food for waders such as Dunlin, Lapwing, Oyster-catcher, Bar-tailed Godwit, Redshank and Ringed and Grey Plover. Keen birders should check the flocks of gulls since this area has regular visits from rare species, especially Mediterranean and Little Gulls.

Other important sites nearby: Radipole Lake (SY 6880) is a reedy lake with interesting birds, including Bearded Tit, Grasshopper and Cetti's Warblers.

Lulworth Cove (SY 8380) is a sheltered spot with fascinating geology, showing buckled strata. Nearby Bindon Hill is also one of a few sites for the rare Lulworth Skipper.

Marbled White *Melanargia galathea*
W 46–56mm
This pretty butterfly is mainly a speciality of south-west England, where it inhabits warm, south-facing slopes on downland. There are also isolated colonies on Gower Peninsula in Wales, and in the North Yorkshire Wolds. They are only on the wing for a short season, from the end of June until mid-August, and like to rest and sunbathe on Scabious and Knapweed flowers.

113 THE LIZARD

Location:	16km south of Helston, Cornwall
Grid Reference:	SW 7014; L203
Visiting:	Footpath from Porth Mellin to Lizard Point, or park in Lizard village
Terrain:	Cliffs, coves, coastal heath
Specialities:	Unique flora; seabirds; migrant birds

This is one of the best sites for unusual plants in the whole of Britain and Ireland, and has become something of a pilgrimage site for

Kynance Cove is a famous site on the Lizard peninsula. Its coastal turf has a rich and unusual flora.

really keen field botanists. Its special nature is partly due to its southerly position, with a warm climate and very mild winters, and partly due to the special geology. In the west, the rocks are mainly serpentine, with granite occurring elsewhere.

A characteristic short acid heath has developed over the granite areas, with Heather, Bell Heather, Cross-leaved Heath, Western Gorse and Purple Moor-grass. Here, in the boggier sites you may see Pale and Common Butterworts, Bog Asphodel, Round-leaved Sundew and Lesser Butterfly Orchid.

On the serpentine, a more alkaline soil develops, with species such as Bloody Cranesbill, Dropwort, and the rare Cornish Heath. Wetter sites here may have Royal Fern, Lousewort and orchids such as Heath Spotted Orchid. Other species to look out for here are Dwarf and Pygmy Rush, Spring Squill and Pale and Common Dog-Violet.

Other special plants of the Lizard include Smooth Rupturewort, Crimson and Upright Clovers, Sea Asparagus, Dyer's and Hairy Greenweeds, Spring Sandwort, Spotted Catsear, Lesser Bird's-foot Trefoil, Autumn Squill, Sand Quillwort, Pillwort, Three-lobed Water Crowfoot, Slender Cicendia and Chaffweed. The alien Hottentot Fig grows on the cliffs near Lizard Point.

Important reserves of the Lizard: Mullion Cliffs/Mullion Island (SW 6717) for seabirds. Predannack (SW 6716), Kynance Cove (SW 6813).

114 BODMIN MOOR

Location:	North-east of Bodmin, Cornwall
Grid Reference:	L200/201
Visiting:	Car parks and footpaths
Terrain:	Upland moor, bog, rivers, woodland
Specialities:	Upland plants, such as Cornish Moneywort and Lesser Bladderwort, and birds, such as Buzzard, Raven, Dipper and Grey Wagtail

Bodmin Moor resembles Exmoor and Dartmoor in that it rises up as a brooding plateau above the surrounding countryside. Like the Devon moors, it too has an acid, Heather-dominated vegetation, with rough grassland and pockets of woodland in valley sites. Outcrops of granite rise as tors above the moorland and many parts of the moor are wet and boggy and very difficult to walk over.

Birds of Bodmin Moor include Buzzard, which can be seen soaring over any part of the moor, Raven, Golden Plover and Curlew. Along the streams and rivers, such as the attractive upper reaches of the River Fowey, there are Grey Wagtail and Dipper. Keep a careful eye out for the latter as it is easily disturbed and all you may see is the flash of its white belly as it flies by. Wet woods are found in some of the valleys and these contain birds such as Redpoll, Marsh and Willow Tits and Grasshopper Warbler, whilst Redstart and Tree Pipit nest in drier woods.

Fox and Badger are common, and Otters can be seen, with luck and patience, on several of the rivers.

Plants include Cornish Moneywort, Lesser Bladderwort, Oblong-leaved Sundew and Pale Butterwort.

115 ISLES OF SCILLY

Location:	Group of islands about 40km south-west of Land's End
Grid Reference:	SV 9010; L203
Visiting:	Spring and summer for spring migrants and flowers. August to October for autumn migrants. By Ferry or helicopter from Penzance
Terrain:	Rocky islands, cliffs, coves, dunes, heath
Specialities:	Seabirds, migrant birds, flowers

In terms of their natural history, the Isles of Scilly are deservedly famous mainly for two things: migrant birds and unusual flora.

Some of the plants found here are uncommon or local elsewhere in Britain, and every year the spring and autumn migrations bring in rare and unusual birds to the scrub, fields and pools. In all, about 375 species of bird have been recorded on the islands. In addition, the islands have several excellent points for watching seabirds, feeding or passing through the coastal waters.

Although the climate is mild, with winter frost rare, it can be very windy and wet, so be prepared with suitable clothing. These islands actually have even milder winters than the Channel Isles, although the summers are cooler.

The following species are commonly found here, but are rare or local elsewhere in Britain: Small Tree Mallow, Western Clover, Hairy Bird's-foot Trefoil, Orange Bird's Foot, Shore Dock, Babington's Leek and Large Cuckoo Pint (Italian Lords and Ladies).

The Eastern Isles, from St Martins, Isles of Scilly. These islands, which in appearance can seem almost sub-tropical, attract many birdwatchers, particularly during spring and autumn migrations, when many rarities regularly turn up.

Seabirds breeding here include British Storm-petrel (over 1,000 pairs), Manx Shearwater (about 300 pairs), Shag (1,200 pairs), Cormorant (about 500 pairs), Lesser Black-backed Gull (about 3,800 pairs) and Great black-backed Gull (about 1,000 pairs). There are also smaller numbers of Guillemot, Puffin, Razorbill and a small colony of the rare Roseate Tern.

The spring migration takes place from March until May, and at this time of year unusual migrants may be spotted almost anywhere, but particularly in areas with low vegetation and the protection of scrub. Hoopoe, Golden Oriole and Woodchat Shrike are fairly regular.

Many American species have turned up, especially in autumn. These have included

159

Pectoral and Buff-breasted Sandpiper, Lesser Golden Plover, Baltimore Oriole and Grey-cheeked Thrush.

In autumn, species such as Little Stint and Curlew Sandpiper are fairly common and Dotterel are regular, especially on St Mary's golf course. Regular songbirds are Redstart, Ring Ousel, Pied Flycatcher and Whinchat. The following are also regular: Icterine, Melodious, Barred and Yellow-browed Warblers, Wryneck, Bluethroat, Red-backed and Woodchat Shrikes, Tawny and Richard's Pipits, Scarlet Rosefinch, Lapland, Ortolan and Snow Buntings, Firecrest and Red-breasted Flycatcher.

Birds of prey also visit in autumn and winter, with Peregrine and Merlin frequent, and the occasional Osprey, Red Kite or Honey Buzzard.

Grey Seals are common around the islands, and Porpoises are not unusual in coastal waters. Another special mammal here is the Lesser White-toothed Shrew, otherwise only found in Britain on the Channel Islands.

Important sites on the Isles of Scilly. St Mary's: The Garrison, Bar Point (SV 9213), Peninnis Point (SV 9109). St Agnes: Horse Point. Bryher: Rushy Pool (SV 8715). Tresco: Great Pool and Abbey Pool (SV 8914). St Martin's. Annet: Small rocky island with the main seabird colonies, particularly British Storm-petrel, Manx Shearwater and Puffin.

*The Great Green Bush-cricket (*Tettigonia viridissima*) is Britain's largest bush-cricket. It prefers coastal sites in south Wales and the south of England. Look for it in hedgerows and bramble patches, or listen for the loud, continuous reeling 'song' of the male.*

12. WALES

A territory ranging from the mountain tops of Snowdonia to the warm coastal limestone of Gower Peninsula, this region is tremendously varied and has many specialities in its flora and fauna.

Amongst plants, the pride of place must surely go to that extraordinary delicate Alpine, the Snowdon Lily (*Lloydia serotina*) named after a 17th-century Welsh botanist Edward Llwyd (Lloyd). Its mountain localities are secret, but it still occurs in places, clinging to inaccessible rocks.

The limestone rocks of the Great Orme still provide a habitat for our only native cotoneaster, and this and similar limestone areas elsewhere in Wales have populations of the very handsome Welsh subspecies of Spiked Speedwell.

Wales, with its damp, oceanic climate, is rich in ferns, and, in addition to the very rare Killarney Fern, still counts among its specialities the Forked Spleenwort and the Oblong Woodsia.

In recent years, a surprising discovery has added to the British flora the early-flowering *Gagea bohemica* at a single, very special locality.

The Pembrokeshire Coast National Park, although a small National Park, contains a great variety of habitat and wildlife, ranging from upland heather moor, to shady oakwoods, to coastal heath and grassland, to rocky cliffs, estuaries, lakes and offshore islands. The Park is well supplied with footpaths and individual nature reserves and is fairly easy of access. Sites 126–9 are important reserves within this National Park.

The famous Pembrokeshire Coast Path is a long-distance trail which hugs the coast along the entire length of the National Park, from Cardigan to Amroth, east of Tenby.

The seas here are clear and relatively unpolluted, and many of the rocky coves and coastal waters attract seals, and porpoises and dolphins are also occasionally seen. The birds of this park include Peregrine, Chough and Manx Shearwater.

The Brecon Beacons National Park covers a large area of southern central Wales, from Llandeilo in the west, to Abergavenny in the east, and stretching north to Llandovery and Brecon. In all it covers 134,400ha and incorporates the four upland areas of (from west to east) Black Mountains on the Powys/Worcestershire border. It rises to over 885m at the peak of Pen-y-Fan, about 8km southwest of Brecon. Sites 130 and 131 lie within this National Park.

Most of the upland in this park carries poor sheep-grazed grassland or heather moor,

The bright-green highland Holly Fern (Polystichum lonchitis) is one of the specialities of Snowdon.

but there are also extensive blanket bogs, many deep valleys with scattered woodland, dark coniferous plantations and the occasional lake or reservoir. Parts of the hills are based on red sandstone, while in other areas limestone provides a contrast. There are extensive underground cave and river systems in the limestone regions such as at Craig-y-Cilau (SO1916).

The birds of Wales include characteristic woodland species such as Buzzard, Pied Flycatcher, Redstart and Wood Warbler. However, the star bird is certainly that beautiful, graceful and rare predator, the Red Kite. The 'hanging' oakwoods of Central Wales are now the stronghold of this bird, which is slowly increasing thanks to vigilant protection and careful land management, and now numbers over fifty pairs. Choughs and Peregrines are regular on certain rocky coasts, and some islands have important colonies of seabirds, notably Manx Shearwater on Bardsey Island.

Amongst mammals, the real Welsh speciality is the Polecat. This ferret-sized predator is widespread in many parts, especially in Central and North Wales. Like many nocturnal mammals it is very difficult to see.

116 SOUTH STACK CLIFFS	
Location:	About 4km west of Holyhead
Grid Reference:	SH 2183; L114
Visiting:	Best spring, summer. Short walk from car park to information centre
Terrain:	Sea cliffs and coastal heath
Specialities:	Nesting seabirds and coastal flowers

This reserve occupies a dramatic site overlooking the Irish Sea and offers excellent views of common and slightly more unusual seabirds at their breeding colonies. However, the reserve, although set up primarily for the birds, has wonderful carpets of coastal wild flowers, especially on the cliff-top heaths.

The cliffs, which rise to 120m in places are home to large numbers of Guillemot – about 2,000 pairs, with smaller numbers of Razorbill, Puffin, Kittiwake, Fulmar, Cormorant and Shag. These can all be watched with ease and there is even a closed-circuit

FIFTY INTERESTING SPECIES TO LOOK FOR

Buzzard	Grey Seal	Mountain Sorrel	Spring Squill
Chough	Polecat	Northern Bedstraw	Thrift
Guillemot	Alpine Cinquefoil	Northern Rock-cress	Welsh Mudwort
Manx Shearwater	Alpine Saw-wort	Oblong Woodsia	Wild Cotoneaster
Peregrine	Bloody Cranesbill	Parsley Fern	Yellow Whitlow-grass
Pied Flycatcher	Field Fleawort	Perennial Centaury	Brown Hairstreak
Raven	Forked Spleenwort	Perennial Knawel	Dark-green Fritillary
Red Kite	*Gagea bohemica*	Rock Cinquefoil	Pearl-bordered
Redstart	Golden Samphire	Roseroot	Fritillary
Rock Dove	Holly Fern	Sea Campion	Purple Hairstreak
Roseate Tern	Killarney Fern	Snowdon Lily	Silver-washed Fritillary
Wood Warbler	Moss Campion	Spiked Speedwell	Small Pearl-bordered
Badger	Mossy Saxifrage	Spotted Rock-rose	Fritillary

Near South Stack on the Anglesey Coast. Clumps of bright-pink Thrift (Armeria maritima) add their colour to this natural rock garden.

television system relaying live coverage of the birds from April to August.

Two star birds of the reserve are Chough, of which there are several pairs, and Peregrine, with a couple of pairs usually present. Other birds here are Raven, Rock Dove and Jackdaw, with Whitethroat and Stonechat on the heath.

Spring finds the cliffs bright with flowers such as Thrift, Bloody Cranesbill, Golden Samphire, Spring Squill, Sea Campion and Kidney Vetch. There are also important tracts of acid maritime heath in this area, notably towards Holyhead Mountain, and these have the rare Spotted Rock-rose and Field Fleawort, very much local specialities.

Adder and Common Lizard are both common, and the butterflies include Small Pearl-bordered, Dark Green and Marsh Fritillaries, Grayling, Common and Silver-studded Blue (the latter at its most northerly site).

Grey Seals can often be seen hauled out on Gogarth Bay.

163

117 NEWBOROUGH WARREN

Location:	Southern tip of Anglesey
Grid Reference:	SH 4164; L114
Visiting:	All year. Permits needed off rights of way
Terrain:	Saltmarsh, dunes, pools, rocks, plantation
Specialities:	In spring, coastal birds, flowers; in winter, waders, wildfowl and raptors

This National Nature Reserve protects one of Britain's finest dune systems and one of the richest examples of dune and coastal sand floras. The area is also good for wintering wildfowl and waders.

The rocky peninsula of Ynys Llanddwyn has flowers such as Spring Squill and Golden Samphire. It is also a breeding ground for Cormorant and Shag. In the winter, this same spot is the best place from which to scan the sea for divers and grebes (notably Slavonian and Black-necked), and Turnstone and Purple Sandpiper feed on the rocks.

The younger dunes themselves are dominated by Marram Grass, and species such as Sea Spurge, Sand Catstail and Wild Pansies can also be seen. Stable dunes have Cuckooflower, Bird's Foot Trefoil, Lady's Bedstraw, Thyme and Meadow Saxifrage.

Behind the dunes, in better vegetated, damper hollows, look out for Grass-of-Parnassus, Round-leaved Wintergreen, Creeping Willow, Yellow Bird's-nest and orchids such as Early Marsh and Northern Marsh and Dune Helleborine.

The saltmarsh along the Cefni Estuary has extensive stands of Sea Rush, with Sea

Pine Marten *Martes martes* L 40–55 (head and body)
This cat-sized weasel relative is an active, mainly nocturnal predator. It is commonest in north and central Wales, in north-west Scotland and in parts of Ireland. Pine Martens inhabit forests (particularly coniferous) and open moorland, and are very good at climbing trees, where they can even catch squirrels. They also hunt on the ground and eat birds, eggs, small mammals, insects and berries.

Aster, Thrift, Annual Sea-blite and Sea Arrowgrass. Wildfowl gather here in considerable numbers in winter. They include Wigeon, Pintail, Goldeneye, Shoveler, Gadwall, Shelduck and the occasional Bewick's or Whooper Swan. Newborough Warren also attracts waders including Curlew, Lapwing, Redshank, Dunlin, Bar- and Black-tailed Godwit, Sanderling and Curlew Sandpiper.

Other important sites nearby: Rhosneigr (SH 3374) has offshore islets with Britain's largest colony of Roseate Tern (about 100 pairs). These can often be seen from the shore fishing along the coast.

118 YNYS ENLLI (BARDSEY ISLAND)	
Location:	About 3km off tip of Lleyn Peninsula, Gwynedd
Grid Reference:	SH 1222; L123
Visiting:	Boat from Pwllheli or Porth Meudwy. Contact Bardsey Island Trust Secretary, 38 Walthew Avenue, Holyhead. Tel: 0407 2633
Terrain:	Rocky island
Specialities:	Breeding seabirds, such as Manx Shearwater, Razorbill and Guillemot; migrant birds

Bardsey is best known for its migrant birds and it contains an important bird observatory and ringing station. However, it is also a breeding site for about 4,500 Manx Shearwater and about half a dozen pairs of Chough. Other species breeding are Peregrine, Fulmar, Kittiwake, Razorbill, Guillemot, Shag, Raven and Oystercatcher. Little Owls have taken up residence in some of the disused Rabbit burrows.

For migrants the best times to visit are April to early June and August to early November. In addition to the more common migrants, such as Ring Ousel, Bardsey regularly turns up the unexpected and the list of species recorded here is long. Regular rarities are Yellow-browed Warbler, Firecrest, Redbreasted Flycatcher, Sooty Shearwater, Leach's Storm- petrel, Little Auk and Sabine's Gull.

The flowers of Bardsey include Western Gorse, Heather, Cliff Spurrey, Thrift, Spring Squill, Lesser Meadow-rue and Wilson's Filmy Fern.

SNOWDONIA NATIONAL PARK

The Snowdonia National Park covers a large area of north Wales, nearly 220,000ha, from the mouth of the Dovey in the south through the mountains of Cadair Idris, north to Snowdon itself, and on almost to Conwy Bay in the north.

The habitats are vary varied, encompassing sheltered valley oakwoods, open estuary, dunes and marshes, inland towering hills and mountains with windswept moorland, and rivers and lakes.

To sample Snowdonia really needs a holiday entirely devoted to this area, so rich and varied is the landscape. The following provides just a selection of sites worthy of visit.

119 YR WYDDFA (SNOWDON)	
Location:	About 6km south of Llanberis, Gwyned
Grid Reference:	SH 6255; L115
Visiting:	Access by track from Pen-y-Pass or Pont Bethania, or by mountain railway from Llanberis
Terrain:	Mountain grassland, cliffs, moor, bog. Wet rocks are often slippery. Take protective clothing and sturdy boots
Specialities:	Mountain flowers and birds

At 1,085m, Snowdon is the highest mountain in Wales and England, and the conditions on this and surrounding mountains are very exposed. This has led to the development of an interesting flora, with several local

165

and rare mountain species, of which the most famous is the Snowdon Lily.

The Snowdon Lily is only found here and on some adjacent mountains, where it is strictly protected. Other mountain flowers of

Snowdon Lily *Lloydia serotina*
This delicate bulbous plant holds a unique position in the British flora. It is the only British mountain plant confined to the Snowdon range in north Wales, and is in fact named after a famous 17th century Welsh botanist, Edward Lloyd (Llwyd), who first discovered it. It is also unique in Britain in being a bulbous mountain plant. It produces its slender stems in June and July, each with a single, delicate, white, six-petalled, lily-like flower. Its habitat is rock crevices between 450 and 750 metres, in several scattered populations on the Snowdon range. It is a widespread mountain plant outside Britain.

Snowdon are Mountain Sorrel, Roseroot, Alpine Saw-wort, Purple and Mossy Saxifrages, Moss Campion, Alpine Cinquefoil, Northern Rock-cress, and Northern Bedstraw. The ferns include Parsley and Holly Fern, and Alpine and Oblong Woodsias.

The boggy patches yield *Sphagnum* moss with Bog Asphodel and cottongrasses, Common Butterwort and Round-leaved Sundew.

The birds are rather few in variety, but make up for that in quality. Look out for Peregrine, Buzzard, Raven, Chough, Ring Ousel and Wheatear.

The mammals include feral Goat and Mountain Hare.

Other important sites nearby: Cwm Idwal (SH 6459) with its splendid corrie and lake has a similar range of rare arctic-alpine plants. These include Snowdon Lily, Mountain Avens, Moss Campion, Mossy, Starry and the rare Tufted Saxifrage, Parsley Fern and Green Spleenwort.

Carneddau NT (SH 6764) covers fine mountain country with Chough, Peregrine and Ring Ousel, and plants including Snowdon Lily.

120 MORFA HARLECH	
Location:	Just north of Harlech, Gwynedd
Grid Reference:	SH 5734; L124
Visiting:	Spring, summer. Permit needed off rights of way
Terrain:	Saltmarsh and dunes
Specialities:	Coastal flowers; winter wildfowl and waders

This beautifully sited reserve lies at the mouth of the Vale of Ffestiniog, a very popular tourist area, and at the opposite side of the estuary from the famous village of Portmeirion. The level saltmarsh and splendid

The crags of this corrie at Cwm Idwal, Gwynedd, support several rare Arctic-Alpine flowers.

dune systems are set against a backdrop of high mountains, with Snowdonia to the north.

The interest here is mainly botanical, with the dunes and dune slacks the main focus. Both this reserve and the nearby Morfa Dyffryn have a wide range of typical dune flowers, with a rich variety of orchids. The species include Maiden Pink, Smooth Catsear, Sharp Rush, Greater Bladderwort, Hound's-tongue, Sea Spurge and Creeping Willow. Amongst the orchids are Bee, Pyramidal, Northern and Early Marsh, and Green-flowered Helleborine.

In winter, the marshes attract wildfowl including Mallard, Wigeon, Teal, Shoveler and Whooper Swan.

Other important sites nearby: Morfa Dyffryn National Nature Reserve (SH 5625) just to the south, has rich dune-slacks with many flowers, including Moonwort and orchids.

121 CADAIR IDRIS	
Location:	5km south-west of Dolgellau, Gwynedd
Grid Reference:	SH 7213; L124
Visiting:	Best early summer. No restrictions, except to some woods. Car park near Minffordd Hotel. Footpath
Terrain:	Mountain, moorland, lake, wood
Specialities:	Mountain birds, mammals and flowers

Cadair Idris is a fine, craggy peak rising to 893m and dominating the countryside of southern Gwynedd. It shows classic glaciated features, with text-book corries (cwms), the

Even though Foxes (Vulpes vulpes) are common in most of the region they are seldom seen, being secretive and largely nocturnal. These are cubs.

main one with towering cliffs rising behind a deep, cold corrie lake (Llyn Cau).

The footpath rises through a moss- and fern-rich oak wood, with Ash, Rowan and Alder. This is the haunt of typical western woodland birds – Buzzard, Redstart, Wood Warbler, Pied Flycatcher and Tree Pipit.

Upland boggy patches have bogmosses, cottongrasses, Round-leaved Sundew and Common Butterwort. On any walk through this countryside it is worth watching the skies and moorland for sight of a Merlin or Raven, whilst the rockier areas have nesting Ring Ousel. Dippers haunt the streams and Common Sandpiper breed close to the lakes.

The most interesting plants here are the Arctic-Alpines such as Purple and Mossy Saxifrages, Moss Campion, and the ferns Green and Forked Spleenwort. Other flowers are Welsh Poppy and Globeflower.

Feral goats can sometimes be spotted on the cliffs and crags and Polecat also inhabit this region, but mainly at lower altitudes.

122 DYFI	
Location:	At mouth of Dyfi (Dovey) estuary, about 16km south-west of Machynlleth
Grid Reference:	SN 6194; L135
Visiting:	Car park, information centre and nature trail at Ynyslas. Public footpaths
Terrain:	Mudflats, saltmarsh, dunes, raised bog
Specialities:	Seabirds, plants

This is an important and very varied reserve with a wealth of characteristic wildlife. It is easy to reach, and makes for a fascinating visit at any season. The sand dunes at Ynyslas have a good range of flowers and put on a good show of orchids in early summer. The estuary attracts plenty of wildfowl in the winter, and the famous raised bog of Cors Fochno (one of Britain's largest) has many special plants.

Towards the sea, the shingle has plants such as Scurvy Grass, Sea Beet and Sea Campion. In the dunes themselves, bound together by Marram Grass and Sea Couch, other species such as Sea Rocket, Sea Spurge, Rest Harrow, Little Mouse-ear and Rue-leaved Saxifrage appear. In the damp dune slacks the orchids emerge – Early Marsh and Northern Marsh, Bee, Pyramidal and Marsh Helleborine. Butterflies here include Grayling and Dark Green Fritillary.

Around 100 Greenland White-fronted Geese arrive on the estuary in October and stay until early April. Other regular wildfowl are Red-breasted Merganser, Shelduck, Pintail, Common Scoter and Goldeneye as well as Red-throated Diver. In late summer it is possible to see Manx Shearwater skimming the waves out over the sea from the coast at Ynyslas. Other birds breeding in the area are Buzzard, Sparrowhawk, Barn Owl and Raven.

Other important sites nearby: Ynys Hir (SN 6896) has bird-rich oakwoods, saltmarsh and bog. Grasshopper Warbler breed here and there are Greenland White-fronted Geese in winter. Badger, Otter and Polecat have also been recorded.

Cors Fochno (Borth Bog) (SN 6392) forms part of above reserve. Access restricted to permit only. Bog Myrtle, Marsh Violet, Round-leaved, Oblong-leaved and Great Sundews. Large Heath butterfly at one of its most southerly sites.

123 DEVIL'S BRIDGE	
Location:	About 16km east of Aberystwyth
Grid Reference:	SN 7477; L135
Visiting:	Car park and footpaths
Terrain:	Rocky gorge, woodland, river
Specialities:	Woodland birds, flowers

The valley of the river Rheidol is very beautiful and well worth exploring, either by car or on the excellent narrow-gauge railway which plies back and forth between Aberystwyth and Devil's Bridge.

Red Kite *Milvus milvus* L 60–70, W 140–165
Only about fifty-five pairs of these magnificent birds of prey breed in Britain, centred in the valleys and hanging oakwoods of central Wales, with recent attempts to introduce them to Scotland and England as well. This graceful, Buzzard-sized bird is unmistakable as it soars over upland moors and woods, revealing its deeply forked tail and angled wings.

At Devil's Bridge itself there is a network of footpaths leading down into the gorge through damp, fern-rich mixed oak woodland. The main trees here are Sessile Oak, Silver Birch and Rowan. Look out for Globeflower and Welsh Poppy. The woods in this area hold good populations of Redstart, Pied Flycatcher, Wood Warbler, Buzzard, Tree Pipit and woodpeckers. In addition, it is worth scanning the skies for a glimpse of a Red Kite, since they often hunt in the vicinity.

Other important sites nearby: Moorland south of Cwmystwyth. About 6km southeast of Devil's Bridge the B4574 forks onto a minor road to Rhyader, following the headwaters of the river Ystwyth. The landscape soon changes to open blanket bog. It is well worth looking in this area (SN 8074) for Red Kite which often glide over the countryside here as single birds or even in small groups. This upland, with its large expanses of bog and rough grassland has the largest Welsh populations of breeding Dunlin and Golden Plover. Other birds to look for here are Raven, Buzzard, Peregrine, Merlin, Hen Harrier, Short-eared Owl, Red Grouse, Wheatear and Ring Ousel.

124 CORS CARON (TREGARON)	
Location:	About 4km north of Tregaron, Dyfed
Grid Reference:	SN 6964; L147
Visiting:	Views from road, but access without permit restricted to one footpath and observation tower. Parking
Terrain:	Raised bog
Specialities:	Bog plants, birds

Cors Caron, which stretches out across the valley of the river Teifi, is almost certainly

the finest raised bog in Wales and England and is gaining ever increasing importance as peatland habitats are steadily disappearing. Unlike many mires however, it is of almost equal interest to botanists and birdwatchers alike, and is close to the heart of Red Kite country.

The vegetation of the bog ranges from wet heath along the margins, to actively growing raised bog at the centre, with hummocks and hollows, to a willow carr bush community. Flowers include Heather, Purple Moor-grass, Cross-leaved Heath, Crowberry, Cranberry, cottongrasses, Bog Asphodel, Bog Rosemary and all three sundews.

Birds breeding here include Water Rail, Moorhen, Coot, Curlew, Redshank, Snipe, Mallard, Teal, Black-headed Gull and Red Grouse. There are also Reed, Sedge and Grasshopper Warblers and Redpolls along the riverbank and in the scrub. Red Kite, Buzzard, Sparrowhawk and Raven occasionally feed over the reserve, particularly in winter, when Peregrine, Merlin and Hen Harrier may also be seen. Whooper Swans also visit in the winter. Other birds to watch for are Barn Owl and Dipper.

The bog also has good populations of mammals, with Otter, Fox, Water Vole and that Welsh speciality the Polecat. Adder, Common Lizard and Slow-worm all occur here as well.

Opposite: the Slow-worm (Anguis fragilis) is a snake-like lizard that lives in a wide range of habitats all over Britain, but is absent from Ireland. If found, a Slow-worm should be handled with care, as if held by the tail the lizard will shed this appendage to make good its escape. A new tail is grown. It is one of the reptiles to be found at Cors Caron.

125 GWENFFRWD/DINAS

Location:	About 12km north of Llandovery, Dyfed
Grid Reference:	SN 7847; L147
Visiting:	Best May–June. Dinas has nature trail. Enquire at Dinas Information Centre for Gwenffrwd
Terrain:	Oakwoods, upland pasture
Specialities:	Red Kite, Peregrine, Merlin, Ring Ousel and other upland birds

These neighbouring reserves contain good examples of so-called hanging oakwoods, growing on the slopes of valleys. This is classic Red Kite breeding country and these splendid birds are occasionally seen in the reserves. However, the visitor is much more likely to see a Buzzard or Sparrowhawk, whilst Peregrine and Merlin are also possibilities, particularly over the adjacent hills and moorland, along with Raven, Ring Ousel and Wheatear.

Kingfisher, Grey Heron, Dipper, Grey Wagtail, Goosander and Common Sandpiper inhabit the rivers and the woods have the usual combination of Redstart, Pied Flycatcher and Wood Warbler.

The woods have a flora rich in mosses and ferns, including Hard Fern, Polypody, Oak Fern, Lady Fern, Lemon-scented Fern and Wilson's Filmy-fern.

Mammals are much more difficult to spot, but include Fox, Badger, Grey and Red Squirrel, and Polecat.

126 ST DAVID'S HEAD

Location:	About 23km south-west of Fishguard, Dyfed
Grid Reference:	SM 7327; L157
Visiting:	Free access
Terrain:	Coastal heath, cliffs
Specialities:	Seabirds, coastal plants

Puffins (Fratercula arctica) are amongst the seabirds breeding on the island of Skomer. At many points on the island they are very tame and can easily be approached and watched bringing fish to and from their nesting burrows. Do not, however, stay too close to their burrows.

St David's Head is popular with tourists because it is easily accessible and gives great views of the coast and out to sea. The cliffs here rise to over 75m and provide breeding ledges for a range of seabirds.

The heath is dominated by Heather, Bell Heather and Western Gorse, and the flowers of the cliffs and coastal grassland include Spring Squill, Cliff Spurrey, Thrift, Sheepsbit, Ox-eye Daisy (dwarf form), Wild Chives, Kidney Vetch, Wall Pepper, Heath Pearlwort and the rare Hairy Greenweed.

Watch the waters below for Grey Seal. They are common in this area and indeed breed in one or two of the more isolated bays.

Birds to look for include Buzzard, Peregrine, Raven, Fulmar, Chough and Rock Pipit. Gannet, Manx Shearwater, Kittiwake, Guillemot and Razorbill can also be seen off-shore.

Other important sites nearby: Ramsey Island, an RSPB reserve (SM 7024), lies just off St David's Head. It has a good colony of Grey Seal, Peregrine and a large Chough population.

127 SKOMER	
Location:	About 17km west of Milford Haven, Dyfed
Grid Reference:	SM 7309; L157
Visiting:	Best April–July. Daily boats in summer form Martin's Haven
Terrain:	Rocky island, grassland, heath, cliffs
Specialities:	Seabirds, especially Manx Shearwater, Puffin, Chough, British Storm-petrel

Skomer is the largest and most accessible of the offshore bird islands of this coast. Boats leave regularly in summer from Martin's Haven and in addition there is a landing fee. Its main claim to fame is the impressive colonies of seabirds, especially the Manx Shearwater population, which stands at over 100,000 pairs. Other seabirds breeding here are British Storm-petrel, Fulmar, Guillemot, Razorbill, Puffin, Kittiwake, Herring, Lesser and Great Black-backed Gulls and Shag.

The cliffs also have Raven, Chough, Buzzard, and Peregrine, and the rough heath has breeding Wheatear, and also both Little and Short-eared Owl.

Although there are so many Manx Shearwater breeding here, it is quite possible to visit during the day and not see a single one. This is because they spend their days out over the open sea, only coming in to their nesting burrows at night. In order to have a 'Shearwater experience', one therefore needs to arrange to stay on the island overnight.

The plants of Skomer are also interesting, and include Tree Mallow, Heath Pearlwort, Rock Sea-spurrey, Sea Beet, Rock Samphire, Thrift, Sea Campion, Sea Squill, Sea Storksbill and Sea Spleenwort.

Grey Seals breed here and can often be spotted, especially around Garland Stone in the north of the island.

Other important sites nearby: Skokholm (SM 7405) has a similar selection of birds, but mostly in smaller numbers. It attracts many migrant birds.

Grassholm (SM 5909) is an isolated rock island best known for its Gannets, which number about 28,600 pairs.

128 STACKPOLE HEAD/BOSHERSTON PONDS	
Location:	About 6km south of Pembroke
Grid Reference:	SR 9895; L158
Visiting:	Mostly accessible
Terrain:	Rocky headland, lake, dunes
Specialities:	Coastal and wetland plants, seabirds

This attractive little complex encompasses an exposed rocky headland, with colonies of seabirds, sheltered sandy coves, and a remarkable drowned valley lake system, with an interesting flora.

The limestone cliffs of Stackpole Head support breeding colonies of Guillemot, Razorbill, Fulmar, Kittiwake and Shag. Other birds to keep an eye open for are Raven, Rock Dove, Chough and the occasional Peregrine. Wheatears are found on the heathy and grassy clifftops.

Cliff flowers here are Sea Campion, Sea and Buckshorn Plantain, Rock Sea-lavender, Sea Pearlwort, Cliff Spurrey, Spring Squill, Golden Samphire, Tormentil, Common Twayblade and the rare Small Restharrow.

The sea thunders against the base of the limestone cliffs at Stackpole Head. The crumbling surfaces provide ideal breeding sites for seabirds, such as Guillemot and Razorbill.

A Kittiwake (Rissa tridactyla) on breeding ledge.

129 OXWICH BAY	
Location:	About 18km south-west of Swansea
Grid Reference:	SS 5187; L159
Visiting:	Footpaths available; otherwise permit required
Terrain:	Shore, dunes, wetland, woodland
Specialities:	Coastal and woodland flowers and birds

Bosherston Lake is an artificial lake which is fed by springs and which rarely freezes over. It has a rather unusual flora, with a good display of water lilies, and species such as Fennel and Curly Pondweed, Spiked Water Milfoil and stoneworts. The margins have Common Reed, Yellow Flag, Purple Loosestrife, Water Mint and Fleabane. Above the lake there is a mixture of limestone grassland with species such as Kidney Vetch, Marjoram and Salad Burnet and heathy patches with Gorse, Bracken and Rosebay Willowherb.

You may see Otter here too and the flash of a Kingfisher.

Oxwich Bay is a prime National Nature Reserve on the fascinating Gower Peninsula, which is within easy reach of Swansea. The area suffers from heavy tourist traffic, especially in summer and on bank holidays and is therefore best avoided at prime times. However, Gower is well worth a visit at any time of year.

A sheltered, sandy bay is backed by a freshwater marsh with a small area of dunes in front. Plants of the marsh include Bulrush and Lesser Bulrush, Flowering Rush, Yellow Flag, Marsh Lousewort, Bogbean, Greater Bird's-foot Trefoil and Lesser Twayblade. The dunes have Marram Grass, Sand Sedge, Sea Holly and Sea Spurge, whilst the slacks are often bright with orchids: Marsh Helle-

Oxwich Wood, Glamorgan, the habitat of a rare whitebeam.

A botanical speciality of the Oxwich area is Yellow Whitlowgrass, which grows nowhere else in Britain. It grows on an old wall near to Oxwich church. Other rarities of the area are Small Restharrow and Goldilocks Aster.

borine, Early and Southern Marsh, Green-winged, Fen and Pyramidal. Other plants of the dune slacks are Creeping Willow and Autumn and Dune Gentian (the latter rare and restricted to this area). On the saltmarsh grow Sea Lavender and Marsh-mallow.

The woods, often pruned by the salty winds, are of Ash and oaks with Small-leaved Lime and the occasional tree of the rare whitebeam, *Sorbus rupicola*.

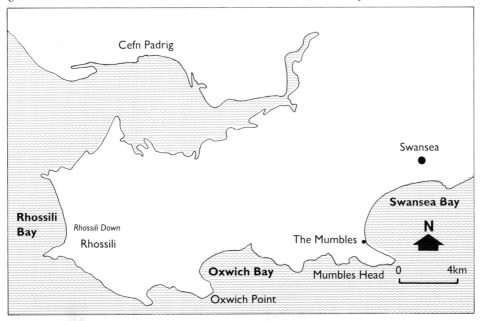

Map of Oxwich Bay and the Gower coast.

In winter, Oxwich Bay attracts Gadwall and Shoveler, with divers and Common Scoter offshore. The rocks around Oxwich Point are a favourite feeding ground for Purple Sandpiper and Turnstone. Breeding birds of the marsh include Water Rail, Teal, Pochard, Reed, Sedge, Grasshopper and Cetti's Warblers. In the woods there are Rooks, Buzzard, Sparrowhawk, woodpeckers and both Marsh and Willow Tits. In spring, Marsh Harrier and Bittern are both fairly regular.

Other important sites on Gower Peninsula: Worm's Head (SS 4088) seabirds. Mumbles (SS 6488) has splendid rock pools and marine fauna. Also rare Hoary Stock.

Port Eynon (SS 4785) for good seabirds and chalk heath flowers.

Llanrhidian Marsh (SS 4894) for wildfowl and waders.

The Black Mountains, Brecon.

BRECON BEACONS NATIONAL PARK

130 CRAIG CERRIG GLEISIAG	
Location:	About 10km south-west of Brecon
Grid Reference:	SN 9723; L160
Visiting:	Access from road. Keep to footpaths. Permit needed off footpaths
Terrain:	Rocky (often dangerous) outcrops, moor, grassland
Specialities:	Upland flowers and birds

This reserve lies at the heart of the National Park and Pen-y-Fan itself is just 5km to the east. The climb is relatively gentle from the road (A470), but it is important to take adequate footwear and water- and wind-proof clothing. There are many areas of craggy

rocks and these have many of the best alpine plants. However, take great care at such sites, because they can be very dangerous.

The vegetation of the upland grassland is dominated by Mat-grass and is rather poor in species. The moorland has Heather and also Bilberry. The main botanical interest lies in the steeper rocks and crags where several arctic-alpine plants grow here near their southern limit in Britain.

Flowers include Purple and Mossy Saxifrages, Green Spleenwort, Parsley Fern, Wilson's Filmy Fern, Globeflower, Northern Bedstraw, Least Willow, Lesser Meadow-rue and Welsh Poppy.

The bird life is rather sparse, but there are typical upland species such as Peregrine, Raven, Buzzard, Ring Ousel, Dipper, Grey Wagtail and Common Sandpiper, and the chance of a Merlin.

131 CRAIG Y CILAU

Location:	About 10km west of Abergavenny
Grid Reference:	SO 1916; L161
Visiting:	By footpath from roads
Terrain:	Limestone and sandstone areas, caves, woods, bog
Specialities:	Rich flora, with Alpines

This site provides a good contrast with the previous one, since it consists largely of a limestone plateau. There are also acid sandstone areas, scrubby woodland, and a bog.

The top of the plateau has millstone grit and supports rough upland grassland and Heather moor, with Bilberry and Crowberry as well.

However, the most interesting flowers are to be found on the limestone crags and cliffs. Here you can see Harebell, Angular

Solomon's Seal, Alpine Enchanter's Nightshade, Mossy Saxifrage, Mountain Melick, Limestone Polypody, Brittle Bladder Fern and Green Spleenwort.

On slightly deeper soils, there are remnants of mixed woodland and scrub, with oak, birch, Wych Elm, Small- and Large-leaved Lime, Beech and Yew. These woods are particularly special as the habitat of four rare whitebeams, including the very rare *Sorbus minima*.

Below the slope is a good example of a raised bog, with fine displays of cottongrasses, Cross-leaved Heath and Round-leaved Sundew.

Peregrine, Buzzard, Raven, Ring Ousel, Wheatear and Whinchat may be seen around the crags or on the moorland, and Redstart, Wood and Willow Warbler, Pied Flycatcher and Tree Pipit in the woodland. The streams have Grey Wagtail and Dipper.

Mammals include Badger, Fox, and, in the caves, hibernating Lesser Horseshoe Bat.

West end of Craig y Cilau, Brecon. Remnants of rich mixed woodland cling to the lower slopes of this reserve.

13. THE ISLAND OF IRELAND

Ireland has a wet climate, but rather mild winters, especially in the south and west. Wetlands dominate in the natural habitats, whether these be the myriad estuaries, lakes and streams, or the extensive areas of sedge and reed, or the large areas of blanket and raised bog, so well developed over much of the interior.

Very little woodland remains in Ireland, most of it having been cleared centuries ago. Where it does remain, it is usually either of oak and birch, with Holly, or dominated by Ash and elm.

There are fine colonies of seabirds, notably Manx Shearwater and British Storm-petrel, on coastal cliffs and islands, and the wetlands attract large flocks of wildfowl and

The Red Squirrel (Sciurus vulgaris) is still more widespread in Ireland than the Grey Squirrel.

waders, among them many thousands of Greenland White-fronted, Pale-bellied Brent and Barnacle Geese. In addition, over 60 per cent of Iceland's Whooper Swans winter in Ireland.

The Irish flora is most famous for its so-called 'Lusitanian' element, comprising a group of species which are almost absent from Britain and which are characteristic of the extreme Atlantic fringe of Europe and west Mediterranean. The best known of these is the Strawberry Tree, still found scattered in the Killarney woods in the south-west. Other members of this group are St Dabeoc's Heath, locally common in Connemara, and Irish Heath, which grows in western Galway and western Mayo. The Dense-flowered Orchid is widespread in the Mediterranean and is here confined to the west of Ireland (except for a single locality in the Isle of Man). Another is the fine Large-flowered Butterwort, locally common in South-west Ireland, but a mountain plant in North-west Spain, the Pyrenees and the French Alps. Two saxifrages, St Patrick's Cabbage and Kidney Saxifrage, are also Lusitanian species which are locally common in South-west Ireland. Finally, Cottonweed, a plant of coastal sand and shingle can be found in one locality in Wexford.

The numerous bogs, especially in the Central Plain, have a restricted flora, but some characteristic plants which are rare in Britain are still quite widespread there. Good examples are the Lesser and Intermediate Bladderworts. Another insectivorous plant, in this case only found in this region in Ireland, is the introduced and strange-looking Pitcher Plant, which grows abundantly on some of these bogs.

NORTHERN IRELAND

The natural history of Northern Ireland, not unexpectedly, has more in common with that of the Irish Republic than that of Britain. It has an imposing coastline with interesting geology, part-icularly around the famous Giant's Causeway, with its step-like columns of basalt. This varied country with its long coast is an ideal habitat for birds such as the Peregrine which often hunts along the shore and selects rocky crags or cliffs for nesting. Elsewhere, the landscape is hilly, with many rivers, loughs and inlets. One of the finest estuaries is Strangford Lough, which attracts large numbers of waders and wildfowl, particularly in winter. The coastal dune systems are also well-developed and have a rich flora.

Northern Ireland is host to a small number of Roseate Tern colonies. This seabird is now endangered internationally and is carefully protected wherever possible.

132 PEATLANDS COUNTRY PARK	
Location:	About 15km north of Armagh, close to south-west shore of Lough Neagh
Visiting:	Car park and information centre
Terrain:	Woodland, bog, lake
Specialities:	Wetland plants, insects

This country park incorporates woodland, bog and lake, around Derryadd Lough. The lake itself is attractive to waterfowl, including diving ducks, particularly in the winter. However, it is perhaps best known for its mire habitats, with typical bog plants. Part of the mire complex is a classic quaking bog, developed over a lake margin.

The boggy areas contain plants such as bogmosses and cottongrasses, along with Bilberry, Bog Myrtle, Bog Rosemary, bladderworts and sundews.

At Mulenakill reserve, within the park, the bog has stands of Royal Fern, with Cranberry, Bog Asphodel, Cow-wheat and Marsh Clubmoss. This is also a site for the Large Heath, a classic bog butterfly whose caterpillars feed on cottongrasses.

To the north of Derryadd Lough lies Annagarriff Wood. This area of woodland and bog has Silver-washed and Marsh Fritillaries and Green Hairstreak. Birds of the wood include Woodcock and Long-eared Owl.

The Wood Mouse (Apodymus sylvaticus) *is the only native small rodent found in Ireland.*

The Mute Swan (Cygnus olor) is the heaviest of flying birds and is common on large bodies of water, such as Lough Neagh.

133 OXFORD ISLAND

Location:	Just north of Lurgan, on south-east shore of Lough Neagh
Visiting:	Parking and footpath, information, hides
Terrain:	Lake, reedbeds, hay-meadow, woods
Specialities:	Water birds

This reserve is centred on a peninsula in Lough Neagh, the largest freshwater lake in Britain and Ireland. The lough itself is one of the best places in Ireland for seeing waterfowl and other waterbirds and can be viewed easily from surrounding roads.

Hay-meadows close to the shore have a rich marsh flora with attractive flowers such as Ragged Robin, Yellow Rattle and Common Spotted Orchid. In May or June the rasping call of the Corncrake can still be heard in some of these hay-meadows, although the birds themselves are rather difficult to spot.

Amongst the waterfowl to be found here, and elsewhere on Lough Neagh, are Shoveler, Wigeon, Teal, Gadwall, Tufted Duck, Pochard, Goldeneye, Pintail, Shelduck, Redbreasted Merganser and Mute, Whooper and

Bewick's Swans. The latter two visit the reserve in autumn and winter and often graze on fields to the south of the peninsula.

Lough Neagh is also a stronghold of nesting Great Crested and Little Grebes. Other birds breeding in the area are Grey Heron, Water Rail, Common Sandpiper, Oystercatcher, Redshank, Ringed Plover, Common Tern and Black-headed, Herring and Great and Lesser Black-backed Gulls.

The mammals include Otter and Mountain (Irish) Hare.

134 STRANGFORD LOUGH	
Location:	Between Newtownards and Downpatrick, to the south-east of Belfast
Visiting:	Spring and early summer for breeding birds; winter for wildfowl. Good views from A20 on eastern shore; several reserves, many hides
Terrain:	Sea-lough with large tidal range; mudflats
Specialities:	Seabirds, including Roseate Tern

Strangford Lough is one of the most important natural history sites in Northern Ireland. It is an inlet of the Irish Sea, but is connected by a narrow channel to the open sea and has a wide tidal range. This means that at each tide, large expanses of mud are exposed, revealing a splendid feeding ground for waders and wildfowl. In addition, the lough has many small islands, particularly on the west side, which provide good breeding grounds for many species. The international rarity and local speciality, the Roseate Tern, also breeds in the area, but the colonies are mostly rather small and isolated.

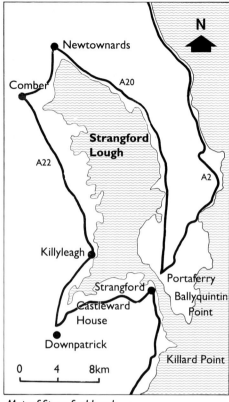

Map of Strangford Lough.

Breeding birds include Redshank, Oystercatcher, Ringed Plover, Shelduck, Tufted Duck, Great Crested and Little Grebes, Red-breasted Merganser, Common, Arctic, Sandwich and Roseate Terns, and Black-headed, Lesser and Great Black-backed, Herring and Common Gulls. Other birds to watch out for are Hooded Crow, Buzzard, Sparrowhawk, Short-eared Owl, Rock Pipit and Black Guillemot.

In winter, the lough attracts large numbers of pale-bellied Brent Geese (maximum 14,500), along with smaller numbers of White-fronted and Greylag, and Mute and Whooper Swans. Joining the huge numbers

181

of Wigeon are Red-breasted Merganser, Goldeneye, Common Scoter and Scaup. Waders are well represented too with Lapwing, Knot, Golden Plover, Oystercatcher, Dunlin, Curlew and Redshank.

Common Seal and Otter can be spotted in the lough, and Porpoises are sometimes seen.

Some important sites on Strangford Lough: Quoile Pondage is a good spot to see wintering geese. Castleward might give views of Roseate Tern. North Strangford Lough: views over mudflats. Castle Espie: good wader and wildfowl watching from hides

135 KILLARD	
Location:	Near Kilclief, about 12km east of Downpatrick
Visiting:	Spring, early summer; winter for migrant seabirds
Terrain:	Grassland, dunes, heath, low cliffs
Specialities:	Coastal flowers, insects and birds

Killard is a fascinating reserve with a good range of coastal habitats, from views out over the open sea, to rocky shore to rich calcareous dune grassland and heath.

Breeding birds include Sand Martin and Fulmar on the cliffs, Shelduck and Common, Arctic and Sandwich Terns.

In winter, there are Guillemot and Razorbill offshore, with occasional Long-tailed Duck and Common Scoter. Waders visiting the reserve in winter include Purple Sandpiper, Turnstone, Golden and Ringed Plover.

Mountain (Irish) Hare can be seen on the grassland and seals often lurk near the rocky bays around Killard Point.

Roseate Tern *Sterna dougallii* L 38
This graceful seabird is restricted mainly to small rocky islands off the coasts of Britain and Ireland. The total population stands at only about 300 pairs, with important sites including Carlingford Lough and certain nearby islands. Differs from Common and Arctic Terns in having an almost entirely black bill (red at base only) and longer tail streamers. Adults have a slight pink flush on the breast in spring, hence the name.

The vegetation of the grassy dune sand is very rich, with Lady's Bedstraw, Spring Squill, and many orchids, such as Bee, Frog, Early Marsh and Northern Marsh, Pyramidal and Green-winged. The grassland is also a good spot for butterflies with Common Blue, Painted Lady and Grayling.

Other important sites nearby: Nearby Gun's Island has tern colonies, with Common and Arctic in approximately equal numbers, and a very small number of Roseate Tern as well.

Other sites nearby: Green Island/Greencastle Point near the border with the Republic of Ireland, has colonies of terns – about 450 Common, 280 Sandwich, sixty Arctic and forty Roseate.

136 MAGILLIGAN POINT	
Location:	About 17km north-west of Coleraine
Visiting:	Only partly open to public; otherwise permit needed
Terrain:	Mudflats and dunes
Specialities:	Dune flowers; seabirds

This reserve, at the mouth of Lough Foyle, has a complete series of dunes, from open shifting sand, through lightly colonized dunes to stable fixed dunes and grassland further inland. There are many colourful plants here, including pearlwort, Adder's Tongue and Grass-of-Parnassus.

In winter, the estuary attracts wildfowl and waders, including over 25,000 Wigeon and about 1,000 pale-bellied Brent Geese, which can be seen feeding out on the mudflats. There are also good views out to sea, with birds such as auks and divers. Watch out over the channel for Great Northern and Red-throated Divers, Black Guillemot and sea ducks.

Other important sites nearby: The Umbra lies close by. It has fine dunes with plants such as Sea Centaury and Moonwort. Also good for butterflies, with Grayling and Marsh, Dark Green and Silver-washed Fritillaries.

Lough Foyle is an area of saltmarsh and mudflats with large numbers of wintering wildfowl and waders, including Pale-bellied Brent and White-fronted Geese, Whooper and Bewick's Swans, Curlew and Bar-tailed Godwit.

Roe Valley Country Park (just south of Limavady) has beautiful valley walks, with woodland flowers and birds.

137 RATHLIN ISLAND	
Location:	Island off the north-east tip of Ireland, north of Ballycastle
Visiting:	By boat from Ballycastle
Terrain:	Steep cliffs, rocky coves, grassland
Specialities:	Seabirds, such as Black Guillemot; flowers

The main attraction of the island is the healthy colonies of seabirds, especially on the cliffs around the West Lighthouse, where they are particularly visible. Cliff-nesters here are Kittiwake (about 6,500 pairs), Fulmar (about 1,250), Guillemot (about 20,000), Razorbill (about 9,000), Shag (about 100), and Black Guillemot (about fifty). Rathlin also has good numbers of all six regularly breeding British gulls.

On the grassy slopes above the northern cliffs there are Puffin (about 3,000) and also Manx Shearwater (about 300). Gannet and skuas are occasionally seen flying over the sea

Common Blue (Polyommatus icarus) on Gorse. This pretty butterfly is common on rough grassland and heaths, throughout Ireland and Britain.

near the island, as are petrels and the rarer Sooty Shearwater.

Other bird specialities of Rathlin Island are Peregrine (several pairs breed here), Chough, Raven and Buzzard, the latter surprisingly scarce over much of Ireland.

The flowers here include eyebrights and Yellow Rattle on the hay-meadows, and Harebell, Bird's-foot Trefoil and Spring Squill on shorter grassland. There are also orchids, including Heath Spotted, Fragrant and Lesser Butterfly, and the area west of Kebble Lough is a good spot to look for these.

Other important sites nearby: Carrick-a-Rede Island, near the mainland opposite Rathlin Island, also has splendid seabird colonie plus Peregrine, Raven and Chough.

Fair Head has cliffs, woodland, and moorland loughs which attract wintering Whooper Swan, Snow Bunting and Twite.

138 THE GIANT'S CAUSEWAY	
Location:	About 16km west of Ballycastle
Visiting:	Car park and causeway
Terrain:	Cliffs, heath, grassland
Specialities:	Amazing geology, fossils; birds

The Giant's Causeway, designated a World Heritage Site, is justly famous for its remarkable hexagonal columns of basalt, which are arranged in a rather step-like formation. Some of these columns are over 12m tall. There are also interesting fossils in some of the rocks here.

Benbane Head, just to the east, has breeding Fulmar, Kittiwake, Shag, Black Guillemot and Rock Pipit. Peregrine, Chough and Rock Dove may all be seen here, and from the cliff-top path. The cliffs also provide a good vantage point for sea-watching. Birds to watch for over or in the sea are Gannet, Manx Shearwater, Guillemot, Razorbill, Eider, and, in winter, divers. Turnstone and Purple Sandpiper feed on the rocks in autumn and winter.

Plants include Spring Squill, Frog Orchid and Sea Spleenwort.

Other important sites nearby: The Bann Estuary, just north-west of Coleraine, has good views over mudflats. It attracts many waders.

The bizarre columns of basalt have made the Giant's Causeway famous as a geological curiosity.

IRISH REPUBLIC

The central part of the Irish Republic is dominated by wetlands and bogs, and by gently undulating hills. Elsewhere, particularly in the west, there are higher hills and an intricate coastline with many islands and inlets. Much of this country is sparsely populated and therefore the wildlife is relatively undisturbed.

Three areas stand out as part-icularly noteworthy: the south-west, around Killarney, with its woodlands and lakes; the very unusual limestone pavement of the Burren with its natural rock-gardens, and the open lakes, shores and hills of Connemara.

The traditional hay-meadows and fields of the west coast and islands recall those of the Outer Hebrides, and similarly hold interesting species, including the elusive and elsewhere rather rare Corncrake. The Chough is another rare species which is still to be seen around the Irish coast, part-icularly in the west and north.

Another rare bird found in both Northern Ireland and the Republic is the beautiful Roseate Tern. One of the largest colonies in

Strawberry Tree (Arbutus unedo) *The fruits of this mainly Mediterranean species inspire its common name.*

Europe, about 300 pairs, is to be found on the tiny rocky island of Rockabill, about 7km off the east coast.

This region is important as the main wintering ground for the Greenland White-fronted Goose, Barnacle Goose and also for the pale-breasted form of the Brent Goose.

FIFTY INTERESTING SPECIES TO LOOK FOR

Barnacle Goose	Whooper Swan	Intermediate	Royal Fern
Brent Goose (pale-	Otter	Butterwort	St Dabeoc's Heath
breasted form)	Mountain (Irish) Hare	Irish Heath	St Patrick's Cabbage
British Storm-petrel	Pine Marten	Irish Lady's Tresses	Strawberry Tree
Chough	Red Squirrel	Irish St John's Wort	Brown Hairstreak
Corncrake	Stoat	Irish Saxifrage	Dark-green Fritillary
Hooded Crow	Blue-eyed Grass	Irish Spurge	Large Heath
Leach's Storm-petrel	Cottonweed	Kerry Lily	Marsh Fritillary
Manx Shearwater	Curved-leafed	Kidney Saxifrage	Pearl-bordered
Merlin	Sandwort	Large-flowered	Fritillary
Peregrine	Dense-flowered	Butterwort	Silver-washed Fritillary
Puffin	Orchid	Lesser Bladderwort	Wood White
Roseate Tern	Filmy Ferns	Mackay's Heath	
White-fronted Goose	Forked Spleenwort	Pipewort	
(Greenland race)	Hydrilla	Pitcher Plant	

139 GLENVEAGH NATIONAL PARK	
Location:	22km west of Letterkenny, Donegal
Visiting:	Open all year. Nature trail
Terrain:	Upland moor, woodland, bog
Specialities:	Moorland birds and flowers

This National Park, at the north-east end of Lough Veagh, is relatively recent, having been founded in 1984. It covers an area of about 9,700ha and incorporates open water of the lake, heather moor, upland grassland, bog and sheltered woods. Glenveagh Castle, which dates from 1870, stands in an imposing position on a headland overlooking the lough and is surrounded by a splendid garden. The garden is well-known for its collection of plants which includes many unusual frost-sensitive species, especially from Chile, Tasmania and Madeira.

Elsewhere, the natural woodland is dominated by oaks and birch. It is damp and rich in ferns, including filmy ferns, and mosses. Woodland birds here include Redstart, Wood Warbler and Siskin. On the hillsides, typical plants are Heather, Tormentil and Purple Moor-grass, with species such as Bog Asphodel in wetter sites. The open moorland has a managed herd of Red Deer and a good population of Red Grouse, as well as other upland and moorland birds such as Raven, Peregrine, Merlin and Stonechat.

Other important sites nearby: Lough Nacung, to the west of the Derryveagh Mountains, has a fine bog around the lake margin. This is a good locality for Mackay's Heath, and has other rarities including Waterwort and Blue-eyed Grass.

140 BENBULBIN	
Location:	About 12km north of Sligo
Visiting:	Road up as far as the mine
Terrain:	Rocky upland, cliffs
Specialities:	Flowers

Benbulbin lies in the Dartry Mountains, a range of mountains lying north of Sligo on the southern shore of Donegal Bay. Like the Burren, it has a fine range of interesting plants, but because it reaches a much higher altitude (Benbulben is 525m), there are more Arctic-Alpines here.

The limestone cliffs cover a large area and not all of the special plants are easy to find. However, two areas are well worth concentrating on. Annacoona cliffs, near Gleniff, and the rocky outcrops above Glenade.

Plants here include Roseroot, Moss Campion, Alpine Meadow-rue, Irish Sandwort, Northern Rock-cress, Mountain Avens, Mountain Scurvy-grass, Hoary Whitlow-grass, Mountain Sorrel, Alpine Bistort, Holly Fern and Green Spleenwort.

The saxifrages include Yellow, Mossy and Purple, and the rare Alpine Saxifrage, unknown elsewhere in Ireland. There is also a distinctive local form of Irish Eyebright.

Other important sites nearby: Slieve League, at the opposite side of Donegal Bay, is a dramatic mountain with steep sea-cliffs, inland crags and well developed blanket bog. It boasts one of the best Arctic-Alpine floras in Ireland. Flowers here include Mountain Avens, Purple, Starry and Yellow Saxifrages, Green Spleenwort and Holly Fern.

Close to Slieve League lies the small island of Rathlin O'Birne. This has about 1,000 pairs of British Storm-petrel, and possibly Leach's Storm-petrel as well.

141 CONNEMARA NATIONAL PARK	
Location:	In County Galway, about 80km from Galway
Visiting:	Open all year. Best spring and summer. Information centre and nature trails
Terrain:	Woodland, poor grassland, moor, blanket bog
Specialities:	Upland birds and flowers

This National Park, just south of Letterfrack, is situated on the northern slopes of the Twelve Bens (or Pins) of Connemara, a group of mountains which rise to 730m, dominating the landscape of Connemara.

This is a good place to see the special local plants of the blanket bogs, which cover so much of the countryside in this part of Ireland. Along with commoner bog plants such as Bell Heather, Cross-leaved Heath, Bog Myrtle, sundews, cottongrasses, Lousewort and Bog Asphodel, a special species here is St Dabeoc's Heath which has its north European outpost in this part of Ireland and is not found elsewhere in Ireland or Britain. The mountains have Purple Saxifrage, Alpine Meadow-rue and Holly Fern. The grass-like Pipewort grows in some of the loughs – it is otherwise found only on Skye and Coll in the British Isles.

Mammals of the park include Red Deer (re-introduced), Badger, Fox and Stoat. The famous Connemara ponies also roam in this area.

Amongst the birds breeding here are Stonechat, Meadow Pipit, Snipe and Woodcock, and birds of prey are well represented, with Kestrel, Sparrowhawk, Merlin and Peregrine.

Other important sites nearby: Errisbeg Bog is a fine blanket bog. Here you can find common bog plants, together with more unusual species such as Dorset Heath (rare in Ireland) and the rare Mackay's and Irish Heaths. Errisbeg Mountain also has Forked Spleenwort, a rare fern. Merlin are frequent.

Lake and blanket bog, with the Twelve Bens in the background, Connemara.

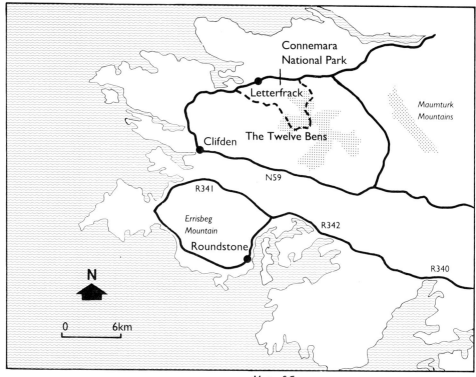

Map of Connemara.

142 THE BURREN

Location:	South shore of Galway Bay, County Clare
Visiting:	Spring–summer; best late May
Terrain:	Limestone pavement
Specialities:	Flowers

The Burren is one of the most outstanding botanical areas in Europe. The great slabs and humps of limestone which rear up from the flat land around ('Burren' means 'great rock'), are weathered into ridges and clefts which are colonized by a fascinating array of flowers. The interest lies partly in the fact that the conditions here allow Arctic-Alpine species to survive and flourish alongside more southern species, creating a beautiful array of often colourful flowers arranged in places almost as in a rock-garden. Small wonder that naturalists travel long distances to admire the plants of the Burren. Indeed, it is almost unthinkable to plan a visit to the west of Ireland without allowing time to browse here.

Bloody Cranesbill is a beautiful Burren flower, found nowhere else in Ireland. Other notable flowers here are Spring Gentian, Mountain Avens, Hoary Rock-rose, Irish and Mossy Saxifrage and the rare orchid Irish Lady's Tresses. The damper crevices have many ferns, including Maidenhair Fern.

The Burren has a distinct pale form of the Grayling. Other butterfly specialities here are

The limestone pavements of the Burren rise up from the surrounding flatter fields. They support a wonderfully rich flora.

143 LITTLE BROSNA RIVER	
Location:	Near Birr, County Offaly
Visiting:	Winter
Terrain:	Flooded meadows
Specialities:	Winter wildfowl, such as Whooper Swan and White-fronted Goose, and waders

Pearl-bordered and Marsh Fritillaries, Wood White, Brown Hairstreak, Dingy Skipper and Small Blue. The latter is much more common in Ireland than in Britain.

Other important sites nearby: Cliffs of Moher, on coast to south-west of Burren. Long, steep cliffs (to 230m) with bird colonies: Kittiwake, Fulmar, Guillemot, Razorbill, Puffin and Shag. Also Peregrine and Chough.

Fanore Dunes, north of Lisdoonvarna has dune and limestone pavement flora, with orchids. Chough.

Poulavallan (woodland), near Carran, is a fine Burren Hazel wood with many ferns.

This river, which is a tributary of the Shannon, forms the border between Tipperay and Offaly, in the centre of Ireland. The river marshes here are used for hay-making and for grazing livestock. In winter, large stretches are flooded, providing attractive feeding grounds for a wide range of migrant birds.

There are Mute and Whooper Swans, which peak at around 200 of each, about 350 Greenland White-fronted Geese, and large numbers of Wigeon, Teal, Pintail and

Chough *Pyrrhocorax pyrrhocorax* L 40
This crow breeds on rocky coasts in the west of Ireland and also in Wales, the Isle of Man and Scotland, but its population is now down to only about 300 pairs, with encouraging signs of a slight recent upturn. It is an acrobatic and noisy Jackdaw-sized bird with a bright-red, long, curved bill and red legs. Choughs need rocky cliffs and crags for nesting and adjacent open rough grazing land for feeding.

Shoveler. The waders are interesting too, with flocks of Golden Plover, Lapwing, Dunlin, Black-tailed Godwit and Curlew.

Other important sites nearby: Mongan's Bog, near Clonmacnoise, is one of the finest raised bogs in Ireland.

Clara Bog is another good raised bog, with associated mineral-rich lakes. Flowers include Royal Fern, Bogbean, cottongrasses, marsh orchids and Marsh Pennywort.

144 NORTH BULL ISLAND

Location:	In the north of Dublin Bay
Visiting:	Access by causeway. Visitor centre
Terrain:	Dunes, saltmarsh, mudflats
Specialities:	Wildfowl, such as Brent Goose, waders, nesting Little Tern

This island, which is about 1km wide and 5km long, is one of the best places to see wildfowl and waders, and is also easily accessible from Dublin.

Many of the species which feed nearby or elsewhere in Dublin Bay use the island for roosting. This is a major wintering area for pale-bellied Brent Geese, which gather here in large numbers (up to about 2,000). Other wildfowl include Shelduck, Wigeon, Pintail and Shoveler.

The waders to watch out for here are Redshank, Oystercatcher, Knot, Dunlin, Black- and Bar-tailed Godwits, Curlew, Grey Plover and Sanderling. There are also Little Terns nesting at this site.

The Mountain (Irish) Hare is common on the grassland and saltmarsh.

Other important sites nearby: Broad Lough, to the north of Wicklow. This is a shingle ridge with lagoons and marshes behind. The reedbeds in this area have Ireland's only breeding Bearded Tits. Little Tern also breed, and wintering species include Greylag Goose, Bewick's and Whooper Swans, Golden Plover and Curlew. Little Gulls are regular passage migrants.

145 WEXFORD WILDFOWL RESERVE	
Location:	North and south sides of Wexford harbour
Visiting:	Open all year. Car park
Terrain:	Mudflats, grassland, channels, reedbeds
Specialities:	Wildfowl

146 KILLARNEY NATIONAL PARK	
Location:	Around Lough Leane just south-west of Killarney, County Kerry
Visiting:	Access from roads
Terrain:	Mixed woods, open water, bog, moorland
Specialities:	Rich flora with several local species

Wexford Wildfowl Reserve, often referred to as Wexford Slobs, is Ireland's best wildfowl reserve. The reserve consists of grassland which has been reclaimed from the sea, on either side of Wexford harbour. There are mudflats, and many drainage ditches and channels cross the fields.

The main interest of this reserve lies in the large numbers of wintering wildfowl and waders. The star species is the Greenland White-fronted Goose, for which this is the single most important wintering ground in the world. The White-fronts gather here in enormous numbers – to a maximum of about 11,000. Other species include pale-bellied Brent Geese (up to 2,000), Bewick's and Whooper Swans, Wigeon, Teal, Shoveler, Pintail, Goldeneye and Scaup (peak in January). More rarely, Barnacle, Pink-footed and Snow Geese turn up. Divers, grebes and Common Scoter are seen on the sea nearby.

Waders include Lapwing, Golden Plover, Oystercatcher, Black- and Bar-tailed Godwit, Curlew, Dunlin, Redshank and Spotted Redshank.

In winter, birds of prey are a regular feature, with Hen Harrier, Kestrel, Sparrowhawk, Peregrine and Merlin.

Other important sites nearby: The Raven is the point just to the east. It has well-developed dunes and pine plantations. Birds include Sparrowhawk and Long-eared Owl. There are Red Squirrels and Irish Hare.

The beautiful mountainous peninsulas of County Kerry jut out into the Atlantic forming Europe's furthest westerly points, well to the west of Portugal! The sea bathing this coast is mild, endowing Kerry with the most oceanic climate in the whole of Britain and Ireland. Rainfall is high and bogs are a prominent feature of the landscape here, but the weather changes often and sunny periods come and go quickly.

The Killarney National Park preserves a special mixture of typical habitats, from open lough, to blanket bog, river, valley woods and rocky upland. The damp mixed oakwoods around the lakes have Yew and Holly, but also the famous Strawberry Tree, a Mediterranean species with characteristic strawberry-like fruits. These woods have a very rich moss and fern flora as well. Other rare or local plants of this area are St Patrick's Cabbage, Blue-eyed Grass, Pipewort, Irish Spurge, Kerry Lily and Large-flowered Butterwort.

Mammals of the region include native and introduced Red Deer, introduced Sika Deer, feral Mink, Irish (Mountain) Hare, Stoat, and Pine Marten, the latter more common here than elsewhere in Ireland and Britain. Ireland's only toad, the Natterjack, occurs around the head of Dingle Bay.

The butterflies here include Marsh and

Silver-washed Fritillaries, Purple and Green Hairstreaks, Large Heath and Wood White.

The large spotted Kerry Slug is an impressive local mollusc. It is a southern species found also in Spain and Portugal.

Other important sites nearby: Glengarriff Woodland, near Glengarriff, has Strawberry Tree and many ferns, including filmy ferns.

Large-Flowered Butterwort
Pinguicula grandiflora
A visit to south-west Ireland in June cannot fail to yield for the botanist one of Ireland's special treasures, the Large-Flowered Butterwort. This bigger and better relative of the Common Butterwort, a widespread plant of boggy places in Britain and Ireland, is happily quite common in parts of Cork and Kerry, and is found north to County Clare. As in the Common Butterwort, the plant has a rosette of pale green, sticky leaves which trap and digest small insects. The flower stalks which grow from the centre of the rosette each have a solitary violet two-lipped flower, in this species as much as 3.5cm across. Large-Flowered Butterwort is a Lusitanian species, also found in Spain and Portugal.

147 DINGLE PENINSULA	
Location:	Peninsula to the west of Tralee, County Kerry
Terrain:	Cliffs, shore, lake, bog, dunes
Specialities:	Seabirds, wildfowl, dune flowers

This peninsula is one of Ireland's most beautiful, with sharply contrasting landscapes all within a comparatively small area. It also has many of the region's characteristic habitats and species, making it an ideal area for the naturalist to explore.

The sheltered bays of Tralee, to the north, and Castlemaine Harbour, at the upper end of Dingle Bay to the south, have rich sand dunes, saltmarsh and mudflats.

Lough Gill, on the east side of Brandon Bay, is a very shallow freshwater lake, with a fringing reedbed. It has dunes to one side and peaty areas on the other, giving it a rather distinctive character. It holds a large colony of Natterjack toads.

The lake attracts winter wildfowl, including Mute, Whooper and Bewick's Swans, Wigeon, Teal, Shoveler, Pochard, Tufted Duck and Coot. Choughs, with their long, red down-curved beaks, are often seen in this area. The dunes here are some of the richest in Ireland for their flora. The Magharee Islands, just north of the lake, have colonies of Cormorant and Shag, and also Common, Arctic and Little Terns. In winter, about 300 Barnacle Geese visit from their northern breeding grounds.

Other important sites nearby: Blasket Islands, which are a group of five rocky islands off Slea Head, have over 40,000 pairs of British Storm-petrel, and also Puffin and Manx Shearwater.

148 THE SKELLIGS

Location:	Islands about 12km off the coast of County Kerry
Visiting:	Arrangement only, by boat from Valencia Island. Best April–August
Terrain:	Rocky island with cliffs
Specialities:	Seabird colonies

Skellig Michael and nearby Little Skellig are famous for their large numbers of breeding seabirds. Skellig Michael, the larger of the two, is an extraordinary island, with its ancient derelict cathedral and stone steps, and is a safe breeding ground for thousands of seabirds. The crevices in the rocks and around the steps are occupied by British Storm-petrel, Manx Shearwater and Puffin. Estimates of their numbers are difficult, but there are thought to be well over 10,000 pairs of British Storm-petrels, 6,500 Puffins and 5,000 Manx Shearwaters, although this could well be a considerable underestimate.

Little Skellig is home to about 22,000 pairs of Gannets, making this one of the largest colonies in Britain and Ireland.

Other breeding birds of the islands include Kittiwake, Guillemot and Razorbill.

Other important sites nearby: Puffin Island lies much closer to the mainland at the north end of St Finan's Bay. Along with its Puffins (about 10,000 pairs) it has probably Ireland's largest Manx Shearwater colony (up to 20,000 pairs) and about 4,000 pairs of British Storm-petrels.

Yellow Horned-poppy (Glaucium flavum). *This attractive shingle plant is rather rare in Ireland. It also grows around the coasts of Wales and southern England.*

193

SECTION III:
FIELD GUIDE TO COMMONER
ANIMALS AND PLANTS

INTRODUCTION

This part of the book offers a concise guide to some of the species most likely to be seen in Britain or Ireland when visiting many of the sites described in Section II.

The species illustrated represent only a small selection of the total flora and fauna of the region, but they do include a good range of some of the commoner animals and plants likely to be encountered. In no sense is this section intended to replace a good, detailed field guide, many of which are now available (*see* Bibliography). Rather, it offers an introduction to the species, which should lead the reader on to study the plants and animals in greater detail.

The groups chosen are those which are most prominent and are likely to be of most immediate interest to the amateur, non-specialist visitor with an interest in general natural history. For this reason, only birds, mammals, reptiles, amphibians, butterflies and flowers are covered here. The wildlife of the region is, however, much richer, and many other groups (such as dragonflies, beetles, spiders and fungi) are equally fascinating and worthy of study. In the site entries, some other groups of animals are occasionally mentioned if the site in question is particularly well known for them. I hope that many readers of this introductory account will go on to deepen their know-

ledge, and therefore their appreciation, of the British Isles' rich wildlife by consulting and becoming familiar with more comprehensive identification guide books.

The descriptions given here follow a standard pattern, with the common name and Latin name given first. These are followed by the length (or height) in centimetres, brief details of the main characteristics used to identify the animal or plant, with notes on its distribution and the habitats in which it is most likely to be seen. Also, particularly for the birds, whether it is a resident breeder or a winter or summer visitor is indicated. The description also indicates if there are similar species with which confusion is possible.

With the aid of these illustrations and notes, the reader should be able to identify some of our the widespread and familiar animals and plants. However, only practice, regular field work and the use of a detailed field guide or flora can give you the knowledge required to name most species you will encounter when visiting a reserve or other wildlife site.

ABBREVIATIONS
L = length in centimetres
H = height in centimetres
F = flowering time (e.g. May–July)
W = wingspan in millimetres

Birds:
R = resident
S = summer visitor
W = winter visitor

Opposite: *a Small White* (Pieris rapae) *on a Fragrant Orchid* (Gymnadenea conopsea).

195

Fulmar *Fulmarus glacialis* **L 46**
A bird of the open seas and sea cliffs, usually spotted gliding on stiff wings over nesting cliffs, with occasional shallow wingbeats. Gull-like in size and colour but method of flight is very distinctive. Locally common at colonies on off-shore islands or at coast. Found all over British Isles, but commonest in north. R.

Cormorant *Phalacrocorax carbo* **L 86**
Hunched black seabird, seen almost exclusively at the coast, although occasionally inland as well, especially in winter. Often perches motionless on rocks, sometimes with wings half open. Swims very low in water, like a diver and submerges regularly to search for fish. Shag is similar, but smaller and is found mainly in the north and west of region. R.

Grey Heron *Ardea cinerea* **L 95**
Large and widespread stately bird found in wetlands throughout the region. Stands still in shallow fresh or sea water and lunges for fish, frogs etc. Flies with slow, deliberate heavy wingbeats with neck tucked into the body and long legs trailing behind. Young birds lack eyestripe and trailing crest feathers on head. Breeds in colonies in waterside trees or sometimes in reedbeds. Flight call is a deep, hollow croak. R.

Mute Swan *Cygnus olor* **L 155**
Large, white waterbird with boat-like swimming motion and heavy, laboured flight. Wingbeats make obvious swishing noise. Common on many lakes, large rivers and on ponds in parks. Holds neck in distinct curve, unlike Whooper and Bewick's Swans (rarer visitors in winter). Latter two have yellow patches on bill, and no knob at the base. R.

Shelduck *Tadorna tadorna* **L 62**
Intermediate in shape and size between ducks and geese. Bright black and white plumage with red legs and bill. Juvenile mostly grey-brown above and whitish below. Common on most coasts, especially on estuaries. Forms large winter flocks. R, W.

Wigeon *Anas penelope* **L 46**
Medium-sized duck with high forehead and short bill. Male very colourful; female similar to Mallard female, but more delicate, with more rounded head and more pointed tail. In flight, the long wings are noticeable, as is the white belly; male in flight has large white patches on wings. Regular winter visitor to muddy shores and lakes, often in large, dense flocks. R, W.

Mallard *Anas platyrhynchos* **L 60**
Largest and best known of all ducks. Male in breeding plumage has shiny green head with yellow bill, reddish-brown breast and curled black central tail feathers. Female has brown camou-flaged plumage. Females make the familiar quack-ing sound. Breeds on nearly all types of still or slow-flowing water. Common in parks. R, W.

Tufted Duck *Aythya fuligula* **L 43**
Small, compact diving duck. Male has charac-teristic black and white plumage; female dark brown, sometimes with white spot at base of bill. Shows white wing bar in flight. Breeds on lakes and reservoirs with open water, both inland and coastal. May gather in large flocks outside breeding season, on lakes and reservoirs. In winter may be tame enough to feed. R, W.

Moorhen *Gallinula chloropus* **L 33**
Common waterbird. Smaller and slimmer than Coot. Bill red with yellow tip and red frontal shield; legs and toes very long and green. Flashes white under tail coverts as tail bobbed. Juveniles brownish with pale chin area, olive green bill. Trails legs in flight and nods head while swim-ming and walking. Breeds at margins of still and slow-flowing water, and in ditches and small overgrown ponds. Common on streams and in ponds in urban parks and gardens. Feeds on adjoining grassland and fields. R, W

Coot *Fulica atra* **L 38**
Black, round waterbird, with bright white shield on forehead. Common on large rivers, lakes and reservoirs. Also found on lakes in parks. Often gathers in large flocks in winter. Dives with a small forward leap. Patters across water surface before take-off. R, W

Fulmar

Cormorant

Grey Heron

Mute Swan

Shelduck

male   female

female

male

Wigeon

male

female

Mallard

male

female

Tufted Duck

Moorhen

Coot

Hen Harrier *Circus cyaneus* **L 46**
Slim and light in flight. Male has ash-grey, almost gull-like plumage, contrasting black tipped wings and dark rump. Female dark brown above, pale yellow-brown beneath, striped wings and tail, clear white rump. Breeds in boggy areas, on heather moor, dunes, marshes and damp meadows, occasionally in young plantations or open country, mainly in the north. In winter regular in open wet areas and cultivated land. Sails and glides with V-shaped wings. R, W.

Buzzard *Buteo buteo* **L 53**
Medium-sized brown bird of prey with short neck and large, rounded head. Wings broad; tail rounded when spread. Characteristic mewing call, especially in spring. Breeds in regions with a good mixture of fields, hedges and woods. Hunts over open country and nests mostly at woodland edge. Often soars and circles. R, W.

Kestrel *Falco tinnunculus* **L 35**
Commonest bird of prey, often seen by main roads; hovers frequently. Small, with long tail, long pointed wings and brown upperparts. Male has speckled red-brown back, grey head, and grey tail with broad terminal band. Female red-brown, with barred upperparts. Juveniles resemble female, but more heavily streaked. Often hunts in open countryside, breeds in trees in fields and at woodland edges, in quarries, in villages and cities, as well as in mountains. R, W.

Pheasant *Phasianus colchicus*
L 82 (male), 58 (female)
Male has striking, colourful plumage and very long, pointed tail; female yellow-brown with dark speckles, tail shorter than male's. Utters loud *kok kok kok* call. Found mainly in cultivated areas, at edges of light woods and in fields. Widespread and common. R.

Oystercatcher *Haematopus ostralegus* **L 43**
Common on most coasts. Large, powerful shorebird with long, red, slightly flattened bill and red legs. Striking black and white plumage. Juveniles with pale throat markings and dark bill tip. In flight shows broad white wing bar and white rump. Call is a loud, fluty whistle. Breeds on

different types of coast, especially on sandy and shingle beaches. Outside breeding season often gathers in large flocks on mudflats or coastal meadows. R, W.

Lapwing *Vanellus vanellus* **L 30**
Striking black and white plumage, visible from distance; long pointed crest on head. Female has shorter crest and paler chin. Call a hoarse *peewee*. Breeds in open lowland habitats such as damp meadows, bogs, fields and farmland. Commonest near coast; large flocks in the autumn. R.

Dunlin *Calidris alpina* **L17**
Commonest European wader. Bill slightly decurved at tip. Large black patch on belly in breeding plumage; winter mostly grey-brown, without black belly patch. Juveniles brown above, with pale feather edges. Flight call is a nasal *trirr* or *krri*. Breeds on upland moors of northern and western Britain and Ireland. Gathers in large flocks on mudflats in autumn and winter. R, W.

Snipe *Gallinago gallinago* **L26**
Medium-sized wader with very long bill. Camouflaged plumage above; brown back with black markings and yellowish streaks. Makes a scratchy call when flushed. Song is a regular, clock-like *ticka-ticka-ticka*, either from a songpost or in flight. Breeds in fens, bogs, damp meadows and other wetland areas with low vegetation. Widespread, but not common. R.

Curlew *Numenius arquata* **L56**
Largest British wader. Long, distinctly decurved bill. Whimbrel is similar but smaller, with shorter bill and dark stripes on crown. Very melodious and atmospheric fluting call and trilling songflight. Breeds mainly on upland moors. Large flocks on mudflats outside breeding season. R, W.

Redshank *Tringa totanus* **L28**
Bright red legs and broad white trailing edge to wings. Juveniles lack red base to bill, have yellower legs, and are more reddish-brown above. A very vocal bird, uttering a loud, fluting '*tleu-hu*' or '*tleu-hu-hu*'. Breeds in open marshes, especially near coasts. Outside breeding season on low-lying coasts, often in large flocks on mudflats. R, W.

male in flight

female

Hen Harrier

Buzzard

female Kestrel
in flight

male

female

Kestrel

male

female

Pheasant

Oystercatcher

Lapwing

summer   winter

Dunlin

Snipe
drumming

Snipe

Curlew

Redshank

Lesser Black-backed Gull
Larus fuscus **L56**
Similar to Herring Gull but with dark slate-grey back and upper wings (wings overlap tail further than Herring Gull's). Legs yellow. In winter, head streaky and legs yellowish-pink. Juveniles difficult to separate from young Herring Gulls, but in second year or older birds the upperparts are darker. Slightly deeper call than Herring Gull. Breeds on low-lying coasts and islands, mainly in west. Outside breeding season mainly at coasts, but regular at inland lakes as well. R, W

Herring Gull *Larus argentatus* **L56**
Commonest large gull. Plumage white except for blue-grey wings and black wing-tips. Large bill is yellow with red spot. Eyes yellow; feet flesh pink. In winter head has brownish streaks. Juveniles speckled brown with broad black terminal tail band. Call is a repeated *kyow*. Breeds in coastal meadows, dunes, on shingle banks and small islands, and in some areas on rock ledges and even in some cities on roofs of houses. Outside breeding season usually at coast. R, W.

Black-headed Gull *Larus ridibundus* **L36**
Commonest gull. Often seen inland as well as at coast. Chocolate brown face mask and red bill. Wing-tips black, legs dark red. In winter head white with dark ear-patch. Juveniles speckled brown above with dark trailing edge to wings and dark tip to tail. In flight narrow, pointed wings show a clear white leading edge. Breeds in colonies at lake margins, and on small islands. R, W.

Kittiwake *Rissa tridactyla* **L 40**
Breeds in large colonies on steep sea-cliffs. Outside breeding season spends most time out to sea. Pure black wingtips without white spots. Juvenile has bold black 'W' mark on wings. Yellow bill, short dark legs. Very noisy at breeding site a loud, penetrating *kiti-wake* call. R, W.

Common Tern *Sterna hirundo* **L 35**
A slim and elegant bird, common in coastal waters. Bill intense red, with black tip. Wings do not extend beyond tail when sitting. Very vocal, with a short, repeated *kick* as flight call. Breeds in colonies on sandy coasts, in dunes, on gravel banks of undisturbed rivers and on low bare banks of lakes and ponds. S.

Guillemot *Uria aalge* **L42**
Common cliff-nesting seabird with narrow, pointed bill. Sits upright. In winter cheeks, chin and neck white, dark line behind eye. Breeds in large, crowded colonies on narrow ledges and small ridges on steep rocky seacliffs. Outside breeding season at sea, far out from land. R, W.

Woodpigeon *Columba palumbus* **L 42**
Very common large pigeon found in open wooded areas and fields, often breeding in trees at field margins. Also seen in urban parks feeding alongside Feral Pigeons and Collared Doves. Bright white patches on wings and neck, visible in flight. Song is familiar far-carrying *goo-goo-gu-gooroo*. Often gathers in large flocks on fields outside breeding season. R.

Collared Dove *Streptopelia decaocto* **L31**
Pale slim, long-tailed dove with dark half collar at back of neck. Breast flushed pink. Usually associated with human activities. Characteristic nasal flight call. Courtship song a monotonous tri-syllabic *coo-cooo, coo*, usually accented on second syllable. Resident in towns and villages, especially where there is an abundance of food such as grain. R.

Barn Owl *Tyto alba* **L35**
A pale owl, usually seen floating over open country at dusk showing long slim wings and very pale underparts. Very vocal at breeding site from February/March onwards, making snarling and screeching sounds throughout the night. Mainly breeds in cultivated areas, choosing church towers, old barns or similar site. Widespread in lowland areas but rather thinly spread. R.

Tawny Owl *Strix aluco* **L38**
Our commonest owl, found in woodland and gardens. Large, round head and dark eyes. Territorial song of male, a shuddering, ghostly hoot, heard mainly in early spring. Female has frequent loud '*ke-wick*'. Breeds in open deciduous and mixed woodland, also in parks, cemeteries and gardens with old trees. R.

1st winter

1st winter

winter

Lesser Black-Backed Gull

Herring Gull

Black-Headed Gull

Kittiwake

Common Tern

winter

summer

Guillemot

Woodpigeon

Barn Owl
in flight

Collared Dove

Barn Owl

Tawny Owl

Swift *Apus apus* L17
Active summer visitor usually seen flying on long, sickle-shaped wings. Blackish plumage with pale chin and neck. Very vocal with a high-pitched shrill scream. Breeds in colonies in buildings such as church towers, chimneys and tower blocks, also under eaves of terraced houses. Very common, especially in towns. Arrives late in spring (late April–May), and departs in August. S.

Kingfisher *Alcedo atthis* L15
Unmistakable bird. Very rapid flight, low and straight over the water; bright iridescent blue back. Female has red base to lower mandible. Loud, high-pitched penetrating whistle *tieht, tji* or *tii-tee*, often rapidly repeated. Breeds on slow-flowing, clear streams and rivers with vertical steep banks. Outside breeding season visits fish ponds, small pools and even coastal waters. R.

Great Spotted Woodpecker
Picoides major L23
Commonest woodpecker. Contrasting black and white plumage, striking white shoulder patches; lower tail coverts bright red, flanks unstreaked. Male has red patch at back of head. Juveniles have red crown. Undulating flight. Hard metallic call *kick* or *kix*, is heard throughout the year. Both sexes drum on dry branches. Breeds in all kinds of woods, and in parks and gardens. R.

Skylark *Alauda arvensis* L17
A common bird of farmland and open grassland. Head has small crest. Trailing edges of wings and outer tail feathers white. Flight call a pleasant hard *chreeoo*; loud trilling song given in ascending flight. Meadow Pipit is much smaller. R.

Swallow *Hirundo rustica* L20
Very slim with unusually long tail streamers. Upperparts and breast band metallic blue, forehead and chin red-brown. Juveniles less brightly coloured and with shorter tail streamers. Flight elegant and rapid, rather more direct than House Martin's. Song a pleasant, halting twittering chatter. Common throughout open countryside and in villages, especially on farms; usually feeds over fields. Nests mainly in buildings such as barns, in a basin-shaped nest. S.

House Martin *Delichon urbica* L13
White rump and pure white underside. More dumpy than Swallow, tail only shallowly forked and without long streamers. Metallic blue-black above, juveniles dark brown, lacking sheen. Common in towns and villages. Usually hunts higher in air than Swallow; always sociable. Nests colonially on the outsides of buildings, usually immediately under the eaves. S.

Meadow Pipit *Anthus pratensis* L14
Small and inconspicuous bird found on moorland, wet meadows, heath, dunes and waste ground. The slightly larger Tree Pipit is very similar, but prefers woodland edge and heath and is absent from Ireland. Meadow Pipit characterized mainly by voice and habitat. Call when flushed is a repeated high-pitched shrill *ist*. Song made up of high, thin notes introduced by an accelerating series of *tsip* sounds. R.

Pied Wagtail *Motacilla alba* L18
Long black tail with white outer feathers; constantly bobs tail. Legs long, thin and black. Female less contrasty and with less black on head. Juveniles brown-grey above, without black. Call is a sharp, repeated *tsick*. Common in open country, especially near water; breeds in towns and villages, farms, gravel pits. R.

Wren *Troglodytes troglodytes* L10
Tiny and squat, with short tail, which is often cocked upwards. Creeps about close to ground. Alarm call a loud, hard *teck teck teck...*, often slurred together. Song very loud and warbling trill. Breeds in woods with thick undergrowth, and in scrub; also in parks and gardens. R.

Dunnock *Prunella modularis* L15
Inconspicuous, resembles female House Sparrow, but has thinner bill. Head and breast slate grey, flanks with dark streaks. High, thin piping alarm call. Song is a pleasant continuous hurried twitter. Common in coniferous and mixed woodland, in parks and gardens with thick undergrowth. Hops on ground in skulking fashion, seldom leaving undergrowth. R.

Swift

Kingfisher

Great Spotted Woodpecker

Skylark
song flight

Skylark

Swallow

House Martin

Meadow Pipit

female

male

Pied Wagtail

Wren

Dunnock

Robin *Erithacus rubecula* **L14**
Rather tame, dumpy bird with orange-red breast
and relatively long legs. Juvenile lacks red, and is
strongly mottled with brown. Breeds in all kinds
of woodland, especially in broadleaf woods with
rich undergrowth. Also in parks and gardens.
Alarm call is a sharp *tick*, often rapidly repeated.
Song is a tuneful and rather melancholy descending series of notes. R.

Blackbird *Turdus merula* **L25**
Very common woodland and garden bird. Male
has shiny black plumage; female dark grey-brown
to blackish-brown with paler, weakly speckled
breast. Juveniles reddish-brown plumage, strongly speckled beneath. Alarm call a metallic *tsink
tsink* and a shrill chatter. Song loud and melodious fluting. R.

Song Thrush *Turdus philomelus* **L23**
Small thrush with brown upperparts and large
dark eyes. Underside covered with small dark
spots. Song loud and variable, made up of musical
phrases, each repeated two or three times (often
more), often delivered from high perch.
Widespread and common in all kinds of tall
woodland, in copses, parks and gardens with old
trees. Often opens snails by banging them against
stones. R.

Mistle Thrush *Turdus viscivorus* **L27**
Noticeably larger than Song Thrush, with longer
wings and tail. Grey-brown above with large spots
below; outer tail feathers tipped white. Resembles
dove in flight, with rounded belly and pale lower
wing coverts; undulating flight. Loud, dry rasping
call. Song reminiscent of Blackbird's, but more
melancholy and less variable. Starts to sing early in
year (February). Found in tall broadleaf and coniferous woodland and wooded fields; also in parks
in some areas. R.

Sedge Warbler
Acrocephalus schoenobaenus **L12**
Small, rather inconspicuous warbler with streaked
plumage and clear white stripe over eye, and dark
crown. Often makes short song-flight, landing
nearby and continuing song. Song usually has

much longer phrases and is faster than Reed
Warbler's; interspersed with long, pleasant trills
and many imitations. Found in reedbeds, marshy
willow thickets, ditches. S.

Reed Warbler *Acrocephalus scirpaceus* **L13**
A plainer bird than Sedge Warbler. Breeds in
reeds and in thick bushes in wetlands. Widespread
and often the commonest warbler in reedbeds.
Song similar to Sedge Warbler's, but quieter, less
penetrating, more continuous and faster. Raw,
scratchy, notes repeated two or three times. S.

Whitethroat *Sylvia communis* **L14**
Lively warbler with chestnut tinge on back (male).
Female drabber, with brownish head. Hurried
rough twittering song, in short flight over bushes.
Relatively long tail with white outer feathers.
Breeds in thorny scrub, in hedgerows, often along
embankments, and gardens. S.

Willow Warbler *Phylloscopus trochilus* **L11**
Slim and delicate warbler breeding in open broadleaf and mixed woods, willow scrub, wooded lake
margins, parks and gardens. Best separated from
very similar Chiffchaff by song. Alarm call is a soft
hoo-eet, usually in two clear syllables. Song is a
fluting, melancholy, descending series of notes. S.

Goldcrest *Regulus regulus* **L9**
Tiny olive green bird, like a diminutive warbler.
Male has bright yellow crown, with a few orange-
red feathers in the centre; female has uniform light
yellow crown. Rarer Firecrest has black stripe
through eye. Juvenile lacks head markings. High-
pitched, fine, call. Song is a short, very high-
pitched, thin phrase, rising and falling. Breeds in
thick coniferous forest or groups of conifers in
mixed woodland, parks and gardens. R.

Blackcap *Sylvia atricapilla* **L14**
Grey-brown warbler with black cap (male), or
chestnut cap (female). Loud, fluting song with
long pauses. Alarm call a hard *tak* or *tzeck*, slurred
to a chatter when disturbed. Breeds in open
broadleaf and coniferous woodland, river-valley
woodland, parks and gardens. S, (W).

female

male

Robin

Blackbird

Song Thrush

Mistle Thrush

Sedge Warbler

Reed Warbler

female

male

Whitethroat

female

female

male

Blackcap

male

Willow Warbler

Goldcrest

Long-tailed Tit *Aegithalos caudatus* **L 14**
Very active, sociable and agile, with a very long, graduated tail, making up more than half its length. Utters constant contact calls while moving through bushes to feed. Breeds in woods with rich undergrowth, especially near water, and in parks and gardens. R.

Blue Tit *Parus caeruleus* **L 11**
Small, compact tit with bright blue and yellow plumage. Juvenile much paler, with greenish brown upperparts and yellow cheeks. Song, soft, pure notes, followed by trills. Breeds in broadleaf and mixed woodland, especially oak, in copses, parks and gardens. Very lively, and rather tame. Often in mixed flocks outside breeding season. R.

Great Tit *Parus major* **L 14**
Striking black and white head, yellow underparts with a broad (male) or narrow (female) black stripe down centre. Juvenile drabber, with yellowish cheeks. Song is a simple phrase consisting of repeated calls. Breeds in all types of woodland, in parks and gardens. Often visits bird tables. R.

Treecreeper *Certhia familiaris* **L 13**
Rather a skulking bird of coniferous and broadleaved woodland, parks and gardens. Bark-coloured plumage and secretive behaviour make it tricky to spot. Often found with tit flocks outside breeding season. R.

House Sparrow *Passer domesticus* **L 14**
Very common bird found close to houses everywhere. Very common in villages, towns and farmyards. Very sociable; often in loose flocks. Hops on ground, and fond of bathing in dust. Several males often perform courtship dance, with wings held low and tail raised. Male has contrasting plumage; female and juvenile drab grey-brown. Familiar chirping song. R.

Chaffinch *Fringilla coelebs* **L 15**
Commonest finch. Male has shiny blue-grey crown, brownish-grey in winter. Female olive brown above, grey-brown below. Bright white wing markings and outer tail feathers prominent in flight. Alarm call a loud, short 'pink', similar to Great Tit. Song is a clear descending phrase, accelerating towards the end. Common in all areas with trees. Feeds mostly on the ground, walking with jerky head movements. Outside breeding season often in large flocks. R

Greenfinch *Carduelis chloris* **L 15**
Large, yellow-green finch, with conspicuous yellow wing patches. Female mainly grey-green with less yellow on wings and tail. Juvenile heavily streaked. Song consists of Canary-like ringing notes and trills, with whistles. Often breeds in light mixed woodland, at woodland edges, in hedges, parks, orchards and wooded avenues; also in gardens, even in urban areas. Sociable. Often visits bird tables. R.

Goldfinch *Carduelis carduelis* **L 12**
Remarkably colourful. In flight, broad yellow wing-bars prominent. Juveniles lack black white and red head colours, but do have the characteristic yellow wing-bars. Song consists of high-pitched, rapidly delivered twittering and trills. Breeds in parks, orchards, hedgerows and gardens. Outside breeding season found in open country and near footpaths. Attracted to thistle and teasel heads. R (S in northern Scotland).

Linnet *Acanthis cannabina* **L 13**
Breeding male has red forehead and breast; duller in winter with no red on head. Female lacks red, is streaked and dark brown above. Juvenile even more heavily streaked. Flight call and song are very nasal in tone. Breeds in open cultivated country with hedges and copses, in cemeteries, vineyards, heathland, parks and gardens, often on the edge of villages. Often in large, dense flocks in open country outside breeding season. R.

Bullfinch *Pyrrhula pyrrhula* **L 15**
Plump and dumpy, with bright rose-red underparts (male); short, black bill. Female brown-grey below. Juvenile brownish, without black cap. In flight, white rump prominent. Soft, quiet call. Breeds in coniferous and mixed woodland, in spruce plantations, in parks and gardens. Normally seen in pairs. Outside breeding season pairs may team up into small groups. R.

Blue Tit

Long-Tailed Tit

Great Tit

Treecreeper

female

male

House Sparrow

female

male

Chaffinch

female

male

Greenfinch

juvenile

Goldfinch

male

female

Linnet

male

female

Bullfinch

Starling *Sturnus vulgaris* **L 21**
Common, noisy and sociable bird. Hunts on ground, with a rather wobbly walk, constantly probing soil with bill. Plumage spotted in winter, becoming shiny in breeding season. Juvenile uniform grey-brown with pale chin and dark bill. In flight shows pointed triangular wings. Song is a varied chatter, made up of whistling, crackling, snapping and rattling calls; incorporates imitations of other birds and sounds. R.

Yellowhammer *Emberiza citrinella* **L 16**
Slim and long-tailed, with cinnamon-brown rump. Male has bright yellow head and breast. Female and juvenile less yellow, and with dark streaks on head and throat. White outer tail feathers obvious in flight. Song is classic short, melancholy phrase l*ittle bit of bread and no cheese*, often shortened. Common almost everywhere in varied cultivated country. In winter seen in small flocks. R.

Reed Bunting *Emberiza schoeniclus* **L 15**
Common in wet areas. Male has black head, chin and throat, with white collar and moustachial stripe. In winter head and neck are mottled brown. Female and juvenile have camouflaged plumage with conspicuous black and white moustache. Song is a short, rather high-pitched stammering phrase. Breeds in overgrown lake and river margins, among reed and sedge beds and damp willow scrub. R.

Jay *Garrulus glandarius* **L 35**
Plump, noisy bird with bright plumage. Striking blue and black barred wing patches. Black moustachial patch. White wing patches and rump, conspicuous in flight. Alarm call a loud, raw scream. Breeds mainly in mixed broadleaf woodland, in wooded parks and gardens, and more rarely in coniferous woods. Flight slow, with irregular wingbeats; often hops on ground when hunting. R.

Magpie *Pica pica* **L 45**
Shiny black and white plumage and long, graduated tail. Juvenile has much shorter tail and more matt plumage. Chattering calls. Breeds in open country among hedges, copses and wooded

avenues and in villages, parks and gardens with trees, and even in urban areas; avoids dense woodland. Usually seen in pairs or small flocks. R.

Chough *Pyrrhocorax pyrrhocorax* **L 40**
Jackdaw-like, black bird with long, curved bright-red bill and red legs. Breeds in mountain districts and steep rocky coasts in Wales, west Scotland and Ireland. R.

Jackdaw *Corvus monedula* **L 33**
Plumage mainly black, with grey nape and back of head. Eye pale. Juvenile has brownish-black plumage. Calls loud *kya* or *kyak*, often repeated. Breeds in variety of habitats including broadleaf woodland nesting in holes in trees, in cliffs and quarries, and in parks. Locally common, but rather patchy. Very sociable. Mostly feed in small flocks in open country. Often join flocks of Rooks to feed on open fields. R.

Rook *Corvus frugilegus* **L 46**
Bare, whitish patch at base of adult's bill. Black, with metallic blue sheen; steep, angled forehead. Belly and thigh feathers tend to be looser than Carrion Crow's. Found in open country with copses, edges of broadleaf and coniferous woodland, parks and even in urban areas. Very sociable. In winter gathers together in large flocks to feed in fields and parks. R.

Carrion Crow/Hooded Crow
Corvus corone **L 47**
Carrion Crow is similar to Rook, but lacks white patch on face. Usually seen singly or in pairs. Hooded Crow has light grey back and underside. and replaces Carrion Crow in North-west Scotland and in Ireland. Common in open country, in moorland, on the coast, in parks and gardens and even in urban areas. R.

Raven *Corvus corax* **L 65**
Largest crow, with very powerful black bill. Plumage black with bluish sheen. In flight, wedge-shaped tail distinctive. Often soars like a bird of prey. Call is a deep, hollow croak. Breeds in a variety of habitats, such as open wooded country, mountains, and rocky coasts. Restricted to north and west of Britain, and to Ireland. R.

Starling

male   female
Yellowhammer

female   male
Reed Bunting

Jay

Magpie

Chough

Jackdaw

Rook

Hooded Crow   Carrion Crow   Raven

Hedgehog *Erinaceus europaeus* **L 25**
Found throughout region. A familiar mammal because it often turns up in gardens, particularly in those with a good growth of shrubs and hedges. Prefers rather dry areas and not usually found in woodland, or on high mountains.

Mole *Talpa europaea* **L 15**
Absent from Ireland. Common, especially in woods and pastures on fertile soils. Not often seen, spending most of its life in underground burrows, but leaves distinctive mounds of crumbled soil. Feeds mainly on earthworms.

Common Shrew *Sorex araneus* **L 12**
Not found in Ireland, although the smaller Pygmy Shrew is. Common in hedges and long grass. Very active and constantly on the move searching for invertebrate food. Sometimes heard making very high-pitched squeaking in roadside verge, for example. Larger Water Shrew is much darker and usually white below, with a fringe of hairs along base of tail.

Brown Long-eared Bat *Plecotus auritus* **W 265**
Second commonest bat in Britain. Absent from far north of Scotland. Likes open woodland, parks and gardens, roosting in winter in caves, hollow trees or buildings. Emerges late in dusk or when dark. Hunts with active, agile flight, often at tree-top height. Often hovers, and picks prey off twigs as well as in flight.

Pipistrelle *Pipistrellus pipistrellus* **W 210**
Easily the commonest bat in Britain and Ireland, but has declined by 60 per cent over the past ten years. Lives in houses, churches, rocks and trees. Emerges early in evening, and often flies backwards and forwards over same area. Feeds on flying insects such as small moths.

Rabbit *Oryctolagus cuniculus* **L 45**
One of our commonest and most familiar mammals. Grazes on meadows, pasture, heath and downland. Breeds in underground burrows. Shorter ears and legs than hares.

Brown Hare *Lepus capensis* **L 65**
Long-legged fast species of open country. Prefers agricultural fields, moorland and dunes. Absent from most of Ireland, and from higher mountains. Slightly smaller Mountain (Irish) Hare replaces it on mountains, and in most of Ireland. The Mountain Hare has somewhat shorter ears. In Britain, Mountain Hares normally turn white in winter.

Grey Squirrel *Sciurus carolinensis* **L 46**
Common mainly in deciduous woodland, parks and large gardens in much of England, Wales and lowland Scotland. Also found in northern and central Ireland. The more delicate **Red Squirrel**, *Sciurus vulgaris,* (L 42) prefers coniferous woodland, although it will also live in deciduous woods, especially where the Grey Squirrel is absent. Common in parts of Scotland, Ireland, and on Isle of Wight.

Bank Vole *Clethrionomys glareolus* **L 14**
Reddish coloured vole, common in gardens, fields, hedges and woods, mainly on dry soils, throughout Britain but absent from most of Ireland. The similar Field Vole, *Microtus agrestis,* has a greyer colour, less prominent ears and a shorter tail.

Water Vole *Arvicola terrestris* **L 30**
Absent from Ireland. Large, almost rat-sized vole of waterways and riverbanks. Swim and dive frequently. Distinguished from Brown Rat by blunt nose, high rump and hairy tail.

Wood Mouse *Apodemus sylvaticus* **L 10**
Agile, mainly nocturnal mouse found in deciduous woods, hedges and large gardens. House Mouse, *Mus musculus,* which also occurs in gardens and hedges, is greyer, with smaller eyes, ears and feet. Both are found throughout Ireland and Britain. The **Yellow-necked Mouse**, *Apodemus flavicollis,* (L12) is larger and brighter, with a yellow collar. Scattered in southern Britain.

Hedgehog

Mole

Common Shrew

Long-Eared Bat

Brown Hare

Pipistrelle Bat

Rabbit

Grey Squirrel

Water Vole

Bank Vole

Wood Mouse

Fox *Vulpes vulpes* **L 110**
Found throughout region. Graceful, dog-like, with russet fur and long, bushy tail. Prefers wooded country or scrubland, with drier soils. Has taken up suburban life in many large cities, such as Bristol, London and Brighton.

Badger *Meles meles* **L 85**
Almost entirely nocturnal and therefore not often encountered, but unmistakable when seen. Travels along regular tracks within woodland. Particularly fond of earthworms. Found throughout, except much of northern Scotland.

Stoat *Mustela erminea* **L 35**
Slim, active hunter, with black tip to tail. Smaller **Weasel**, *Mustela nivalis*, lacks black tip, and is absent from Ireland. In the north, changes to partial white coat in winter. Feeds on small mammals, to size of Rabbit.

Otter *Lutra lutra* **L 120**
Beautifully graceful swimmer, found in clean rivers, estuaries and on some coasts. Only common on the more remote rocky coasts of Scotland and Ireland, but beginning to return to some traditional lowland haunts. Similar introduced **American Mink**, *Mustela vison*, which is now common in some river systems, is like a small, dark Otter.

Wild Cat *Felis silvestris* **L 100** (not illustrated)
Restricted in British Isles to central and northern Scotland, but slowly spreading southwards. Seldom seen, because of shy behaviour and nocturnal tendencies, but good populations in many highland areas. Resembles large tabby, with bushy tail.

Grey Seal *Halichoerus grypus* **L 300**
Found mostly on exposed rocky coasts, with isolated bays, mainly on western seaboard of Britain and Ireland. Grey colour, with larger head, and longer snout. The **Common Seal,** *Phoca vitulina* (L 160), is more typical of sandy bars and estuaries and is found in the Wash area as well as in the north and west. Variable in colour, with small, rounded head.

Roe Deer *Capreolus capreolus* **L 110**
Smallest native deer, found in woods, heaths and fields. Most often seen early in the morning, moving out of woodland to feed on grassland nearby. **Muntjac,** *Muntiacus reevesi*, and **Chinese Water Deer,** *Hydropotes inermi*, are both even smaller and are introductions from China. Muntjac are found in woods, especially in the midlands, and Chinese Water Deer in wet woods in parts of Hampshire.

Fallow Deer *Cervus dama* **L 150**
Commonest deer of woodland and parkland scattered throughout region. Mainly nocturnal and herds difficult to spot in woodland. Dark and light colour forms are common. The otherwise similar Sika Deer, *Cervus nippon*, has unflanged antlers and is smaller. It is introduced in some parts of England and Scotland.

Red Deer *Cervus elephas* **L 250**
Largest deer. Commonest on the open hills and moors of Scotland, where they are managed as game. However, also found scattered elsewhere, where they are often more at home in woodland.

Fox

Badger

Stoat

Otter

Grey Seal

male   female

Roe Deer

female

male

male

female

Red Deer

Fallow Deer

Warty Newt *Triturus cristatus*   **L 14**
Rather local. Absent from Ireland. Large, dark, with rough, warty skin. Brown-grey above with dark spots. Belly orange or yellow, with dark patches. Breeding males have large crest with bluish streaks along it. Likes still water with good underwater plant growth.

Smooth Newt *Triturus vulgaris*   **L 11**
Commonest newt. Smooth-skinned, yellow or olive-brown, with small dark spots, merging into lines on back and also stripe on side of head. Yellow or orange below with dark spots. Breeding males have continuous crest on tail and body and fringes on hind toes. Often found on land, under stones and logs as well as in water.

Palmate Newt *Triturus helveticu*   **L 9**
Absent from Ireland. From Smooth Newt by smaller size, paler colour and shorter head. Pale yellow on centre of underside, with few or no spots. Breeding males have very low crest and filament at end of tail. Hind feet strongly webbed and dark; centre of tail orange.

Common Toad *Bufo bufo*   **L to 15**, usually smaller
Absent from Ireland. Heavy, dark and warty. Mainly nocturnal, hiding by day. Walks, but will also hop when frightened. Eggs (spawn) laid in long strings in water.

Natterjack *Bufo calamita*   **L 8** (not illustrated)
At north-west limit of range; local and mainly coastal in Britain and south-west Ireland. Brown, grey or greenish; usually has yellow stripe down centre of back. Runs in short bursts. Nocturnal and very loud and vocal in breeding season. Sings in chorus with loud ratchet-like croak.

Common Frog *Rana temporaria*   **L 10**
Smooth-skinned and very variable in colour; grey, brown, olive or yellow. Black spots on back and flanks. Underside white, yellow or orange. Call is a weak croak and usually made under water. Lives in damp grassland. Usually only found in water when breeding or hibernating. Spawn laid in clumps.

Sand lizard *Lacerta agilis*   **L 9** (excl. tail)
Rare and local. Short legs and short, broad head. Colour very variable but males have green or yellow-green flanks; females grey or brown. Eye-spots on sides. Found only on sandy heaths and some coastal dunes, in south of England.

Viviparous (Common) Lizard *Lacerta vivipara*
L 6.5 (excl. tail)
Found throughout Britain and Ireland. Rather rounded head and thick neck. Usually grey- or olive-brown, with scattered dark spots or lines. Found in a range of habitats but prefers field edges, heaths, dunes, hedges and embankments.

Slow Worm *Anguis fragilis*   **L 30**
Absent from Ireland. Snake-like lizard, without visible legs. Brown, grey or copper-coloured. Young are very distinctive, gold, with dark sides and central black stripe. Lives in fields, heaths, open woods, hedges and embankments, and often remains hidden beneath logs or stones. Likes to eat slugs.

Grass Snake *Natrix natrix*   **L 120**
Absent from Ireland. Large, non-venomous snake with thick body and rounded head. Usually olive-grey, green or brown, with dark bars on sides and small spots on back. Yellow collar, sometimes absent. Often found near water. Swims well and eats frogs, toads, newts, fish, and also young birds and small mammals. The **Smooth Snake**, *Coronella austriaca* (L 60) is rare and local, restricted in British Isles to small area of southern England. Small non-venomous snake with rather small head and pointed snout. Grey, brown or pinkish, with dark belly. Dark spots along back. Stripe from neck through eye. Feeds largely on lizards.

Adder *Vipera berus*   **L 65**
Absent from Ireland. Only venomous snake found here. Thick body and flat head. Usually has dark obvious zig-zag stripes on back on grey, brown or reddish background. Inhabits mainly heaths, moors and bogs. Feeds mainly on small mammals.

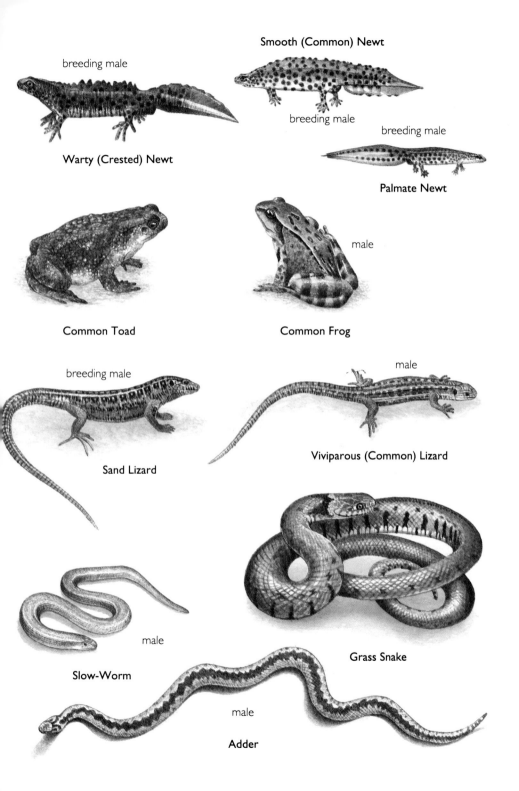

Smooth (Common) Newt

breeding male

breeding male

breeding male

Warty (Crested) Newt

Palmate Newt

Common Toad

male

Common Frog

breeding male

male

Sand Lizard

Viviparous (Common) Lizard

Grass Snake

male

Slow-Worm

male

Adder

Large White *Pieris brassicae* **W 55**
One of our commonest butterflies, found throughout the region, including Orkneys and Shetland. Seen from February to November. Only absent from highest mountains. Often breeds in gardens, on cabbages, sprouts and related plants, and on nasturtiums. Also lays eggs on Wild Mignonette.

Small White *Pieris rapae* **W 45**
Very common species, again found throughout, but not in Orkneys or Shetland. Mainly seen April to October. Lays eggs on cabbages and relatives, but also on nasturtium, and the wild Garlic Mustard and Charlock.

Orange-tip *Anthocaris cardamines* **W 40**
Common, but absent from much of northern, central and western Scotland. Female lacks orange tips to wings. On the wing between April and June. Mainly found along hedgerows and woodland edges, but also in gardens. Main food plant is Lady's Smock.

Brimstone *Gonepteryx rhamni* **W 55**
Striking species. Male bright yellow, female paler. Common only in southern half of Britain, especially in limestone areas. Scattered and rarer in Wales and Ireland (common on Burren), and absent from Scotland. Can be seen at almost any time of the year. Larval food plants are Buckthorn and Alder Buckthorn. Adults are attracted by flowers of Buddleia and Teasel.

Small Copper *Lycaena phlaeas*
W 25 (male) 30 (female)
Common on rough grassland and heath throughout region, except for Scotland where it is scattered. Very territorial, chasing other species that stray too close. On the wing between April and October. Eggs are laid on Common and Sheep's Sorrel.

Holly Blue *Celastrina argiolus* **W 30**
The only blue regularly seen in suburban gardens. Also a very tame species. Found only in the southern half of Britain, and scattered in Ireland. Populations vary from year to year. Often seen flitting around Holly or Ivy in gardens, from March to September. Eggs also laid on Gorse, Dogwood and Spindle.

Common Blue *Polyommatus icarus* **W 28**
Commonest blue over country as a whole. Found everywhere except high mountains. Prefers grassland, pasture, heath and dunes. Female is usually brown, but a blue form occurs in Ireland and North-west Scotland.

White Admiral *Ladoga camilla* **W 52**
Found mainly in large, shady woods in southern and central England. One of the few species actually increasing. Swift tree-top flight and elusive habits make this beautiful species hard to spot. Flies late June to August. Larvae feed on Honeysuckle.

Peacock *Inachis io* **W 55**
One of our most beautiful and commonest butterflies. Common in lowland habitats and gardens throughout England, Wales and Ireland, but rather rare and patchily distributed in most of Scotland. May be seen at almost any time of the year. Adults hibernate in winter. Larvae feed on Stinging Nettles.

Red Admiral *Vanessa atalanta* **W 55**
Another common species, mostly seen from April to October. Red Admirals migrate here from the continent, then raise a brood here using nettles and Pellitory of the Wall as larval food plants. Adults love to feed on garden flowers, especially Buddleia.

Large White

Small White

male

female

Orange Tip

male

female

Brimstone

Small Copper

Holly Blue

female

male

Common Blue

White Admiral

Peacock

Red Admiral

Small Tortoiseshell *Aglais urticae* **W 47**
Very common and familiar butterfly found throughout the region, in most habitats and in gardens. Adults are attracted by Buddleia, Michaelmas Daisies and Ice Plant, and may be seen at almost any time of year. Larvae feed on nettles.

Comma *Polygonia c-album* **W 50**
A smart, active butterfly restricted to southern England, where it is common in woods and gardens. Slowly spreading north. Larval food plant is the Hop, or nettles.

Small Pearl-bordered Fritillary
Boloria selene **W 38**
This small fritillary is a western speciality, but is declining. Look for it in woodland clearings and grassland in southern and south-western England, western Wales, Lake District, and western and central Scotland. Flies mainly in May and June. Absent from Ireland and most of eastern England. Larvae feed on Marsh and Dog Violets. The similar, Pearl-bordered Fritillary, *B. euphrosyne*, has a similar range, with an outpost in the Hazel scrub of the Burren in Ireland.

Ringlet *Aphantopus hyperantus* **W 42**
Scattered mainly in lowland sites, in open woodland and damp grassland, especially in Ireland and southern England. More scattered further north. On the wing for a short season in July and August. Very pretty species, with several eye spots. Rather weak flight. Larvae feed on grasses such as Cock's Foot and Wood False Brome.

Meadow Brown *Maniola jurtina* **W 46**
Possibly our commonest species. Likes grassland, hedgerows and open woodland. Flies from mid-June to September. Very variable, with the brightest and largest in the north and west. Eggs laid on grasses such as meadow grasses, rye-grasses and bents.

Gatekeeper *Pyronia tithonus* **W 35**
Bright, active brown. Locally common in southern half of Britain, but absent from Scotland and most of Ireland. Flies from late July to early September. Caterpillars feed on meadow grasses, bents, fescues or Couch. Brighter colour than Meadow Brown, and has small, white spots on hind wing.

Wall Brown *Lasiommata megera* **W 40**
This is a common species of grassland and hedgerows in lowland England and Ireland. Likes to sunbathe on open ground or on stones. Mostly seen flying betwen May and September. Larvae feed on grasses such as Cock's Foot, Wavy Hairgrass, Tor Grass and Wood False Brome.

Speckled Wood *Pararge aegeria* **W 40**
This is an attractive species of woodland and glades, including conifer plantations. Common in Ireland, Wales and southern England; scattered in Scotland. May be seen between late March and October. Larvae feed on grasses such as Yorkshire Fog, Cock's Foot and Wood False Brome.

Small Heath *Coenonympha pamphilus* **W 30**
Very widespread on dry grassland and heaths throughout the region, except Orkney and Shetland. Up to about 750 m on mountains. Fly betwen mid-May and mid-July, or in August and September.

Small Skipper *Thymelicus sylvestris* **W 22**
Common in much of England, but absent from Scotland and Ireland. Habitat is open, fairly tall grassland, heath, and woodland glades. Eggs laid on Yorkshire Fog. Adults fly between late June and early August. The slightly smaller Essex Skipper, *Thymelicus lineola*, is common on grassland in the south and east of England. It is slightly smaller and has black undersides to the tips of its antennae (those of Small Skipper are orange).

Small Tortoiseshell

Comma

Small Pearl-Bordered Fritillary

Ringlet

Meadow Brown

Gatekeeper

Wall Brown

Speckled Wood

Small Heath

Small Skipper

Norway Spruce *Picea abies* H to over 5000
Widely planted conifer, native to Europe. Also naturalized in this region. The christmas tree. Along with the American Sitka Spruce, *Picea sitchensis*, used for timber plantations. Spruce trees have quite long cones which hang down from the branches, unlike the rather similar Silver Fir, whose cones sit upright. Fir is naturalized in some parts of Britain, but it is not a major plantation tree.

Alder *Alnus glutinosa* H 2000
Tree or shrub of wet habitats, with rounded, rather blunt leaves. Male flowers in drooping, yellow catkins; female flowers in 'cones'. Often found in groves alongside rivers, or on boggy ground elsewhere. The similar Grey Alder, *Alnus incana*, with more pointed leaves, is not native but is sometimes planted, particularly in Scotland and Ireland.

Pedunculate (English) Oak
Quercus robur H 3000
Familiar tree of heavier clay-rich soils throughout the region, especially in lowlands. Acorns on long stalks. The similar Sessile Oak, *Q. petraea*, dominates on more acid soils, particularly in the north and west of England, in Wales, Scotland and in Ireland. Acorns have very short stalk.

English Elm *Ulmus procera* H 3000
Fine, tall tree, commonest in southern and south-west England. Much less common in the north of England and East Anglia. The small-leaved Elm, *U. minor*, is more common in the Midlands and in south-east England. It is very variable, and often reproduces by suckering, to give cloned populations of identical trees. Both species have been badly affected by Dutch Elm Disease.

Sycamore *Acer pseudoplatanus* H 3000
Familiar tree found throughout the region. Not native, but probably introduced as early as the 15th century, and now very common. Sycamore likes deep well-drained soil. It is also very tolerant of high winds and spray from the sea.

Beech *Fagus sylvatica* H 3000
Fine spreading tree, with smooth, grey bark. Forming woods on shallow, well-drained soils, especially on chalky areas in southern England. Beech woods are open habitats, often with little in the way of shrubs growing below the trees. The triangular nuts, known as Beech mast, are produced in the autumn, in varying amounts. In mast years, these seeds provide food for many birds and mammals.

Silver Birch *Betula pendula* H 3000
Pretty tree with silvery bark and drooping branches. Male flowers hang down as catkins. Grows especially on poor and sandy soils, including heaths. Throughout, but rather thinly scattered in Ireland. The similar Downy Birch, *Betula pubescens*, tends to be found on wetter soils and is particularly common in the highlands of Scotland.

Holly *Ilex aquifolium* H 1000
Widespread prickly tree with leathery, green leaves and bright red berries (when ripe). Absent from extreme north-east of Scotland, Orkney and Shetland. Holly sometimes forms a shrub layer in woods.

Hazel *Corylus avellana* H 600
Widespread shrub, often found as woodland undergrowth, especially in coppiced woods, but also in the open (as in the Burren) and in hedges. Edible nuts attract mammals such as squirrels and mice.

Ash *Fraxinus excelsior* H 4000
A large tree, common throughout, except in the highlands and far north of Scotland. Ash has large, pinnate leaves, smooth bark and large, black buds. Found as scattered trees, or as a component of mixed deciduous woods. Ash prefers calcareous soils, and moist or wet habitats.

Common Alder

Norway Spruce

Sycamore

English Oak

English Elm

Holly

Common Beech

Silver Birch

Hazel

Common Ash

Greater Stitchwort *Stellaria holostea* **H 60**
Common hedgerow plant with large white flowers. Found throughout, but not in Orkney, Shetland and Outer Hebrides, rare in west of Ireland. Similar Lesser Stitchwort, *S. graminea*, has smaller flowers and prefers dry, acid heathland.

White Campion *Silene alba* **H 80**
Common as a weed in rough places and roadsides in lowland areas. Common in many areas, but rare in Ireland, Wales and south-west England. Very similar, except for colour, to the Red Campion. Hybrids occur, with pink flowers, where the two overlap. These hybrid plants are often very pretty, and are themselves fertile, forming obvious patches along roadside verges, hedges and woodland margins.

Red Campion *Silene dioicais* **H 80**
A beautiful flower of hedgerows and woodland edges. Also rare in Ireland, central Scotland and the East Anglian fenland.

Sea Campion *Silene maritima* **H 20**
This pretty coastal flower has large white flowers, each with a swollen calyx. It grows in low cushions on sea-cliffs and shingle. The similar Bladder Campion, *Silene vulgaris*, is a taller species which grows inland on disturbed sites such as roadsides.

Marsh Marigold *Caltha palustris* **H 50**
Like a large buttercup with glossy leaves and large flowers. Found In marshes, wet woods and along the banks of streams. Throughout region, but rather scattered in South-west Ireland.

Wood Anemone *Anemone nemorosa* **H 30**
A common woodland spring flower, also found in hedges and in mountains to about 800 m, Wood Anemones make a beautiful sight in the spring, appearing like white stars on the woodland floor, mostly before the canopy has come into leaf. Rare in southern Ireland, north Scotland and fenland.

Lesser Celandine *Ranunculus ficaria* **H 25**
Another common spring flower found throughout the region, but rather scattered in southern Ireland. Pretty, star-like yellow flowers and heart-shaped glossy leaves.

Lesser Spearwort *Ranunculus flammula* **H 50**
A widespread flower of damp and wet habitats throughout the region. Rather a grass-like growth, and small yellow flowers. It often spreads along the ground by runners. The leaves have a sharp, burning taste, and both this species and the next are poisonous to cattle. Greater Spearwort, *R. lingua*, has larger flowers and grows taller. It can be seen in lowland areas, in fens and marshland. Both spearworts flower in summer and early autumn.

Meadow Buttercup *Ranunculus acris* **H 90**
One of three common buttercups. Found everywhere in damp meadows and pasture, even in high mountains. Flowers late spring and summer. The other common species are Creeping Buttercup, *R. repens*, and Bulbous Buttercup, *R. bulbosus*. The former has a ridged stem and the latter has sepals which turn back along stem.

Common Poppy *Papaver rhoeas* **H 60**
A familiar field and roadside weed, found throughout, but rather rare in the north and west of both Britain and Ireland. The scarlet petals often have a dark spot at the base. The Long-headed Poppy, *P. dubium*, has paler flowers. It is found in similar habitats but gets further north and west.

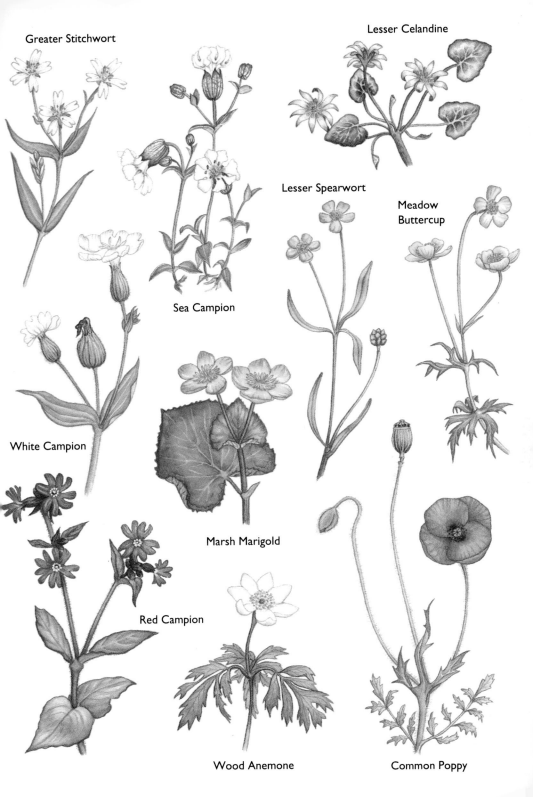

Greater Stitchwort

Lesser Celandine

Lesser Spearwort

Meadow Buttercup

Sea Campion

White Campion

Marsh Marigold

Red Campion

Wood Anemone

Common Poppy

Rowan *Sorbus aucuparia*   H 1500
This slender tree has clusters of white flowers in the spring, and attractive red berries in the autumn. It is characteristic of woods and rocky sites throughout the region, particularly on acid soils, but is rare over much of lowland England. Grows at altitudes of up to over 900 m, which is higher than any other British tree species.

Blackthorn *Prunus spinosa*   H 400
Very widespread shrub with spiny twigs. Often encouraged and planted in hedges since it provides a good thorny protective barrier, along with hawthorns. The white flowers brighten up hedgerows in spring. Carries blue-black sloes in autumn. Often grows at field and woodland edges, and even on exposed coasts, where wind-pruning keeps it low-growing and dense. Blackthorn bushes provide an important safe nest-site for many birds.

Hawthorn *Crataegus monogyna*   H 500+
A common shrub or small tree of woodland, hedgerows, heath and scrubland. Bears clusters of white flowers in spring, and oval red berries, called haws, in the autumn. The haws are eaten by birds and small mammals in the autumn and winter. The similar Midland Hawthorn, *C. laevigata*, which is local in Wales and southern England, has less deeply lobed leaves.

Dog Rose *Rosa canina*   H 300
This spiny shrub with large pink or white flowers is one of the commonest of our wild roses. It grows throughout the area, except in the far north. Many birds feed on the smooth red hips, especially in harsh weather in autumn and winter.

Bramble *Rubus fruticosus*   H 200
Familiar hedgerow shrub with sharp thorns and tangled growth. Found everywhere, except highlands of Scotland, in woods, field margins and waste ground.

Tormentil *Potentilla erecta*   H 30
Very widespread throughout region. Bright yellow flowers with four petals and leaves with three leaflets each. Commonest on acid soils such as heathland.

Meadowsweet *Filipendula ulmaria*   H 100
Found in wet places throughout the region, especially when these are not mown or grazed frequently. Cream-coloured flower heads. Leaves have distinctive smell of oil of wintergreen. Likes fertile soils bordering rivers, lakes or streams, but avoids those which are waterlogged through the year.

Gorse *Ulex europaeus*   H 200
Very spiny shrub with masses of yellow flowers in late winter and early spring. Characteristic of heaths and rough grassland, in all parts of the region. Also found on roadsides, railway embankments and sea cliffs, and along rides in coniferous plantations.

Broom *Cytisus scoparius*   H 200
Not spiny, but has gorse-like yellow flowers. Flowers borne on long, green stems. Flowers in spring and early summer. Broom is common on heaths and rough grassland.

Tufted Vetch *Vicica cracca*   H 200
One of the commonest and most widespread of the vetches. Each flower stalk has many purple flowers. Found in hedgerows, scrub, embankments, woodland margins, rough grassland and also coastal shingle.

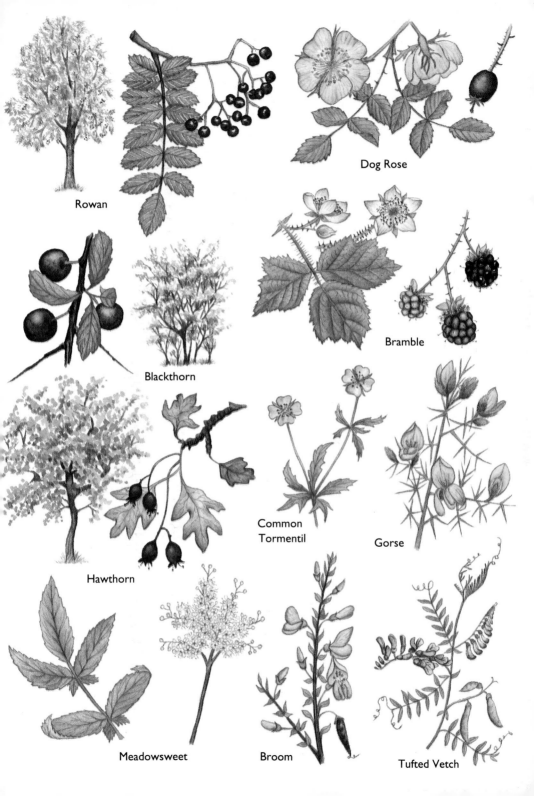

Rowan

Dog Rose

Blackthorn

Bramble

Hawthorn

Common
Tormentil

Gorse

Meadowsweet

Broom

Tufted Vetch

Wood Sorrel *Oxalis acetosella* **H 15**
Pretty white flowers with lilac veins, appearing in spring and early summer. The clover-like leaves are very characteristic. A common woodland plant, also found amongst rocks and in hedgerows.

Common Mallow *Malva sylvestris* **H 80**
A rather stocky plant with pretty, large purple flowers and large round leaves. Most often seen as a weed along roadsides and on waste ground. Found throughout, but much less common in Ireland, Wales and Scotland.

Common Dog-violet *Viola riviniana* **H 30**
The commonest wild violet, with a pale spur to the relatively large flower. It grows in woods, heath and grassland throughout the region. The Early Dog-violet, *V. reichenbachiana*, is similar, but has a dark spur. It is most common in the chalky woods of southern and eastern England. It is one of our earliest woodland species, with flowers appearing in March.

White Bryony *Bryonia dioica* **H 600**
A climber found in hedges and woodland edges in the lowlands of England and Wales. Virtually absent from Ireland, Wales the south-west and north-west of England, and from Scotland. Female plant has bright red berries in the autumn.

Purple Loosestrife *Lythrum salicaria* **H 120**
A beautiful flower of wet habitats in all areas except for much of northern and eastern Scotland. Purple Loosestrife brightens many a swampy or fenland habitat, especially when clumps grow close together. The flowers are attractive to many insects, including butterflies.

Great Willowherb *Epilobium hirsutum* **H 150**
A tall, hairy plant with pretty pink flowers in the summer. Found in wet habitats in Ireland, Wales and England, but absent from much of Scotland. Often grows along river banks and in fenland habitats.

Rosebay Willowherb
Chamaenerion angustifolium **H 120**
This showy flower adds colour to waste ground, embankments and roadsides in many parts of the region. Absent from much of Ireland and northern Scotland. A classic weed species which rapidly colonizes as the community develops further. Often associated with building sites and waste land. Tends to avoid wetter soils and prefers rather acid conditions.

Cow Parsley *Anthriscus sylvestris* **H 100**
Common throughout the region. This pretty umbellifer, also known as Queen Anne's Lace, has delicate white flowers. Found in hedges, at woodland edges and along roadsides. Flowers in late spring.

Wild Angelica *Angelica sylvestris* **H 200**
The leaves and stems of this tall flower have a rather purplish tinge. Another characteristic feature are the slightly inflated leaf-stalks. A plant of marshes, wet woods and damp grassland. Grows throughout the region, up to about 900 m in Scotland.

Hogweed *Heracleum sphondylium* **H 200**
Flowers after Cow Parsley in summer. Large, flat white heads of flowers. Hogweed grows along roadside verges and similar sites throughout the region, up to about 1000 m in Scotland. the related Giant Hogweed, *H. mantegazzianum*, lives up to its name, growing to 5 m tall. It is a garden escape, but is found scattered in the wild as well. Its sap can cause blisters on the skin, in sunlight.

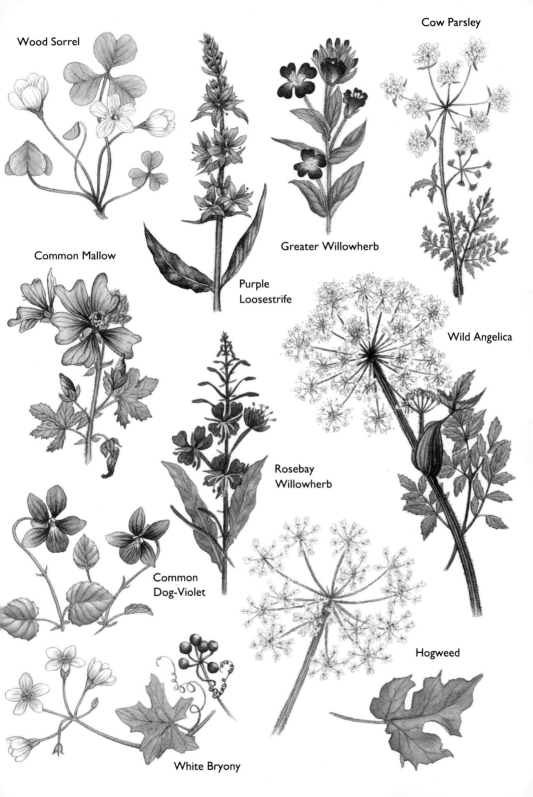

Wood Sorrel

Cow Parsley

Common Mallow

Greater Willowherb

Purple Loosestrife

Wild Angelica

Rosebay Willowherb

Common Dog-Violet

Hogweed

White Bryony

Bell Heather *Erica cinerea*   H 60
Found on dry heaths and moorland throughout the region, except central England and central Ireland. The similar Cross-leaved Heath, *Erica tetralix*, which is a flower of wet heath and bog, is softly hairy.

Heather *Calluna vulgaris*   H 60
The dominant plant of upland moors and lowland heath alike. Beautiful purple (occasionally white) flowers, often colouring whole hillsides. Heather moor is mainly a carefully managed and maintained artificial habitat which is systematically burned to encourage re-growth of relatively pure stands of Heather, mostly to provide ideal habitat for Red Grouse. This habitat covers huge areas of upland Britain. Older, taller Heather encourages other species as well, including the rare Merlin.

Bilberry *Vaccinium myrtillus*   H 60 ·
A tough shrub with rather shiny, toothed leaves, pale red flowers and black berries. Common on heather moors and in acid woods. Avoids the limestone of central, southern and eastern England.

Primrose *Primula vulgaris*   H 10
A common and very pretty spring flower of woods, hedges and grassland. In the south-east of England, Primroses tend to be associated with woods, but in the west they are also a feature of grassland. Local in south and west Ireland. One of our most familiar wild flowers.

Cowslip *Primula veris*   H 20
The flowers are a deeper colour than those of Primrose and are held up on long stalks. A plant of lime-rich grassland and road verges. The larger Oxlip, *Primula elatior* has paler flowers. Cowslip has a very limited distribution, growing only in certain East Anglian woods.

Yellow Loosestrife *Lysimachia vulgaris*   H 120
This fine flower grows alongside streams, rivers, lakes and in fens. It belongs to the same family as Primrose, although it has a very different growth habit and general appearance. Its closest relatives are in fact the Yellow Pimpernel and Creeping Jenny. It does not occur in northern Scotland.

Thrift *Armeria maritima*   H 25
The delicate pink flowers on soft cushions enliven many cliffs and saltmarshes all around our coasts. However, Thrift is also found on some inland mountains in northern England and Scotland, up to a height of 1250m.

Bogbean *Menyanthes trifoliata*   H 40
Scattered throughout, but especially common in the north and west, mostly in acid lakes, ponds and bogs. The large three-lobed leaves are highly distinctive.

Cleavers *Galium aparine*   H 120
Leaves, stems and fruits all tend to stick to clothing because of their hooked hairs. Found throughout in hedges, woods and waste land. Absent from Scottish highlands.

Field Bindweed *Convolvulus arvensis*   H 75
A common weed of the lowlands; rarer in the north and west. Flowers are white or pink. The coastal Sea Bindweed, *Calystegia soldanella*, has heart-shaped leaves. Hedge Bindweed, *Calystegia sepium*, and Large Bindweed, *Calystegia silvatica*, have much larger flowers.

228

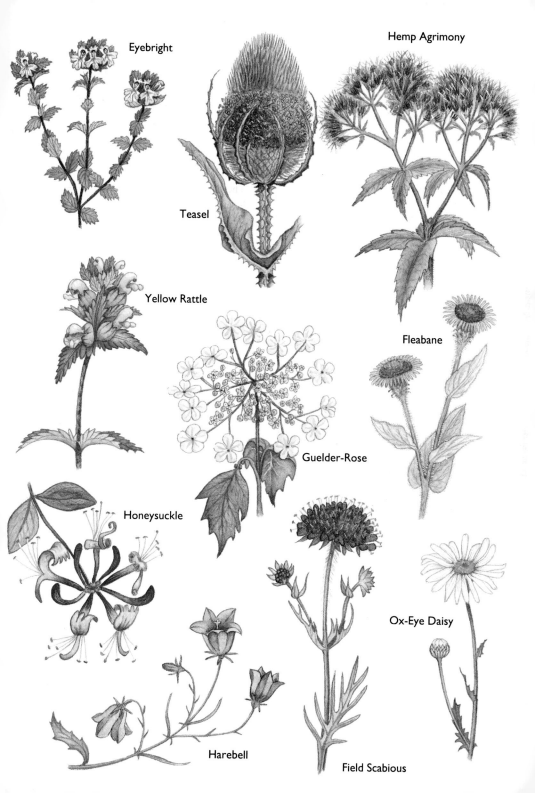

Eyebright

Hemp Agrimony

Teasel

Yellow Rattle

Fleabane

Guelder-Rose

Honeysuckle

Ox-Eye Daisy

Harebell

Field Scabious

Bugle *Ajuga reptans* **H 30**
Resembles Selfheal, with its spikes of blue flowers. However, the flowers of Bugle lack an upper hood. May also be confused with Water Mint, but has no minty smell. Found throughout region, in damp woods and meadows.

White Dead-Nettle *Lamium album* **H 60**
A common plant throughout lowland areas but rare in much of Ireland and Scotland. Grows in hedges, fields and waste places. Red Dead-nettle, *Lamium purpureum*, is also a common weed; it is smaller and has pink flowers.

Yellow Archangel
Lamiastrum galeobdolon **H 60**
Looks like a nettle with yellow flowers. Likes wet woodland and other well-shaded moist habitats. Flowers in late spring and early summer. Rare in Scotland and Ireland, and commonest in southern and eastern England.

Betony *Stachys officinalis* **H 60**
A tall-stemmed flower of open woods, heath and grassland, especially on limestone soils. Widespread, but rather rare in Scotland and Ireland, and probably decreasing in most lowland areas. Formerly collected and used as a medicinal herb.

Selfheal *Prunella vulgaris* **H 30**
A very common flower of woodland, grassland, limestone pasture and old lawns. Grows throughout the region. Often found growing alongside Daisy which has a similar ecology. With its creeping habit and vegetative reproduction it is well suited to survive even quite close regular grazing or mowing.

Wild Thyme *Thymus praecox* **H 10**
A creeping aromatic flower of dry grassland, dunes and heath. In southern and eastern England the Larger Thyme, *Thymus pulegioides*, also occurs. It has a longer flowering stem.

Water Mint *Mentha aquatica* **H 90**
Common in shady, wet and marshy habitats throughout, although rarer in northern Scotland. Occasionally grows partly submerged in the water, but usually grows some way from the water's edge. Forms patches as it grows by sending out rhizomes, and also spreads by stem fragments floated to other sites. Gives of a distinct minty smell when the leaves or stems are crushed. The flowers are insect pollinated and attract butterflies.

Common Toadflax *Linaria vulgaris* **H 60**
Bright yellow flowers, each with a spur, and pale green somewhat feathery foliage. Common Toadflax grows throughout Britain in grassland and on roadsides. Uncommon in northern Scotland and Ireland.

Foxglove *Digitalis purpurea* **H 150**
Very well-known flower of acid soils, especially where the ground has been disturbed, such as river banks, rocky ledges and hedgerows. Also likes burned areas within acid woodland and recent plantations. The seeds of Foxglove, which are produced in huge quantities, need disturbed soil in which to germinate and grow. Rare in lime-rich areas of south-east England, and in central Ireland; commonest in upland regions. The leaves are poisonous to grazing animals.

Germander Speedwell
Veronica chamardrys **H 25**
Common in hedges and in grassland and limestone pasture. It likes lightly grazed habitats, where there is some disturbance to the soil. The Heath Speedwell, *Veronica officinalis*, has lilac-coloured flowers on a long spike. It is found in drier habitats than the previous species, referring heaths, dry woods and dry grassland.

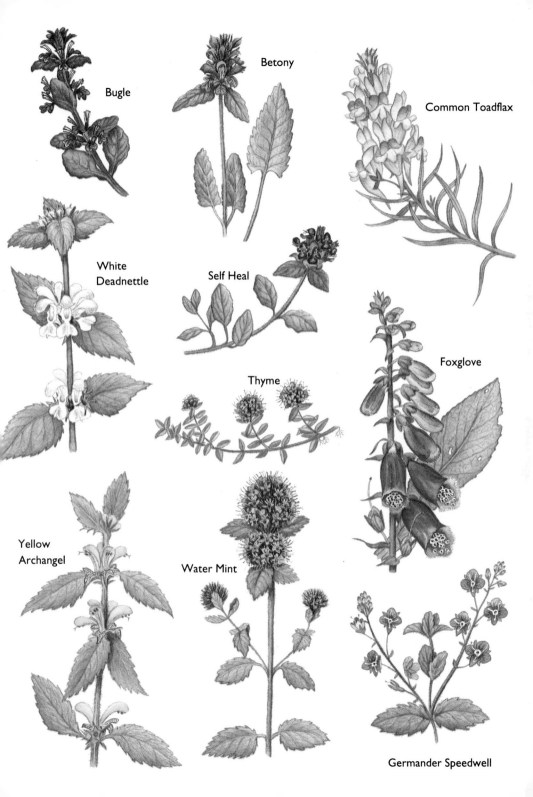

Bugle

Betony

Common Toadflax

White Deadnettle

Self Heal

Thyme

Foxglove

Yellow Archangel

Water Mint

Germander Speedwell

Eyebright *genus Euphrasia*
These small, pretty flowers are tricky to identify to species level, although the genus itself is really rather distinctive. The commonest is *E. nemorosa*, a plant of grassland, heaths, grassy hedgerows and wood margins, especially in England and Wales. It is much more local in Scotland and Ireland. The Eyebright flowers in late summer.

Yellow Rattle *Rhinanthus minor* **H 50**
A common flower of grassland throughout the region, although rather patchy in East Anglia. It likes well-established, unfertilized traditional pastures and hay-meadows. Since this habitat is threatened in many of the more intensively farmed areas, this species has suffered a decline in recent years. Yellow Rattle is a semi-parasite which uses several host species, including grasses and legumes, from which it takes nutrients.

Honeysuckle *Lonicera oericlymenum*
H many metres
This climber rambles over hedgerows and trees throughout Britain and Ireland. It also grows as a more compact shrub on the woodland floor. In the north it tends to grow on south-facing slopes in woodland, and on north-facing slopes in more open habitats. Honeysuckle is a common colonizing species in broad-leaf plantations, on light, acid soils. It has beautiful, scented flowers which attract moths in summer evenings.

Harebell *Campanula rotundifolia* **H 30**
The pretty sky-blue bell-like flowers are held up on thin stalks. A common flower of grassland. In Ireland, restricted to north and west, including the Burren. The woodland Giant Bellflower, *C. latifolia*, is frequent in central and northern England. It has large flowers, about 4cm long. In southern and eastern England, the Nettle-leaved Bellflower, *C. trachelium*, also occurs in woods.

Teasel *Dipsacus fullonum* **H 150**
Tall and prickly, this is an unmistakable flower, found on roadside verges, embankments and by footpaths, mainly in the southern half of the region. Absent from most of Ireland, north-western Britain and Scotland. Flowers are very attractive to butterflies, especially Peacocks, and the seed-heads to Goldfinches.

Guelder Rose *Viburnum opulus* **H 350**
A shrub with pretty clusters of white flowers, and bright red berries in autumn. Found in wet woods and in fen carr. Only scattered in Ireland and Scotland.

Field Scabious *Knautia arvensis* **H 100**
A flower mainly of limestone and chalk grass-lands, found everywhere except the west and north of Scotland and Ireland. Attracts adult Marbled White butterflies in south-western England.

Hemp Agrimony
Eupatorium cannabinum **H 120**
A flower of wet habitats, such as damp woods, marshes, and fens. Also found at the coast, particularly in Scotland. The flower heads look very soft, and have a pinkish colour. Rather rare in much of Ireland and Scotland.

Blue Fleabane *Erigeron acer* **H 40**
A rather scruffy looking flower of banks, walls, dunes and dry grassland, usually on lime-rich soils. Commonest in southern and eastern England, and northern and southern Wales.

Oxeye Daisy *Leucanthemum vulgare* **H 80**
This large-flowered daisy is a common flower of grassland throughout the region. The common Scentless Mayweed, *Tripleurospermum inodorum*, has similar, but less flat flowers. A weed of arable crops and waste ground.

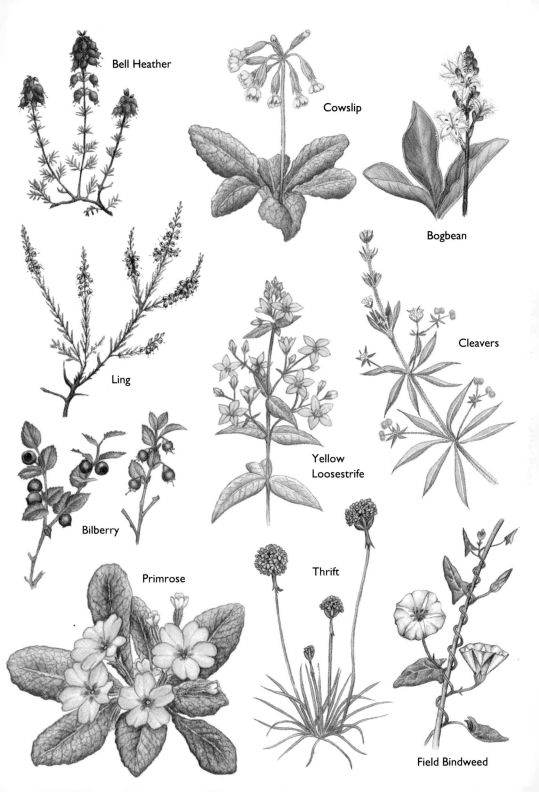

Bell Heather

Cowslip

Bogbean

Ling

Yellow
Loosestrife

Cleavers

Bilberry

Primrose

Thrift

Field Bindweed

Common Ragwort *Senecio jacobaea* **H 150**
Bright yellow flowers and divided leaves typify this very common pasture weed. Also grows on dunes, in limestone quarries, on rocky sites and screes and all kinds of waste ground and open spaces. It is very poisonous to grazing mammals, including rabbits, and it therefore grows well even in heavily grazed sites, whether these be fields grazed by horses and cattle, or open, rabbit-grazed turf. The Cinnabar Moth, *Tyria jacobaeae*, is often found on this plant, which is sometimes stripped of its foliage by the yellow and black striped caterpillars.

Spear Thistle *Cirsium vulgare* **H 150**
A common weed in pastures. It is also avoided by many grazing animals, because of the sharp spines which cover its stem and leaves. It colonizes parts of fields, particularly when they are overgrazed, and is also resistant to drought. This thistle has large, purple flowers. Each plant produces up to 8000 seeds, each borne on a feathery parachute, and dispersed on the wind. The fruiting heads often attract small seed-eating birds, such as Goldfinches.

Creeping Thistle *Cirsium arvense* **H 120**
This is the other very common thistle, which grows in similar habitats to the Spear Thistle, and it spreads mainly by thin roots, which spread out from the original plant.

Common Knapweed *Centaurea nigra* **H 60**
A very common summer flower found in roadside verges, grassland and hedgerows. The Greater Knapweed, *Centaurea scabiosa*, which is common in lowland Britain, and in the Burren of Ireland, has larger flower heads and dissected leaves.

Common Dandelion
Taraxacum officinale **H 20**
One of our best-known flowers, found wherever there is wasted ground or disturbed soil. The leaves make characteristic rosettes, which are often seen on lawns, and the bright yellow rounded inflorescence turns into a soft mass of fluffy seeds – the so-called dandelion clock. Dandelions are quick to colonize new habitats by seed.

Bluebell *Hyacinthoides non-scripta* **H 50**
A common flower of woodland, scrub and hedgerows throughout the region. In many southern, deciduous woods, especially ancient woods, it forms carpets of blue flowers in the spring. Like many woodland species, Bluebells are adapted to develop and flower before the main leaf cover reduces the sunlight reaching the woodland floor. This is one of the region's most typical flowers, being otherwise absent from most of Europe, except north-west France.

Yellow Iris *Iris pseudacorus* **H 150**
A fine, tall flower of wetlands throughout the region. Unmistakable, with large bright yellow flowers, and flat rather spear-like leaves. Often grows along river banks and at the margins of ditches.

Ramsons *Allium ursinum* **H 45**
Common late spring flower of wet, but well-drained woodlands, especially on limestone. Rare in much of Ireland and in north-east Scotland, and generally rather local in the east. The leaves smell strongly of garlic when crushed, and they add a fine flavour to sandwiches! Ramsons produces heads of white, star-shaped flowers in the late spring.

Lords and Ladies *Arum maculatum* **H 50**
Common in woods and hedges, but absent from most of northern and central Scotland. The similar Italian Lords and Ladies, *Arum italicum*, has an orange spadix and bears its leaves in the autumn and winter.

Common Spotted Orchid
Dactylorhiza fuchsii **H 70**
This is one of our commoner orchids. It grows in woods, marshes and meadows throughout the region. It has oval spots on its leaves. More acid sites, especially in the north and west, are the choice of the Heath Spotted Orchid, *Dactylorhiza maculata*. This has leaves with round spots, and a narrower spur on the flowers.

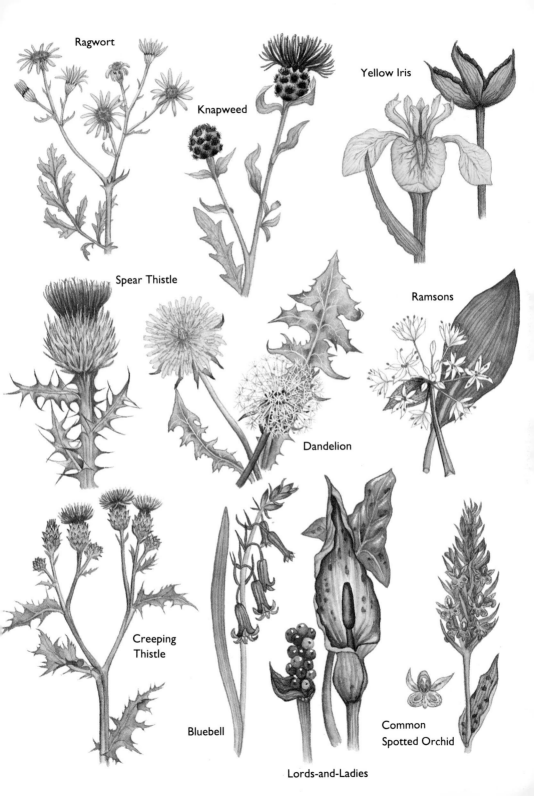

Ragwort

Knapweed

Yellow Iris

Spear Thistle

Ramsons

Dandelion

Creeping
Thistle

Bluebell

Common
Spotted Orchid

Lords-and-Ladies

USEFUL ADDRESSES

An Taisce (National Trust for Ireland)
The Tailors' Hall
Back Lane
Dublin 8

Botanical Society of the British Isles
c/o Natural History Museum
Cromwell Road
London SW7

British Butterfly Conservation Society
Tudor House
Quorn, nr Loughborough
Leicestershire LE12 8AD

British Trust for Ornithology
The Nunnery
Nunnery Place
Thetford
Norfolk IP24 2PU

Irish Wild Bird Conservancy
Royal Irish Academy
19 Dawson Street
Dublin 2
Eire

National Trust
36 Queen Anne's Gate
London SW1H 9AS

Royal Society for Nature Conservation
The Green
Witham Park
Waterside South
Lincoln
Lincolnshire LN2 7JR

Royal Society for the Protection of Birds
The Lodge
Sandy
Bedfordshire SG19 2DL

Wildfowl and Wetlands Trust
Slimbridge
Gloucestershire GL2 7BT

BIBLIOGRAPHY

BIRDS
Complete Book of British Birds (AA/RSPB 1988).
Gooders, J. Field Guide to the Birds of Britain and Ireland (Kingfisher Books 1986).
Heinzel, H., Fitter, R. & Parslow, J. The Birds of Britain and Europe (Collins 1972).
Morrison, P. Bird Habitats of Great Britain and Ireland (Michael Joseph 1989).
Parslow, J. (ed.) Birdwatcher's Britain (Pan Books/Ordnance Survey 1983).
Ratcliffe, D.A. Bird Life of Mountain and Upland (CUP 1990).
Redman, N. and Harrap, S. Birdwatching in Britain (Christopher Helm 1987).
RSPB Where to go Birdwatching (BBC Books 1987/9).
Singer, D. Field Guide to the

Birds of Britain and Northern Europe (The Crowood Press 1991).

FLOWERS
Halliday, G. & Malloch, A. Wild Flowers: Their Habitats in Britain and Northern Europe (Peter Lowe 1981).
Perring, F. & Walters, M. British Wildflowers (Macmillan 1989).
Polunin, O. Collins Photoguide to Wild Flowers of Britain and Northern Europe (Collins 1988).

REPTILES AND AMPHIBIANS
Arnold, E.N. & Burton, J.A. A Field Guide to the Reptiles and Amphibians of Britain and Europe (Collins 1978).

BUTTERFLIES
Chinery, M. Butterflies and

Day-flying Moths of Britain and Europe (Collins 1989).
Higgins, G. & Riley, N.D.A Field Guide to the Butterflies of Britain and Europe (Collins 1970).
Thomas, J. & Lewington, R. The Butterflies of Britain and Ireland (Dorling Kindersley 1991).
Whalley, P. The Mitchell Beazley Pocket Guide to Butterflies (Mitchell Beazley 1981).

GENERAL
Beames, I. Exploring Britain's Wildlife (David & Charles 1988).
Botting, D. Wild Britain (Ebury Press 1988).
Guide to Britain's Nature Reserves (Macmillan 1984).
Nature Atlas of Great Britain (Pan/Ordnance Survey 1989).

INDEX

Numbers in bold refer to main entries.

Aberlady Bay 20, 66
acid rain 17
acidification 9
Adder 15, 35, 136, 141, 163, 171, 183, 214
Adonis Blue 106–108, 119, 123
Ailsa Craig 59, 64
Ainsdale Dunes 72
Alder 220
Alexanders 91
Alpine Bartsia 53, 67, 68, 84
Alpine Cinquefoil 53, 84, 166
alpine flowers 7, 38, 48, 53, 55, 80
Alpine Lady's Mantle 45, 49, 51–53, 61
Alpine Saw-wort 35, 36, 53, 166
Angelica 19, 99, 101, 125, 226
Arctic Skua 32, 33, 152
Arctic Tern 32
Argyll 14, 48
Argyll Forest Park 48
Arne 153
Arran 64, 65
Arundel 110, 132
Ashbourne 10, 86, 140
Ashdown Forest 115, 116
Ashton Wold 16
Aston Rowant 135
Autumn Crocus 131
Autumn Lady's Tresses 108
Avocet 91, 95, 113, 152, 153
Avon 125, 142, 143
Avon Gorge 143
Axmouth 155
Badger 77, 115, 131, 136, 158, 162, 169, 171, 177, 187, 212
Balranald 42, 43
Bardsey Island 162, 165
Barn Owl 18, 110, 123, 132, 169, 171, 200
Barnacle Goose 61, 63, 185
Bass Rock 12, 63, 66
Beachy Head 108, 109
Bearded Tit 90, 91, 97, 110, 156
Bee Orchid 72, 74, 121
Beech 220
beechwoods 15
Beinn Eighe 38
Bell Heather 228
Ben Lawers 9, 51, 53–55, 54
Ben Lui 53
Ben Nevis 8
Benacre 97
Benbulbin 186
Bens of Connemara 8
Berkshire 125
Betony 123, 136, 141, 145, 230
Bewick's Swan 91, 110, 152, 192
Bilberry 228

Bird's Eye Primrose 31, 32, 67, 68, 78, 84
Bird's Nest Orchid 103, 131, 134, 144
Bittern 22, 68, 75, 76, 90, 91, 94, 97, 110, 111, 176
Black Grouse 16, 17, 41, 47, 48, 53, 58, 60, 78
Black Guillemot 19, 33, 36, 38, 41, 181, 183, 184
Black Redstart 71, 87, 107, 146
Black Tern 94, 95, 122, 152
Black-necked Grebe 117
Black-tailed Godwit 18, 19, 61, 66, 91, 94, 100, 109, 113, 132, 144, 152, 153, 164, 190
Black-throated Diver 22, 39, 41, 53, 81
Blackthorn 15, 21, 105, 108, 135, 155, 224
Blakeney 92–95, 95
Bloody Cranesbill 74, 87, 157, 163, 188
Blue-eyed Grass 186, 191
Bluebell 112, 137, 141, 143, 144, 148, 234
Bodmin Moor 13, 158
Bog Asphodel 44, 114, 115, 135, 140, 151, 157, 166, 171, 179, 186, 187
Bog Myrtle 53, 78, 120, 169, 179, 187
Bog Rosemary 59, 60, 171, 179
Bogbean 45, 80, 112, 140, 174, 190, 228
Border Loughs 80
Bosherston Ponds 173
Box Hill 106, 115
Brambling 16
Brandon Mountain 8
Braunton Burrows 146
Brecon Beacons 8, 139, 161, 176
Brent Goose 109, 110, 153, 155, 185
Bridgwater Bay 20, 147
Brimstone 117, 137, 216
British Storm-petrel 127, 193
Broom 14, 224
Brown Argus 52, 63, 102, 107, 119, 123, 131, 135, 140, 145
Brown Hairstreak 143, 162, 185, 189
Brown Hare 53, 210
Brownsea Island 154, 155
Bryher 160
Buckholt Wood 133, 134
Buff Wood 103
Bugle 31, 32, 39, 145, 230
Bunowen Bay 8, 8
Burnham Beeches 135
Burnham Overy Staithe 19, 19
Burren 8, 9, 38, 67, 87, 185, 188, 189, 216, 218, 220, 232, 234
Buzzard 198

Cadair Idris 167
Caenlochan 55
Caerlaverock 20, 59, 61, 62
Cairngorms 8, 51, 57, 58
Cairnsmore of Fleet 60
Candytuft 102, 135
Cannock Chase 139, 140
Capercaillie 17, 40, 48, 51–53, 55, 58
Carlton Bridge 11
Carneddau 166
Carrot 109, 143
Castle Hill 109
Castor Hanglands 137
Cavenham Heath 98, 99
Cetti's Warbler 96, 97, 110, 112, 127, 142, 143, 151, 176
Chalkhill Blue 107–109, 115, 119, 135
Channel Islands 119, 121, 127, 160
Cheddar Gorge 144, 145
Cheddar Pink 142–145, 145
Chequered Skipper 41
Chiddingfold Forest 116
Chiltern Gentian 135
Chilterns 9, 15
Chough 19, 67, 68, 161–163, 165, 166, 172, 173, 184, 185, 189, 190, 208
Cirl Bunting 18, 127, 142, 143, 151–153
Cissbury Ring 109
Clara Bog 190
Cleavers 228
Cley 92–94
Cliffs of Moher 19, 189
Clo Mor 38
Cloudberry 61, 78, 86
Clouded Yellow 119
Colne Estuary 104
Comma 117, 137, 218
Common Blue 125, 182, 183, 216
Common Dormouse 123
Common Frog 71, 214
Common Gull 181
Common Mallow 226
Common Poppy 222
Common Ragwort 234
Common Sandpiper 22, 43, 46, 68, 168, 171, 177, 181
Common Scoter 22, 36, 47, 54, 63, 110, 153, 176, 182, 191
Common Seal 32, 182, 212
Common Shrew 210
Common Tern 55, 105, 109, 122, 155, 181, 200
Common Toad 214
Compton Down 121
Connemara 8, 87, 178, 185, 188
Connemara National Park 187
conservation 10, 12, 21, 24, 39, 89, 112, 173
coppicing 9, 16
Corn Cockle 12

Corncrake 13, 18, 40–42, 44, 180, 185
Cornflower 12
Cors Caron 170
Cotswolds 9, 129
County Clare 8, 188, 192
Covehithe 97
Cow Parsley 19, 226
Cowslip 89, 90, 102, 121, 133, 228
Craig Cerrig Gleisiag 176
Craig y Cilau 162, 177
Cranberry 59, 78, 140, 171, 179
Cranham Common 134
Creeping Thistle 234
Crested Tit 17, 51, 52
Curlew 198
Cwm Idwal 166, 167
Dandelion 234
Dark Green Fritillary 41, 52, 54, 68, 72, 89, 121, 123, 135, 143, 145, 146, 162, 169, 185
Dark Red Helleborine 31, 87
Dartford Warbler 15, 115, 118–121, 127, 153
Dartmoor 8, 13, 42, 85, 139, 148–150, 158
Dawlish Warren 153
Derbyshire 8, 79, 87
Devil's Bridge 169, 170
Dinas 171
Dingle Peninsula 8, 192
Dingy Skipper 117, 119, 140, 189
Dipper 21, 22, 46, 59, 61, 68, 87, 131, 136, 139, 140, 149, 150, 151, 158, 171, 177
Ditchling Beacon 109
Dog Rose 224
Dolphin 161
Donegal 8, 63, 186
Dormouse 123-125, 131
Dotterel 14, 51, 52, 58, 146, 160
Dovedale 140
Dovey 20, 165, 168
Downs 9, 15, 106, 108, 118, 122
Drigg Dunes 71
Duke of Burgundy 75, 119, 123, 130, 136
Dune Helleborine 72, 82, 164
Dungeness 106, 107
Dunnet Head 36
Dyfi 168
Early Marsh Orchid 72, 74
East Anglia 9, 10, 14, 19, 97, 102, 232
Eastern England 17, 23, 90, 218, 228, 230
Eastern Scotland and Highlands 51
Ebbor Gorge 145
Eden 20, 55
Edible Dormouse 125
Egyptian Goose 91

Eider **31**, 32, 36, 41, 43, 45, 47, 54, 56, 57, 63, 66, 71, 77, 81, 104, 109, 153, 184
Elmley Marshes **113**
English Elm 220
Epping Forest 105
Eskmeals Dunes 71
Essex Skipper 107, 218
Everlasting Pea **20**
Exe Estuary 20, 142, 152
Exmoor 8, 13, 85, 139, 150, 151, 158
Eyebright 121, 133, 135, 145, 184, 186, 232
Fair Isle 34
Fallow Deer 91, 107, 115, **116**, 119, 130, 131, 136, 141, 212
Fanore Dunes 189
Farne Islands 77, 82
Farne Islands 10, 13, 16, 21, 22, 69, 75, 76, 80, 84, 90, 91, 95, 96, 98, 99, 101, 146, 152, 175
Fetlar 32, 33
Field Bindweed 228
Field Fleawort 102, 122, 163
Field Scabious 232
Firecrest 16, 17, 71, 104, 117, 119, 146, 160, 165, 204
Firth of Forth 12
Flamborough Head 85
Fleabane 119, 174, 232
Forest of Dean 129, 130
Fort William 8, 46
Fox 39, 46, 54, 77, 79, 98, 102, 115, 124, 131, 136, 158, **168**, 171, 177, 187, 212
Foxglove 141, 230
Frensham Country Park 115
Frith Wood 134
Frog Orchid 33, 35, 184
Fulmar 196
Gait Barrows **74**
Gannet **12**, 13, 19, 31, 32, 33, 34, 45, 59, 63, 85, 107, 127, 172, 173, 183, 184, 193
Garganey 18, 22, 91, 94, 112, 127, 138, 144, 152
Gatekeeper 218
geology 9, 22, 23, 156, 179, 184
Germander Speedwell 230
Giant's Causeway, **184**
Gibraltar Point 77, 89
Glanville Fritillary 119, 121
Glengarriff Woodland 192
Glenveagh National Park 186
Gloucestershire 129, 131
Goatfell 64, **65**
Goldcrest 17, 48, 131, 140, 204
Golden Eagle 13, 14, 19, 35, 38, 39, 43, 45–47, 49, 51, 52, 55, **57**, 58, 60, 67, 68
Golden Oriole 90, 91, 159
Golden Plover 14, 19, 35, 46, 53, 55, 59, 60, 65, 74, 77, 82, 84, 86, 112, 113, 152, 153, 158, 160, 170, 182, 190, 191

Golden Samphire 104, 113, 122, 163, 164, 173
Goldeneye 22, 36, 47, 50, 66, 73, 74, 95, 100, 104, 109, 117, 122, 144, 153, 155, 164, 169, 180, 182, 191
Goosander 22, 59, 73, 79, 104, 117, 122, 130, 144, 151, 171
Goshawk 16, 17, 78, 120, 121
Grass of Parnassus 54, 66, 72, 78
Grass Snake 113, 214
Grassholm 173
Grasshopper Warbler 95, 97, 130, 137, 152, 158, 169, 171
Grayling 15, 54, 63, 98, 115, 116, 131, 147, 155, 163, 169, 182, 183, 188
Great Black-backed Gull 71, 159, 173
Great Skua 13, 19, 31, 33
Great Spotted Woodpecker 50, 69, **130**, 153, 202
Great Willowherb 76, 110, 125, 226
Greater Stitchwort 222
Green Hairstreak 75, 89, 135, 140, 179, 192
Green-flowered Helleborine 72, 167
Greenshank 38–41, 46, 53, 55, 71, 73, 82, 94, 110, 113, 132
Grey Mare's Tail 61
Grey Seal 32, 34, 78, 143, 162, 172, 212
Grey Squirrel 210
Grey Wagtail 21, 22, 46, 61, 87, 136, 139, 140, 145, 149, 150, 151, 158, 171, 177
Grizzled Skipper 109, 119, 140
Guelder Rose 86, 232
Guillemot 200
Gwenffrwd 171
Hadrian's Wall 77, **80**
Hampshire 9, 14, 118–121, 123–125, 212
Harbottle Crags 79
Harebell 61, 108, 121, 133, 136, 141, 177, 184, 232
Hartland Point 146, 147
Harvest Mouse 123, **133**
Haweswater 57, 70
Hawfinch 87, 105, 119, 120, 131, 135, 136, 140
Hawthorn 224
Hayley Wood 9, 16, 90, **102**, **103**
Hazel 220
Headley Heath 115
Heather 228
Heath Fritillary 107, 143
Hebrides 13, 40, 41, 44, 47, 185, 222
Hemp Agrimony 74, 97, 99, 101, 110, 125, 232

Hen Harrier 14, 17, 35, 47, 49, 59, 61, 73, 77, 81, 89, 100, 112, 113, 170, 171, 191, 198
Herb Paris 103, 131
Hereford 129, 136
Heron, Grey 22, 110, 149, 171, 176, 181, 196
Hickling Broad 95, 96
High Brown Fritillary 68, 75, 143, 149
Hoary Whitlow Grass 84
Hobby 15, 90, 99, 114, 115, 118–121, 126, 153
Hogweed 226
Holkham 91, 92
Holly Blue 126, 131, 216
Holly Fern 41, 46, 49, **161**, 166, 186, 187
Honey Buzzard 16, 118–121, 160
Honeysuckle 112, 155, 216, 232
Hooded Crow 41, 181, 185, 208
Irish Lady's Tresses 41, **42**, 188
Irish Republic 8, 25, 182, 185
Irish Spurge 185, 191
Islay 47, 63
Isle of Noss 33
Isle of Wight 119, 121, 210
Isles of Scilly 142, 158–160
Jay **30**, 50, 179, 208
Jersey 126, 127
Kerry 191-193
Kerry Lily 191
Kestrel 18, 43, 47, 79, 110, 115, 120, 145, 149, 187, 191, 198
Killard 181, 182
Killarney National Park 191
King's Lynn 15
Kingfisher 22, 110, 131, 136, 140, 144, 149, 171, 202
Kingley Vale 108, 135
Kittiwake 200
Knapweed 133, 234
Knot 20, 66, **73**, 74, 82, 87, 89, 104, 113, 147, 182, 190
Lake District 8, 11, 57, 67, 68, 70, 218
Langstone Harbour 20, 122
Lapland Bunting 14
Large Blue 118, 143
Large Copper 91, 99
Large Heath 32, 41, 46, 52, 59, 60, 78, 139, 169, 179, 185, 192
Large-flowered Butterwort 178, 185, 191, **192**
Lathkill Dale 86, 87
Leach's Storm-petrel 19, 31, 32, 35, 74, 165, 186
Leigh Woods 143
Leighton Moss 75, 76
Lesser Black-backed Gull 200
Lesser Celandine 103, 145, 222
Lesser Spearwort 145, 222
Lesser White-toothed Shrew 160

Levisham Moor 82
Lindisfarne 77, 81, **82**
Little Brosna River 189
Little Gull 87, 122
Little Owl 18, 98, 126
Little Ringed Plover 89, 107, **138**, 139
Little Skellig 193
Little Tern 89, 107, 113, 155, 190, 192
Loch Druidibeg 43, 44
Loch Gruinart 47
Loch Leven 55, **56**
Loch Lomond **49**, 50
London 105, 117, 200, 212
Long-eared Bat 210
Long-eared Owl 17, 46, 97, 137, 140, 179, 191
Long-tailed Duck 36, 38, 54, 57, 66, 81, 122, 151, 182
Lords and Ladies 158, 234
Lough Neagh 179-181
Lullington Heath 109
Lulworth Skipper 143, 156
Lundy 142, 143, 146
Lyme Regis 155
machair 10, 18, 40, 42–44
Magillicuddy's Reeks 8
Magilligan Point 183
Malham Tarn 84
Mandarin 110, 126
Manx Shearwater 13, 19, 32, 33, 41, 46, 74, 146, 159–162, 172, 173, 178, 184, 192, 193
Marbled White 18, 109, 115, 119, 121, 133, 143, 145, 147, 155, **156**, 232
Marsh Clubmoss 179
Marsh Fritillary 22, 41, 123, 143, 163, 179, 185, 189, 191
Marsh Frog 113
Marsh Harrier 22, 76, 90, 94, 97, 144, 176
Marsh Helleborine 72, 74, 146, 169, 174
Marsh Marigold 19, 76, 80, 145, 152, 222
Marsh Sow-thistle 97
Marsh Warbler 130
Martagon Lily 131
Martham Broad 95
Martin Down 118, 123
Martin Mere 72, 73
Meadow Brown 218
Meadow Buttercup 222
Meadowsweet 19, 76, 99, 101, 110, 145, 224
Mediterranean Gull 107
Merlin 14, 35, 38, 39, 43, 46, 47, 59–61, 73, 77–79, 81, 82, 86, 89, 100, 112, 132, 160, 168, 170, 171, 177, 185–187, 191
Mezereon 86, 134, 140
Midlands and Welsh Borders 129
Milk Parsley 95, 96

Minchinhampton Common 133
Minsmere 96, 97
mires 10, 120, 140, 171
mixed fen 21
mixed planting 17
Mole 210
Monkshood 129, 130, 137
Morfa Harlech 166
Moss Campion 39, 41, 45, 46,
   49, 55, 58, 166, 168, 186
Mossy Saxifrage 39, 78, 79, 87,
   140, 166, 168, 177, 188
Mountain Avens 31, 32, 37, 38,
   45, 46, 53, 55, 84, 166, 186,
   188
Mountain Hare 14, 35, 39, 52,
   56, 58, 59, 166, 210
Mountain Ringlet 52, 54, 68, 70
Mountain Sorrel 58, 65, 166,
   186
Mountains of Mourne 8
National Parks 11, 24, 27
Natterjack 15, 21, 23, 61, 71,
   89, 191, 214
nature reserves 7, 12, 24, 27,
   118, 161
Neolithic 9, 12neutral rocks 9
New Forest 24, 118–121, 125,
   126
Newborough Warren 164
Nightingale 97, 98, 103, 115,
   117, 119, 123, 125, 137, 152,
   155
Nightjar 15, 17, 90, 98, 115,
   118–121, 123, 126, 130, 153
Norfolk Broads 16, 24, 90, 95,
   96
North and South Downs 9, 106
North Bull Island 190
North Hoy 35
North Meadow 123
North Norfolk Coast 90
North Scotland 222
North York Moors National
   Park 78
North-east England 77
North-west England 67
Northern Bedstraw 55, 81, 84,
   166, 177
Northern Brown Argus 52, 63
Northern Ireland 8, 24, 179,
   181, 185
Northern Marsh Orchid 33, 43
Northern Rock-cress 33, 41, 45,
   46, 166, 186
Northern Scotland 31, 206, 212,
   226, 228
Northumberland 77, 79
Nuthatch 70, 105, 110, 126,
   131, 135, 136, 145, 149
Old Man of Storr 44, 45
Orange-tip 76, 216
Orkney 14, 31, 32, 35, 36, 218,
   220, 222
Osprey 22, 51, 52, 58, 95, 139,
   144, 160

Otter 32, 39–42, 77, 130, 131,
   143, 149, 169, 171, 181, 182,
   185, 212
Ouse Washes 19, 100, 101, 137
Oxeye Daisy 135, 232
Oxford Island 180
Oxlip 90, 91, 103, 228
Oxwich Bay 174–176
Oystercatcher 20, 42, 54, 61,
   71, 87, 89, 104, 113, 139,
   147, 153, 156, 165, 181, 182,
   190, 191, 198
Pagham Harbour 20, 106, 109,
   110
Painswick Hill 134
Painted Lady 126, 147, 182
Palmate Newt 214
Pamber Forest 123, 124
Parsley Fern 166, 177
Peacock 76, 117, 137, 216
Peak District 11, 86
Peak National Park 85
Pearl-bordered Fritillary 41, 52,
   60, 68, 117, 131, 140, 143,
   162, 185, 218
Peatlands Country Park 179
Pedunculate Oak 103, 135, 136
Pembrokeshire Coast 161
Pennines 8, 9, 78, 81, 86
Pennington and Keyhaven
   Marshes 19
Peregrine 9, 10, 13, 14, 19, 35,
   39, 41, 43, 44, 46, 47, 53, 58,
   59, 61, 65, 67, 70, 81, 100,
   144, 160–163, 165, 166,
   170–173, 177, 179, 184–187,
   189, 191
Peterborough 16, 137
Pewsey Downs 122
Pied Flycatcher 69, 70, 85, 104,
   108, 109, 129–131, 136, 139,
   146, 149–151, 160, 162, 168,
   170, 171, 177
Pied Wagtail 202
Pine Marten 17, 38, 39, 51, 52,
   68, 69, 164, 185, 191
Pink-footed Goose 68
Pintail 18–20, 61, 73, 100, 104,
   109, 113, 131, 144, 147, 151,
   153, 155, 164, 169, 180,
   189–191
Pipewort 40, 187, 191
Pipistrelle 210
plantation 17, 48, 77, 82, 91,
   139, 164
Polecat 130, 131, 162, 168, 169,
   171
Poulavallan 189
Primrose 31, 32, 36, 37, 67, 68,
   78, 84, 90, 117, 134, 137,
   145, 146, 228,
Ptarmigan 14, 38, 39, 49–53, 55,
   58, 65
Puffin 19, 31, 35, 36, 38, 41, 77,
   85, 127, 146, 159, 160, 162,
   173, 189, 192, 193

Puffin Island 193
Purple Emperor 107, 108, 117,
   119, 124
Purple Hairstreak 105, 107, 119,
   130, 137, 143, 162
Purple Loosestrife 21, 76, 95,
   98, 101, 110, 155, 174, 226
Purple Sandpiper 14, 36, 52, 63,
   82, 164, 176, 182, 184
Pygmy Shrew 210
Pyramidal Orchid 72, 87, 133
Queendown Warren 112
Rahoy Hills 46, 47
Ramsons 137, 148, 234
Rannoch Moor 52
Rannoch-rush 52
Rathlin Island 183, 184
Raven 14, 36, 41, 49, 50, 53, 60,
   65, 67, 70, 131, 139, 144,
   149, 151, 158, 163, 165, 166,
   168–173, 177, 184, 186, 191,
   208
Razorbill 13, 35, 36, 38, 85, 127,
   146, 159, 162, 165, 172, 173,
   174, 182-184, 189, 193
Red Admiral 216
Red Campion 19, 86, 222
Red Data Book 12
Red Deer 14, 38–40, 45, 51, 53,
   56, 58–60, 143, 151, 186,
   187, 191, 212
Red Grouse 13, 14, 38, 46, 49,
   53, 55, 58, 60, 77–79, 82, 84,
   85, 86, 139, 170, 171, 186
Red Kite 13, 16, 160, 162,
   169–171
Red Squirrel 17, 48, 55, 68, 69,
   77, 78, 119, 127, 155, 171,
   178, 185, 210
Red-breasted Merganser 22, 36,
   43, 47, 48, 54, 61, 66, 74,
   104, 109, 113, 122, 153, 156,
   169, 180–182
Red-necked Phalarope 31–33,
   40, 41, 43, 32
Red-throated Diver 13, 14, 22,
   32, 33, 46, 74, 81, 109, 153,
   169, 183
Redgrave 101
Redstart 39, 50, 69, 71, 84, 85,
   87, 97, 104, 105, 107–109,
   115, 120, 126, 129–131, 135,
   136, 139, 140, 146, 149–151,
   160, 162, 168, 170, 177, 186
Redwing 39, 52, 39
Reed Bunting 110, 153, 208
Rhum 40, 43, 45, 46
Ribble 20, 73
Ribble Estuary 73
Ring Ouzel 14, 39, 44, 50, 55,
   58, 59, 65, 70, 78, 79, 84–86,
   92, 104, 109, 139, 146, 149,
   160, 166, 168, 170, 171, 177
Ringed Plover 18, 20, 42, 71, 89,
   104, 107, 109, 113, 138, 139,
   181, 182

Ringlet 52, 54, 68, 70, 142, 218
River Spey 6
Rock Dove 19, 32, 36, 64, 163,
   173, 184
Rock Pipit 19, 32, 63, 64, 155,
   172, 181, 184
Rodborough Common 132
Roseate Tern 159, 162, 164,
   179, 181, 182, 185
Rosebay Willowherb 21, 174,
   226
Roseroot 34–36, 39, 53, 58, 61,
   166
Rowan 44, 86, 130, 135, 140,
   151, 168, 170, 224
Royal Fern 44, 150, 157, 179,
   185, 190
Roydon Common 15
Ruddy Duck 110, 138, 141, 143,
   144, 151
Ruff 18, 55, 73, 91, 94, 100, 113,
   132, 153
Rutland Water 129, 138
Saltfleetby-Theddlethorpe
   Dunes 88
Salthouse 90, 92-94
Sand lizard 15, 72, 118, 153,
   214
Sanderling 54, 61, 66, 74, 164,
   190
Sands of Forvie 56
Sandwich Tern 182
Savi's Warbler 91, 95, 97, 112
Scaup 47, 54, 61, 81, 182, 191
Scotch Argus 41, 52, 58–60, 68
Scots Lovage 19, 34, 36, 59, 64
Scottish borders 8
Scottish Crossbill 13, 17, 31, 39,
   51, 52, 57
Scottish Highlands 7, 68
Scottish Primrose 36, 37
Sea Campion 15, 38, 63, 162, 196
Sea Spleenwort 19, 41, 64, 173,
   184
Selfheal 121, 230
Seven Sisters 109
Severn 11, 130, 136
Shag 19, 127, 146, 159, 162,
   164, 165, 173, 183, 184, 189,
   192, 196
Shelduck 19, 43, 55, 61, 71, 81,
   89, 104, 109, 113, 122, 138,
   144, 147, 153, 156, 164, 169,
   180–182, 190, 196
Shetland 14, 32, 33, 34
Shorelark 91
Short-eared Owl 59, 68, 73, 77,
   79, 81, 89, 113, 132, 170,
   173, 181
Short-toed Treecreeper 119
Shropshire 22, 139
Shrubby Cinquefoil 67, 68, 81
Sika Deer 130, 153, 191, 212
Silver Birch 91, 220
Silver-spotted Skipper 119, 123,
   136

Silver-studded Blue 15, 115, 116, 126, 145, 163
Silver-washed Fritillary 108, 123, 124, 143, 162, 183, 192
Siskin 17, 48, 51, 52, 131, 186
Skokholm 173
Skomer **172**, 173
Skye 40, 44–46, 187
Slapton Ley 151
Slavonian Grebe 51, 52, 81, 110, 122, 151, 153
Slieve League 8, 186
Slimbridge 129, 131, 132
Slow-worm 113, **170**, 171, 214
Small Blue 102, 119, 121, 123, 130, 135, 146, 189
Small Copper 15, 54, 63, 76, 98, 216
Small Heath 15, 79, 98, 218
Small Pearl-bordered Fritillary 41, 52, 68, 117, 131, 140, 143, 162, 218
Small Skipper 218
Small Tortoiseshell 76, 218
Smew 95, 97, 100, 104, 109, 117, 144, 151
Smooth Newt 89, 214
Smooth Snake 15, 118, 153, 214
Snow Bunting 14, 39, 51, 52, 58, 89, 160, 184
Snowdon 161, 162, 165, 166
Snowdon Lily 161, 162, **166**
Snowy Owl 31, 32
Somerset Levels 19
Sooty Shearwater 165, 184
South Downs 9, 106, 108
South Stack 162, **163**
South Walney 71
Southern England 9, 15, 22, 111, 118, 119, 125, 218, 220
Southern Scotland and Borders 59
Sparrowhawk 16, 39, 43, 46–48, 61, 76, 89, 98, 110, 114, 115, 120, 126, 131, 132, 135–137, 140, 142, 145, **148**, 149, 151, 153, 169, 171, 176, 179, 181, 187, 191

Spear Thistle 234
Speckled Wood 137, 155, 218
Spoonbill 94
Spotted Orchid 34, 43, 65, 76, 103, 133, 135, 141, 157, 234
Spotted Redshank 61, 71, 87, 89, 94, 113, 132, 144, 191
Spring Gentian 78, 81, 188
Spring Squill 15, 35, 36, 157, 163–165, 172, 173, 182, 184
St Abb's Head 59, 63
St Catherine's Point 121
St David's Head 172
Stackpole Head 173, 174
Staines Reservoirs 117
Stinking Hellebore 131
Stoat 115, 131, 136, 185, 187, 191, 212
Stodmarsh 106, **111**
Stone Curlew 15, 18, **90**, 91, 98
Stonechat 15, 49, 96, 115, 120, 126, 149, 153, 163, 186, 187
Strangford Lough 20, 179, 181, 182
Studland Heath 153, 154
Sunart Woods 46
Swallowtail 90, 91, 95, **96**
Swithland Wood 140
Sycamore 134, 220
Symonds Yat **131**
Tawny Owl 69, 97, 149, 200
Teasel 206, 216, 232
Tennyson Down 121
Tentsmuir Point 54
Thatcham Reedbeds 125
The Burren 8, 9, 67, 185, 186, 188, 218, 220, 232, 234
The Fleet 155, 156
The Giant's Causeway 184
The Lizard 142, 156, 157
The Long Mynd 139
The Naze 104
The Needles 121
The Skelligs 193
Therfield Heath 102
Thrift 15, 19, 20, 63, 64, 71, 82, 88, 104, 113, 122, 127, 146, **163**–165, 172, 173, 228

Thursley Common 113
Tormentil 14, 15, 34, 71, 139, 141, 148, 173, 186, 224
Tree Pipit 14, 69, 98, 115, 120, 135, 168, 170, 177, 202
Treecreeper 206
Tregaron 170
Tring 125
Tufted Vetch 43, 125, 224
Turnstone 20, 36, 63, 87, 104, 113, 147, 164, 176, 182, 184
Twelve Bens **8**, **187**
Twite 13, 14, 31, 32, 35, 36, 42, 49, 89, 184
Tyne and Wear 77
Upper Teesdale 78, 80, **81**
Viviparous Lizard 13, 15, 214
Walberswick 97
Wall Brown 218
Warty Newt 214
Wash 11, 89, 212
Water Lobelia 22, 44, 67, 68
Water Mint 76, 155, 174, 230
Water Rail 22, 75, 76, 97, 110, 125, 151, 171, 176, 181
Water Shrew 210
Water Vole 171, 210
Weasel 115, 131, 136, 212
Welney **101**
Wenlock Edge 139
West Sedgemoor 152
Western Scotland and Islands 40
Wexford Wildfowl Reserve 191
Wheatear 14, 35, 53, 64, 77, 79, 84, 85, 98, 139, 149, 166, 170, 171, 173, 177
Whimbrel 31–33, 61, 71, 94, 104, 147, 152, 198
Whinchat 15, 79, 85, 98, 139, 141, 143, 149, 160, 177
White Admiral **106**, 107, 117, 119, 123, 124, 126, 131, 135, 145, 150, 216
White Bryony 108, 226
White Campion 222
White Helleborine 102, 131
White-fronted Goose 185, 191

White-tailed eagle 19, 40, 41
White-toothed Shrew 160
Whooper Swan 36, 43, 81, 164, 167, 184, 185
Wicken Fen 10, 16, 90, 96, 98
Wicklow Mountains 8
Wigeon 196
Wild Cat 14, 38–41, 52, 212
Wild Gladiolus 119, 120
Wild Thyme 15, 21, 87, 102, 121, 123, 135, 136, 145, 230
Windsor Great Park 125, 126
Wistman's Wood 148, 150
Witcombe Wood 134
Witley Common 115
Wood Anemone 103, 124, 137, 145, 148, 222
Wood Sandpiper 32, 94
Wood Sorrel 124, 137, 145, 226
Wood Warbler 39, 48, 50, 69, 87, 120, 129–131, 135, 136, 139, 140, 149–151, 162, 168, 170, 171, 186
Wood White 117, 137, 155, 185, 189, 192
Woodcock 39, 46, 65, 131, 135, 137, 179, 187
Woodlark 15, **17**, 90, 91, 115, 120, 121, 126
Woodwalton Fen 99
Worcestershire 161
Wryneck 63, 85, 87, 92, 109, 127, 160
Wyre Forest 129, **136**, 137
Yarner Wood **150**
Yellow Archangel 112, 135, 155, 230
Yellow Iris **11**, 234
Yellow Loosestrife 68, 125, 228
Yellow Rattle 81, 99, 132, 136, 146, 180, 184, 232
Yellow-necked Mouse 124
Ynys Enlli 165
Yorkshire Dales 78
Yr Wyddfa 165
Ythan 20, 56

Photographic Acknowledgements

Peter Brough 42, 45, 124, 160, 163; RJ Chandler 4–5, 30, 32, 147, 190; Paul Doherty, 31, 58, 60, 63, 101, 105, 108, 110, 115, 116, 129, 138, 153, 180; Andrew N Gagg 10, 11, 20, 37, 39, 54 (upper and lower), 72, 74, 79, 86, 87, 96, 103, 107, 113, 119, 132, 136, 137, 143, 145, 156, 157, 166, 185, 192; Alan Hamilton 184; E & D Hosking 182; David Goodfellow 27, 80, 82, 111, 144, 148, 159, 172, 174 (left and right), 194; Paul Kirby 12, 23, 36, 38, 43,52, 56, 64, 66, 88, 126, 161; John Measures 133; Nature Photographers 51, 57, 112, 118, 124, 125, 156, 164, 169; M Sanders 65; Peter Sell 6, 48, 49, 69, 75, 100, 131, 175, 176, 177; Roger Tidman, 34, 40, 44 (left and right), 59, 67, 73, 76, 85, 90, 96, 97, 106, 121, 128, 130, 133, 141, 142, 148, 152, 168, 171, 178, 179, 183; Martin Walters 2–3, 14, 15, 17, 18, 21 (upper and lower), 47, 91, 102, 150, 189; PF Yeo 8, 16, 19, 77, 81, 84, 94, 95, 167, 187.